# Leading Health Care Transformation

"Readers should go broad and go deep with this book. Readers who do both will find this book a valuable framework for approaching the complexities of leading health care organizations today…it will provide a framework for approaching the work, and that framework is one likely to lead to business success and personal satisfaction."

—*From the Foreword by Thomas H. Lee, MD, Chief Medical Officer, Press Ganey and Senior Physician, Brigham and Women's Hospital*

The U.S. health care system continues to undergo transformation, with a rate of change that has accelerated in recent years. This rapidly evolving field requires a new level of astute clinical leadership. The bottom line is that physician leadership will be the key ingredient for any dramatic change in our health care system and a fundamental driver of outcomes for patients and communities.

*Leading Heath Care Transformation* prepares physician leaders with the evidence, tools, and ideas to make and lead systemic improvement. This second edition provides fresh insights, new evidence, and modern topics with revised and updated chapters. Each chapter is complete with contemporary evidence, pragmatic case studies, lessons learned, and action steps for physician leaders.

This second edition of *Leading Health Care Transformation* is a succinct and practical primer on 16 key topics in health care transformation. Physician leadership is critical to transform care; this book will help guide the way.

# Leading Health Care Transformation

## A Primer for Physician Leaders

Second Edition

Maulik Joshi, DrPH
Aaron George, DO

Foreword by Thomas H. Lee, MD

Routledge
Taylor & Francis Group
A PRODUCTIVITY PRESS BOOK

First published 2024
by Routledge
605 Third Avenue, New York, NY 10158

and by Routledge
4 Park Square, Milton Park, Abingdon, Oxon, OX14 4RN

*Routledge is an imprint of the Taylor & Francis Group, an informa business*



ISBN: 978-1-032-51562-5 (hbk)
ISBN: 978-1-032-51563-2 (pbk)
ISBN: 978-1-003-40283-1 (ebk)

DOI: 10.4324/9781003402831

Typeset in Garamond
by SPi Technologies India Pvt Ltd (Straive)

# Contents

**Foreword** ........ **xiii**
**About the Authors** ........ **xvi**

**1 The Health Care Landscape** ........ **1**
Introduction ........ 1
First Curve to Second Curve ........ 2
Leading Transformation ........ 5
Key Factors Driving Transformation ........ 6
High Cost of Care ........ 6
Shifting Demographics: Patients and Workforce ........ 7
Transition to Value-Based Reimbursement ........ 8
Variable Quality Outcomes ........ 11
Expansion of Coverage ........ 13
Impact of the COVID-19 Pandemic ........ 15
Advances in Health Information Technology ........ 15
Shift from Defined Benefit to Defined Contribution Health Plans ........ 17
Action Steps and Strategies to Lead as a Physician Leader ........ 17
Conclusion ........ 20
Note ........ 20
References ........ 20

**2 Effectively Implementing Quality and Safety Improvement....25**
The Evidence....25
The Model for Improvement....25
Lean....28
Six Sigma....32
International Standards Organization 9001....33
Case Study: Enhancing Vaccine Access....35
Lessons Learned....37
Action Steps and Strategies to Lead....40
References....42

**3 Building a Culture of Safety....45**
The Evidence....45
Transparency around Safety Events....50
AHRQ Surveys on Patient Safety Culture (SOPS)....50
Safety Attitudes Questionnaire....53
Case Study: Improving Organizational Culture of Safety....53
Lessons Learned....56
Action Steps and Strategies to Lead....57
References....58

**4 Principles and Practices of High Reliability Organizations....60**
The Evidence....60
Preoccupation with Failure....61
Reluctance to Simplify....62
Sensitivity to Operations....62
Commitment to Resilience....63
Deference to Expertise....63
Case Studies....64
Preoccupation with Failure: Investigating Near Misses and Good Saves....65

Reluctance to Simplify: Thorough Root Cause Analysis and Event Investigation ......66
Sensitivity to Operations: Daily Organization Huddle ......67
Commitment to Resilience: Simulation ......69
Deference to Expertise: Executive Rounding ......70
Lessons Learned ......71
Action Steps and Strategies to Lead ......72
References ......73

**5 Key Quality, Safety, and Efficiency Measures ......74**
The Evidence ......74
Data for Performance Measurement: The Basics ......77
Types and Dimensions of Measures ......78
Criteria and Standards ......80
Data Sources ......80
Metrics of the Future ......83
Effective Strategies: Using Data to Drive Performance Improvement ......84
Selecting Measures ......85
Case Study: Reducing Unnecessary Testing ......87
Lessons Learned ......91
Action Steps and Strategies to Lead ......92
References ......94

**6 Using Data for Feedback and Improvement ......98**
The Evidence ......98
Step 1: Data Collection: Objectives, Sources, and Methods ......99
Step 2: Displaying the Data ......103
Physician Profiling ......104
Dashboards ......105
Run Charts ......106
Step 3: Analyzing the Data ......107
Step 4: Implementing Improvement Cycles ......110

Case Study: Improving and Enhancing Surgical Recovery....110
Lessons Learned....114
Action Steps and Strategies to Lead....115
References....116

**7 Physician Champions....119**
The Evidence....119
Characteristics of Effective Champions....120
Case Study: Identifying and Developing Champions....126
Lessons Learned....129
Action Steps and Strategies to Lead....130
References....131

**8 Leading Effective Teams: For Clinical Care and Performance Improvement....133**
The Evidence....133
Clinical Care Teams....134
Performance Improvement Teams....135
Strategies for Success....137
Effective Strategy: TeamSTEPPS....137
Effective Strategy: Understanding the Stages of Team Formation....140
Case Study: Reduction of Central Line Associated Blood Stream Infections....142
Lessons Learned....146
Action Steps and Strategies to Lead....147
References....148

**9 Spreading and Sustaining Improvement....150**
The Evidence....150
Preparing for Spread....151
Establishing an Aim for Spread....154
Developing a Spread Plan....154
Effective Strategies for Executing and Monitoring Spread....157
Sustaining Improvement....159

Case Study: On the CUSP: Stop CAUTI ..........163
Lessons Learned ..........168
Action Steps and Strategies to Lead ..........170
References ..........171

**10 Engaging Patients and Families in Safety and Quality ..........174**
The Evidence ..........174
Effective Strategies for Patient and Family Engagement ..........176
Strategies at the Direct Care Level ..........176
Strategies to Engage Patients in Organizational Design and Governance ..........179
Working with Patients/Family Advisors ..........180
Case Study: Developing a Patient and Family Advisory Council ..........184
Lessons Learned ..........186
Beyond the Bedside ..........187
Engage Patients as Partners ..........188
Provide Meaningful Opportunities for Patients and Families to Contribute ..........188
Patient and Family Engagement as a Strategy to Eliminate Harm ..........189
Barriers to Engagement ..........189
Action Steps and Strategies to Lead ..........192
References ..........193

**11 Health Equity and Addressing Disparities ..........195**
The Evidence ..........195
Effective Strategies ..........199
Cultural Awareness ..........199
Stratify Data to Identify Areas of Need ..........200
Community Partnerships ..........202
Case Study: A Health Equity Report ..........203
Lessons Learned ..........204
Action Steps and Strategies to Lead ..........205
References ..........207

**12 Addressing Variation in Utilization....................208**
The Evidence....................208
Understanding Warranted vs. Unwarranted Variation....................209
Choosing Wisely®....................211
The Safer Dx Checklist....................212
Strategies for Success....................213
Case Study: Reducing Opioid Overprescribing....................218
Lessons Learned....................225
Action Steps and Strategies to Lead....................227
References....................228

**13 Improving Care Coordination and Reducing Readmissions....................231**
The Evidence....................231
Boston Medical Center Reengineered Discharge....................233
Care Transitions Program....................234
Transitional Care Model....................235
Strategies for Success....................236
Identify Patients at High Risk for Readmission....................237
Build Self-Management Skills....................237
Discharge Planning....................238
Follow-Up and Community Resources....................239
Case Study: Increasing Access and Improving Care Coordination....................240
Case Study: Improving Access and Preventive Care....................243
Lessons Learned....................246
Action Steps and Strategies to Lead....................247
References....................249

**14 Population and Community Health....................252**
The Evidence....................252
Population-Based Payment Models....................255
Per Member Per Month....................255
Policy Implementation and Implications....................256
The Affordable Care Act....................257

Accountable Care Organizations ............................... 258
Social Determinants of Health .................................. 258
Community Engagement ........................................... 262
Data Utilization ..................................................... 264
Case Study: Improving Models for Managing Chronic Kidney Disease ................................................ 265
Action Steps and Strategies to Lead ............................ 269
References ............................................................. 271

**15 New Payment Models: Value-Based Purchasing ..................................................... 272**
The Evidence ........................................................... 272
Pay-for-Performance ............................................... 274
Accountable Care Organizations and Shared Savings .............................................................. 275
Identifying an Attributed Patient Population ............ 277
Structure of Risk Sharing ......................................... 278
Bundled Payments .................................................. 279
Capitation .............................................................. 281
Case Study: Bundled Payments ................................... 282
Lessons Learned ....................................................... 288
Information Technology ........................................... 289
Data and Analytics .................................................. 289
Care Management ................................................... 290
Action Steps and Strategies to Lead ............................ 291
References ............................................................. 293

**16 The Physician Leader Role in Emerging Models of Care, Disruption, and Innovation ........ 295**
The Evidence ........................................................... 295
Retail Medicine ....................................................... 297
Mobile Health ......................................................... 299
Artificial Intelligence ............................................... 301
Case Study: Responding to New and Disruptive Models of Care ......................................................... 302
Lessons Learned ....................................................... 306

Action Steps and Strategies to Lead....307
References....309

**17 Compendium of Action Steps....311**
Chapter 1: The Health Care Landscape....311
Chapter 2: Effectively Implementing Quality and Safety Improvement....312
Chapter 3: Building a Culture of Safety....314
Chapter 4: Principles and Practices of High Reliability Organizations....315
Chapter 5: Key Quality, Safety, and Efficiency Measures....316
Chapter 6: Using Data for Feedback and Improvement....317
Chapter 7: Physician Champions....318
Chapter 8: Leading Effective Teams: For Clinical Care and for Performance Improvement....318
Chapter 9: Spreading and Sustaining Improvement....319
Chapter 10: Engaging Patients and Families in Safety and Quality....320
Chapter 11: Health Equity and Addressing Disparities....321
Chapter 12: Addressing Variation in Utilization....322
Chapter 13: Improving Care Coordination and Reducing Readmissions....323
Chapter 14: Population and Community Health....324
Chapter 15: New Payment Models: Value-Based Purchasing....325
Chapter 16: The Physician Leader Role in Emerging Models of Care, Disruption, and Innovation....326

**Index....327**

# Foreword

There is a changing-of-the-guard in leadership in health care underway, and it is picking up steam. The generation passing from the stage has had many "accidental leaders," who found themselves in senior positions because they were trusted by their colleagues but often did not have expertise in management or strategy. Some of them turned out to have the skills needed to guide their organizations through the clinical and financial challenges of the COVID pandemic, the social unrest that followed the murder of George Floyd, and the 500-year weather events that seem to be occurring with every year or so now. But others did not. And the turnover among leaders has been accelerating due to retirement and the search for leaders who might be able to do a better job.

The generation that is replacing them has a better grasp of the breadth and depth of the skills needed to lead health care organizations today. These leaders know that they must understand the health care landscape, which is rapidly evolving due to medical progress, rising costs and complexity, social and cultural changes, and rapid information flow. They cannot simply say, "This is what we do," and expect hard work will be supported and rewarded.

These leaders must understand organizational culture, and what it takes to make the principles of high reliability the norms among their colleagues. They have to understand how "safety" means more than protecting patients from physical harm; it also entails protecting them from emotional harm, financial harm, and social harm. The goal of Zero Harm has to include Zero Inequity and Zero Disrespect.

This second edition of *Leading Health Care Transformation* can be read in two ways—and both can strengthen the skills of leaders during the complex times ahead. The first way is what I would call "Focused Skimming." Readers should look carefully at the Table of Contents to take in the range of topics that will be discussed. They should go to the last chapter, and skim through the Compendium of Action Steps. This will help readers build their sense of what cross-cutting skills are going to prove most important—e.g., understanding culture, truly listening to colleagues, setting priorities, and driving improvement.

With that sense of the types of skills they need, readers can then plunge more deeply into individual chapters and topics. Recognizing that few readers are going to consume every word on every page in the order they appear, my recommendation is look at each chapter, and ask if this topic is already one of your strengths? If so, you might spend less time on it and more on the chapters focusing on topics that you are less comfortable with.

This advice may seem paradoxical, at first—the suggestion to spend more time on the issues that interest you less. But the fact is that every one of these chapters is focused on a topic that is essential to leaders in health care today and understanding the action steps in each chapter is essential to success.

In short, readers should go broad and go deep with this book. Going broad means grasping the full range of areas of expertise needed by complete leaders in health care today. Going deep means resisting the temptation to avoid detail on topics that are not already areas of strength and plunging in instead.

Readers who do both will find this book a valuable framework for approaching the complexities of leading health care organizations today. A painful reality is that complex problems virtually never surrender to simple solutions. There are no single magic bullets that will make everything right. This book will not make the complex challenges less complex. But it will provide a framework for approaching the work, and that framework is one likely to lead to business success and personal satisfaction.

**By Thomas H. Lee, MD**
*Chief Medical Officer, Press Ganey*
*Senior Physician, Brigham and Women's Hospital*

# About the Authors

**Maulik Joshi, DrPH,** is the President and CEO of Meritus Health, Inc., which includes the proposed Meritus School of Osteopathic Medicine (MSOM) and Meritus Medical Center (MMC). The mission of Meritus Health is to improve the health of our community by providing the best health care, health services, and medical education.

Meritus Medical Center is a regional health system with 3,000+ employees and 500+ medical staff. MMC includes a 327-bed medical center, a 190-provider Meritus Medical Group, Meritus Home Health, and 25% ownership of Maryland Physicians Care, a 250,000 Medicaid member health plan. Meritus Medical Center serves over 200,000 people in western Maryland, southern Pennsylvania, and the eastern panhandle of West Virginia. The proposed Meritus School of Osteopathic Medicine is seeking accreditation and working to have its first matriculation of medical students in the Fall of 2025. MSOM's mission is to prepare future generations of physicians who are professionally accomplished, socially responsible, and community oriented.

Previously, Maulik was the COO and executive vice president at the Anne Arundel Health System (AAHS). Prior to AAHS, he was at the American Hospital Association as associate executive vice president and president of the Health Research and Educational Trust. He has also worked at the Institute for

Healthcare Improvement, the Agency for Healthcare Research and Quality, the University of Pennsylvania Health System, and the HMO Group.

Maulik holds a doctorate in Public Health and a master's degree in Health Services Administration from the University of Michigan. He was editor in chief of the *Journal for Healthcare Quality*. He has co-edited the *Healthcare Quality Book: Vision, Strategy and Tools* (fifth edition, published in 2022) and coauthored *Healthcare Transformation: A Guide for the Hospital Board Member*. Maulik has authored a combination of over 50 peer-reviewed articles, commentaries, and perspectives. He is adjunct faculty at the University of Michigan School of Public Health at the Department of Health Management and Policy, where he teaches annually. He has served on the board of trustees for Anne Arundel Medical Center and the board quality and patient safety committee for Mercy Health System and Advocate Health System, among others.

**Aaron George, DO,** is Associate Dean for Clinical Education for the Proposed Meritus School of Osteopathic Medicine. Previously, Dr. George served as the chief medical officer of Meritus Health, Inc. He holds a medical degree from the Philadelphia College of Osteopathic Medicine in Philadelphia and completed his residency in family medicine at Duke University Medical Center in Durham, North Carolina. Dr. George was an Andlinger fellow in health policy with the Center for Public Health in Vienna, Austria, where he focused on models of care delivery. In addition, he is a clinical associate professor at Penn State College of Medicine, where he teaches coursework on the history of medicine. Dr. George is an author and speaker on population health, medical education, and physician leadership development throughout the spectrum of clinical training. Dr. George is board certified in Family Medicine by the American Board of Family Medicine.

# *Chapter 1*

# The Health Care Landscape

## Introduction

Health care has observed massive shifts since the turn of the century, and the rate of change continues to increase. The passage of the Affordable Care Act in 2010 brought expanded health insurance coverage to millions of previously uninsured Americans. In the decade that followed, the burden of chronic disease within the American public worsened, the COVID-19 pandemic challenged the mettle of organizations small and large, and inequity across populations widened. Under these pressures, the transition from volume-based care to value-focused delivery systems has been more prolonged than predicted. New models of care continue to emerge that harness technology and deploy novel strategies to improve quality, reduce costs, and enhance the patient experience of care. The transformation of the U.S. health care system remains inevitable. Given the seismic changes from recent government-mandated reforms and health care crisis, the

DOI: 10.4324/9781003402831-1

speed and extent of that transformation will be dependent upon the emergence of transformational clinician leadership.

## First Curve to Second Curve

The health care industry is transitioning from a "first curve" business model, one based on volume, to a "second curve" business model based on value (Figure 1.1). This shift is driven by many factors and is most notably due to the high, growing, and unsustainable cost of health care. As payment incentives shift to reward value, health care organizations are

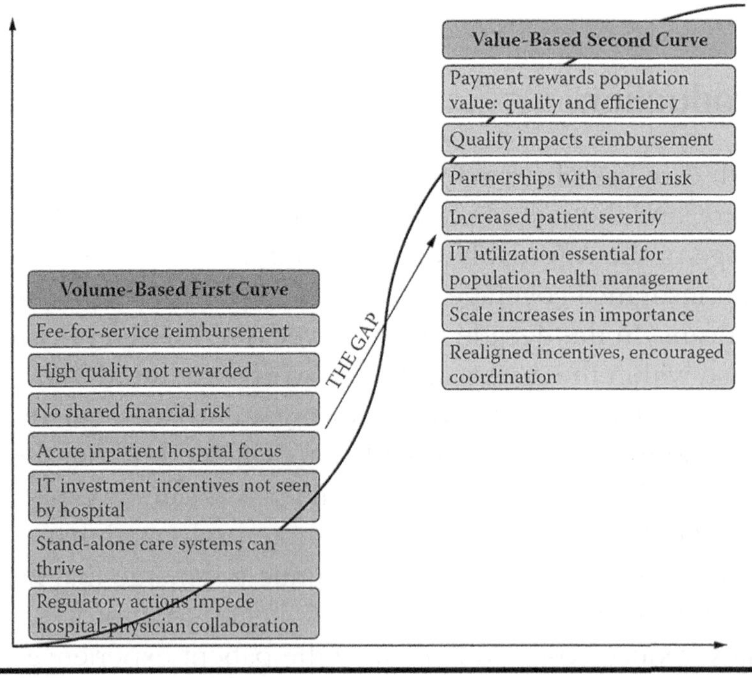


**Figure 1.1 First-curve to second-curve transition. (American Hospital Association. Committee on Performance Improvement, Jeanette Clough, Chairperson. Hospitals and Care Systems of the Future. Chicago: American Hospital Association, September 2011, adapted from Ian Morrison.)**

changing their business models to deliver second-curve outcomes: High-quality, low-cost, patient-centered care.

Organizations that do not adapt to a new second-curve business model will not make the leap from the first curve. This was evident in the movie rental business where Blockbuster thrived in the first-curve transaction-based business model (where more stores and supply of movies maximized revenues), but did not succeed in the second-curve business model (where bricks and mortar did not matter and having a "capitated" model like Netflix led to financial success).

As the system shifts from the first curve to the second curve, the biggest challenge for health care leaders is navigating "life in the gap," the period of transition between the two operational models. Organizations that transition to the second curve ahead of the payers in their market may experience reductions in revenue in the short term. Alternatively, those organizations that do not prepare for the second curve will find that they are unable to transition quickly enough once payers more consistently reward providers based on quality and cost.

In search of value, many organizations have invested in strategy and infrastructure that has not yet realized sizable financial gains, marked increases in quality, or decreases in cost. In other words, we have not yet witnessed the health care equivalent of a Netflix level of disruptive innovation. Yet organizations that remain in the gap are already considering moving beyond the second curve and seeking to redefine value itself. Such forward thinking organizations have spent the past decade following playbooks such as that devised in 2011 by the American Hospital Association Committee on Performance Improvement (AHA CPI). This identified a set of core competencies and must-do strategies for hospitals to transition from the first curve to the second-curve business model. Figure 1.2 lists those ten must-do strategies, emphasizing the first four as the most important.

| Must-Do Strategies |
|---|
| 1. Align hospitals, physicians, and other clinical providers across the continuum of care. |
| 2. Utilize evidence-based practices to improve quality and patient safety. |
| 3. Improve efficiency through productivity and financial management. |
| 4. Develop integrated information systems. |
| 5. Join and grow integrated provider networks and care systems. |
| 6. Educate and engage employees and physicians to create leaders. |
| 7. Strengthen finances to facilitate reinvestment and innovation. |
| 8. Partner with payers. |
| 9. Advance an organization through scenario-based strategic, financial, and operational planning. |
| 10. Seek population health improvement through pursuit of the Triple Aim. |

**Figure 1.2 Must-do strategies. (American Hospital Association. 2011. Committee on Performance Improvement, Jeanette Clough, Chairperson. Hospitals and Care Systems of the Future. Chicago: American Hospital Association, September 2011.)**

| Core Competencies |
|---|
| 1. Design and implement patient-centered, integrated care. |
| 2. Create accountable governance and leadership. |
| 3. Strategic planning in an unstable environment. |
| 4. Internal and external collaboration. |
| 5. Financial stewardship and enterprise risk management. |
| 6. Engagement of full employee potential. |
| 7. Collection and utilization of electronic data for performance improvement. |

**Figure 1.3 Core competencies. (American Hospital Association. Committee on Performance Improvement, Jeanette Clough, Chairperson. Hospitals and Care Systems of the Future. Chicago: American Hospital Association, September 2011.)**

The AHA CPI also identified seven core competencies for organizations to develop to survive and thrive in the era of value-based health care (Figure 1.3). One may feel these references are dated, but are in fact relevant a decade later.

## *Leading Transformation*

There is certainly lots of talk directed at reform, but why do organizations need to change? This chapter provides an overview of the key factors driving transformation including the following:

- High and increasing cost of care
- Shift in demographics of patients and workforce
- Evolution of patient expectations and the rise of consumerism
- Transition to value-based reimbursement
- Variable quality and patient-safety outcomes and persistent disparities in care
- Expansion of coverage and access to care
- Advances in health information technology
- Shift from defined benefit to defined contribution health plans
- Novel and emerging markets
- Competition among various groups, including arrival of nontraditional health care entities

These are turbulent and exciting times, and the health care industry is in need of diverse leaders who can effectively navigate the rapid and often-disruptive changes underway in hospitals and health systems. While the delivery system is changing, the face of leadership is also changing. As physicians and health systems become aligned, organizations are adopting hybrid leadership models that include both clinical and administrative leaders. In all new models of alignment, physicians are taking on leadership roles that require skill sets and tools, and they are increasingly faced with the many challenges inherent in health care transformation.

The chapter concludes with six leadership competencies to successfully lead health care transformation:

1. Effectively communicate the imperative for and steps to achieve health care transformation
2. Understand the relationship between cost and quality in practice and how to drive value
3. Build, deploy, and lead improvement teams across all dimensions of care
4. Lead effective and coordinated multidisciplinary care teams
5. Leverage data to improve clinical and organizational practice
6. Realize the role of patient as consumer

## Key Factors Driving Transformation

### *High Cost of Care*

The United States spends far more on health care than any other country and yet does not consistently deliver superior quality or achieve better outcomes when compared to less-expensive heath care systems. In 2021, the United States spent $4.3 trillion on health care, which accounted for 18.3% of gross domestic product (GDP), equating to per capita spending of $12,914. Further estimates suggest that health care spending will grow 5.1% per year over the coming decade, with projections that the total spend will exceed $6 trillion by 2030 (CMS 2021).

In addition to contributing to a large portion of GDP, numerous studies have demonstrated that U.S. health care spending drastically exceeds that of other countries, both per capita and as a percentage of GDP. A 2021 study by the Commonwealth Fund compared U.S. spending and health care outcomes to that of ten other industrialized countries.[1]

Findings from this study showed that despite outspending other nations, devoting nearly twice as much of its GDP to health care, the United States ranks last overall on health care outcomes including mortality and life expectancy. This study and others have controlled for differences in national income, an older population, and both supply and utilization of hospitals and doctors (Schneider et al. 2021).

The high cost of health care has important implications. For individuals, the high cost of care can pose a significant financial burden, particularly for those without insurance. For employers providing health insurance coverage, the high and increasing cost of care adds significantly to the cost of business. As a result, over the past decade employers have shifted costs to employees through new benefit designs (i.e., high deductible health plans), raised premiums, and dropped employee-sponsored coverage (Claxton et al. 2022). At the state and federal levels, the cost of public insurance programs, including Medicare and Medicaid, contributes significantly to state and federal budget challenges and crowd out other spending, notably on education, transportation, and other government priorities (NASBO 2022).

Growth in U.S. health care costs continues to outpace GDP growth and represents a significantly larger portion of U.S. spending and GDP as compared with other industrialized nations.

## Shifting Demographics: Patients and Workforce

Impending demographic shifts will significantly impact the demand for care, both the amount and type (i.e., acute vs. long term). How the U.S. health care system adapts to this shift in demand will be a challenge for providers and patients in the coming decades. For the next 20 years, about three million members of the baby boom generation will enter retirement age each year. The U.S. Census Bureau estimates that by 2029, 71 million Americans will be 65 or older, a 73% increase from 2011. This will result in a massive shift in insurance coverage from commercial plans to Medicare. The solvency of Medicare is already a highly charged political issue, and this will further aggravate an already financially strapped program.

The aging population will also impact the type of care delivered. Over a quarter of those over the age of 65 are living with multiple chronic conditions, and this number increased from 21.8% in 2001 to 27.2% in 2018 (Boersma et al. 2020). Providers and health care organizations must develop new models to effectively care for patients with chronic conditions, including coordinating services across the continuum of care and ensuring effective care transitions from one provider to another. Likewise, during that time, as the burden of illness has increased, so too has the complexity of treatment options as well as the rate of best practice revisions.

In addition to growth in demand for care, the demographic shift will also exacerbate existing staffing shortages. The past decade has witnessed staffing shortages and early retirements across nearly every aspect of health care, impacting physician, nursing, and direct care numbers. Further estimates suggest that by 2034, the shortfall of physicians in the workforce could be as large as 124,000 (AAMC 2021). Additionally, health care organizations must grapple with the consequences of management and leadership retiring at a faster rate than perhaps ever before.

## Transition to Value-Based Reimbursement

Historically, the U.S. health care system has been financed primarily through fee-for-service reimbursement. Hospitals and physicians were paid for the number of services, tests, and procedures provided, regardless of the value of those services. The fee-for-service reimbursement structure provides perverse incentives for care providers and is a key driver of the high, unsustainable cost of health care in the United States (The Miller Center 2014). To incentivize hospitals and clinicians to provide high-quality care, which may actually include fewer tests and procedures, the reimbursement structure must change to reward the desired behaviors. In an attempt to both contain costs and improve quality, private and public insurance programs alike are implementing "value-based payment," a methodology that rewards quality through incentives and transparency (Health Affairs Research Brief 2022).

Generally, payment reform initiatives, including bundled payments, value-based purchasing (VBP), pay-for-performance (P4P), capitation, and others, attempt to align incentives to provide care that is necessary, appropriate, timely, and cost-effective. Such initiatives have been underway for years, albeit in pilot or relatively small-scale efforts. The Affordable Care Act sought to accelerate the implementation of value-based payment programs through applying VBP to the Medicare and Medicaid reimbursement structure and through providing funding to support research in the private sector related to VBP (Kaiser Family Foundation 2013b). Given that one of every five dollars spent on health care within the United States is done through Medicare, CMS plays a key role in incentivizing high quality and value in care delivered. Thus, CMS announced the ambitious goal to have all participants of traditional Medicare in an accountable care relationship with a health care provider by 2030 (Health Affairs Forefront 2022). This coincides with goals set out in the CMS National Quality Strategy depicted in Figure 1.4. Many of these mirror strategies and competencies that are laid out in Figures 1.2 and 1.3 (Schreiber et al. 2022). In response, physician leaders should look into these strategies as they develop their respective approaches to improvement, as providers are called to find new ways to deliver high-quality care in a cost-efficient way.

| CMS National Quality Strategy Goals |
|---|
| **1. Embed Quality into the Care Journey:** Incorporate quality as a foundational component to delivering value as a part of the overall care journey. Quality includes ensuring optimal care and best outcomes for individuals of all ages and backgrounds as well as across service delivery systems and settings. Quality also extends across payer types. |
| **2. Advance Health Equity:** Address the disparities that underlie our health system, both within and across settings, to ensure equitable access and care for all. |
| **3. Promote Safety:** Prevent harm or death from health care errors. |
| **4. Foster Engagement:** Increase engagement between individuals and their care teams to improve quality, establish trusting relationships, and bring the voices of people and caregivers to the forefront. |
| **5. Strengthen Resilience:** Ensure resilience in the health care system to prepare for, and adapt to, future challenges and emergencies. |
| **6. Embrace the Digital Age:** Ensure timely, secure, seamless communication and care coordination between providers, plans, payers, community organizations, and individuals through interoperable, shared, and standardized digital data across the care continuum. |
| **7. Incentivize Innovation and Technology:** Accelerate innovation in care delivery and incorporate technology enhancements (e.g., telehealth, machine learning, advanced analytics, new care advances) to transform the quality of care and advance value. |
| **8. Increase Alignment:** Develop a coordinated approach to align performance metrics, programs, policy, and payment across CMS, federal partners, and external stakeholders to improve value. Strive to create a simplified national picture of quality measurement that is comprehensible to individuals, their families, providers, and payers. |

**Figure 1.4 CMS national quality strategy goals. (CMS. *CMS Quality Workgroup*, 2022; Schreiber et al. 2022.)**

The transition from volume to value is a key driver of rapid transformation. Those who do not transform quickly enough to produce value through more efficient care processes will no longer flourish. Value-based purchasing models aim to incent and reward safe, high-quality, patient-centered care. To reward such behavior, hospitals and payers must have systems that accurately measure and track such indicators. Successful value-based purchasing programs are contingent on identifying, tracking, and tying payment to those quality and patient satisfaction indicators that produce the most value for the health care system. As such, the ability to use data and measurement to drive decision-making will be a key competency for leaders in the transition from volume- to value-based payment.

## *Variable Quality Outcomes*

Despite spending significantly more on health care than any other industrialized nation, the U.S. health care system's quality outcomes lag behind those of many other industrialized counties. Some organizations and systems within the United States provide some of the highest quality care in the world. As a whole, however, compared to other Organization for Economic Cooperation and Development (OECD) countries, the quality of care in the United States is more highly variable and not notably superior to other far less-expensive systems. For example, the avoidable mortality rate, defined as deaths before age 75 from conditions that are either preventable through effective public health and primary prevention or treatable when detected, are higher in the United States than essentially every other OECD country. Where the United States has a rate of 272 per 100,000, essentially all others are under 200, with Spain at 144 (Radley et al. 2022). Additionally, the U.S. infant mortality rate has actually increased from 5.4 deaths per 1,000 live births in 2014 to 5.7 in 2019. This compares to the mean of all OECD countries at 4.2 per 1,000, and countries such as Italy with 2.4, Japan 1.9, and Iceland 1.1 per 1,000 (OECD 2021). Particularly, given the expense of the U.S. health care system, the underperformance on numerous quality indicators continues to be a challenge for providers and patients alike.

In addition to variation in quality, there is also great variation in the cost of care across the United States. Furthermore, this variation in cost frequently does not correlate with quality, generating concerns and questions around the efficiency and effectiveness of the system as a whole. Numerous studies have documented widespread and significant variations in the cost of care (Cooper et al. 2022). Similarly, there is a large body of literature documenting variation in treatments, procedures, and surgeries given a particular diagnosis (Song et al. 2022).

Identifying and explaining variation in cost and quality of care helps to identify irregularity and incompatibility as well as opportunities for innovation and improvement (Wheeler 2000).

Along with regional and small area variations in cost and quality, the United States also experiences significant disparities in care across racial, ethnic, and other demographic indicators. In 2002, the Institute of Medicine defined health care disparities as "racial or ethnic differences in the quality of health care that are not due to access-related factors or clinical needs, preferences and appropriateness of the intervention." Disparities in both health care and health outcomes are well documented. Examples include the following:

- The infant mortality rate for non-Hispanic black babies is greater than twice that of non-Hispanic white babies (10.8 vs. 4.6) (Ely & Driscoll 2020).
- Asian-American screening rates are lower compared with Americans overall for cervical cancer (75.4% vs. 83.0%), breast cancer (64.1% vs. 72.4%), and colorectal cancer (46.9% vs. 58.6%) (Lee et al. 2021).
- Lower household income is directly related to an increased risk in chronic conditions in children.
- Rural Americans are more likely to have chronic illnesses such as high blood pressure, heart disease, and diabetes, while simultaneously they have less access to health care services such as for mental health (Coughlin et al. 2019).

Not only is there a moral imperative to eliminate disparities, but there are also financial and efficiency incentives, as disparities impact the quality and cost of care as well. Racial and ethnic minorities are more likely to experience medical errors, adverse outcomes, longer lengths of stay, and readmission and are also less likely to receive evidence-based care for certain conditions (HRET 2013). An analysis by the Kaiser

Family Foundation suggests that 30% of direct medical costs for African-Americans, Hispanics, and Asian-Americans are excess costs due to health inequities (Kaiser 2023c). These disparities lead up to a 15-year difference in life expectancy between the most advantaged and disadvantaged citizens (Chetty et al. 2016). Identifying the causes of both variation and disparities in care and, more importantly, identifying solutions to address these inequities are keystones of twenty-first-century medicine. The very definitions of the delivery of quality, safety, and value in health care are now increasingly recognizing variables that encompass the social determinants of health and commitment to health equity.

## *Expansion of Coverage*

In 2010, President Obama signed the Affordable Care Act (ACA) into law, marking the largest expansion of health insurance coverage in the United States since the creation of Medicare and Medicaid in 1965. As a result, over the decade that followed the rate of uninsured within the U.S. population decreased from a high of 18.0% in 2013 to an all-time low of 8.8% by the end of 2021. The same time period saw very little change with regard to the number of covered lives with the private insurance market. This translates to an estimated 35 million Americans who gained coverage through expansions initiated by the Affordable Care Act, including 21 million people enrolled in Medicaid expansion coverage (Lee et al. 2022).

While the coverage expansions increase access to care for millions of Americans, this large influx of users presents challenges for the health care–delivery system. The United States is currently experiencing a shortage of primary care physicians, particularly for adults. Growing demand—including from aging baby boomers, insurance expansions, and increases in the number of individuals living with diabetes and obesity—will continue to accelerate the demand for primary care physicians (NRMP 2023). Traditionally, solutions to the primary care physician shortage have focused on educating more physicians. More recent policy recommendations focus on changing care-delivery models to empower other personnel to practice at the top of their licenses; enable non-licensed health personnel to function as patient navigators, panel managers, and health coaches to address preventive and chronic care needs; increase capacity for patient self-care and utilize technology to add capacity (Bodenheimer & Smith 2013). Regardless of the policy changes implemented, the imperative remains the same—adding 35 million more new lives to the current health care system will require significant transformation in the way care is delivered, coordinated, and financed.

In addition to the large influx of patients, the coverage expansions in the Affordable Care Act have had significant financial impact on the delivery system. As more individuals now have insurance, either through public or private exchange plans or through Medicaid, hospitals have witnessed their uncompensated care and need for charity care decrease (Karpman et al. 2021) Additionally, many of the newly insured have defined contribution plans, one form of which is a high deductible health plan. These plans require patients to pay for a greater percentage of their care up to a given deductible, which has shifted the cost burden to consumers. Compared with more traditional insurance, these plans require the delivery system to have a more active role in collecting copays and other payments from patients directly. Overall, the expansion of health insurance coverage has many financial impacts on the delivery system including new revenue streams, and thus far has had a positive impact on enhancing the delivery system.

## *Impact of the COVID-19 Pandemic*

The global health care system, as well as the global economy as a whole, was sizably disrupted by the impact of the 2020 COVID-19 viral pandemic and the subsequent response. Health systems were forced to rapidly alter traditional operations, while the health care workforce faced unprecedented challenges in the call to care for a new influx of patients. At the organizational level, these unexpected circumstances were compounded by supply chain disruption alongside staffing shortages due to early retirement and exodus from the profession by nurses, physicians, and workers at all levels. The financial implications of the COVID-19 pandemic were tremendous, and the American public faced some conflicting messaging that shed layers of distrust against the U.S. health care system. Ultimately, this period echoed all the greater need for systems and those leading health systems to be adaptive, responsive, and prepared for change. The health care ecosystem that has emerged for the decade of the 2020s is one that has been transformed by the pandemic. In spite of the noted detrimental impact, there are positives in terms of the witnessed acceleration of digital health infrastructure, promotion of the need for improvement within the realm of public health, and necessity for all health care organizations to face disruption and innovation.

## *Advances in Health Information Technology*

The United States made significant investment in the adoption and use of Health Information Technologies (HIT) with over $35 billion of support through the Health Information and Technology for Economic and Clinical Health Act (HITECH Act) in 2009. Prior to this, as recently as 2008, 34% of physicians' offices had adopted any Electronic Health Record (EHR), less than 2% of acute care hospitals had a comprehensive EHR, and only between 8% and 12% of all hospitals had even a basic EHR system (Jha et al. 2009). It is staggering to consider how far that digital gap has been improved over the past decade. By 2021, among all non-federal acute care hospitals, 96% have adopted an EHR, and office-based physicians had a 78% rate of having EHR capability (AHA 2022). Though EHR implementation has accelerated over the past decade, the touted benefits of HIT (e.g., cost-saving efficiencies, sophisticated analytics, and modeling capabilities) are in many instances still unrealized. Challenges remain concerning integrating new technology into existing workflows, data extraction for analysis and quality improvement, efficacy of technologies, and continued resistance to adoption. Technologies such as electronic prescribing, computerized decision support, computerized physician order entry, and health information exchanges hold potential to reduce inefficiencies and produce cost savings; however, leaders will continue to face challenges over the next decade in the advancement of these technologies.

In addition to these more traditional technologies, there are numerous disruptive technologies affecting the health care system as well. Telehealth, the use of electronic information and telecommunications technologies to support long-distance clinical care, is changing the way patients access care. Specifically, as telehealth becomes more effective and widespread, it is beginning to challenge the way health care is delivered in small and rural communities.

Another disruptive technology is the rise of mobile health and the opportunities for remote monitoring of a host of vital signs and patient activities. These enable consumers to track their diet, exercise, and sleep patterns and also their own biometrics and, in many cases, to self-diagnose and treat minor illnesses or injuries. The combination of rapid expansion of technology along with a movement toward greater consumer engagement in health care creates exciting opportunities in this space. As with any disruptive technology, there are risks and opportunities. Managing and capitalizing on the rise of mobile health technologies is an important role for clinical leaders in the twenty-first century.

### *Shift from Defined Benefit to Defined Contribution Health Plans*

Another factor that is having a significant impact on patients and their decisions to seek care is the shift in insurance from defined benefits to defined contribution health plans. This shift has been driven largely by the reforms implemented under the Affordable Care Act, specifically the public and private insurance exchanges. Across all health plans, however, as health care costs increase, insurers are finding new ways to design plans that shift costs to consumers. This shift to defined contribution plans has increased consumers' financial responsibility for care, thus making them more cost conscious. This in turn has driven the rise of consumerism and retail in health care. As consumers have more "skin in the game" financially, they are increasingly looking for the best value for what they pay. Faced with these new financial incentives, consumers are becoming more engaged in the process of seeking care and are driving the delivery system to demonstrate value.

## Action Steps and Strategies to Lead as a Physician Leader

The collective impact of these forces is rapidly driving the U.S. health care system to be financially unsustainable and increasingly difficult for patients and consumers to navigate. For the United States to continue to provide affordable and high-quality care, nothing short of complete transformation is required. Leadership will be required at all levels, but especially from physicians stepping into new leadership roles across the continuum of care. Here are six key competencies for physicians to serve as clinical leaders to successfully lead health care transformation:

1. **Effectively communicate the imperative for health care transformation and the steps to achieve change**. The forces driving transformation are many, varied, and complex. Leaders must be able to effectively communicate to staff, leadership, governance, and their communities the imperative for transformation. They must be effective in translating how national drivers have a local impact and how changes and decisions, often very difficult ones, relate to a larger context driving change. Effectively conveying the reason behind the need for change, forming a call to action for any involved from patients to team members, is the first step in engagement.
2. **Understand the relationship between cost and quality in practice and how to drive value**. The health care system of the future will be based on value—a combination of cost and quality. Clinical leaders must be proficient in measuring and managing costs and quality and understanding the relationship between the two to drive value. It is no longer an option for clinicians or patients to ignore costs. Costs must become a part of a larger conversation on how to create the most high-quality, value-driven health care system.
3. **Build, deploy, and lead improvement teams across all dimensions of care**. The ability to build teams and implement improvement cycles is a critical element of success. Physician leaders must be proficient in the systems and tools of quality improvement and create a culture of continuous improvement, safety, and

accountability. These physician leaders must also be able to teach those skills to others and build organizations focused around continuous improvement in all dimensions of care—quality, efficiency, and finance.

4. **Build and lead effective multidisciplinary teams**. Siloed care is a way of the past. The health care organization of the future will deliver care through multidisciplinary teams. Physician leaders must enable all clinical team members to practice at the top of their license and build a culture of transparency and open communication. Teams must be able to communicate effectively internally and with external organizations and partners, particularly about care transitions.
5. **Leverage data to improve clinical and organizational practice**. Health care is becoming a data-driven industry. Leaders must track and understand data related to quality, cost, efficiency, patient experience, and more. Effective physician leaders will use data to drive decision-making and to create a culture of transparency and continuous improvement.
6. **Realize the role of patient as consumer**. Delivery systems are increasingly recognizing the potential of patients and families as engaged and active participants in care. In addition to improving patient satisfaction and experience, patient- and family-engagement initiatives have been linked to high quality, lower cost, and improved outcomes in care. Beyond patient and family engagement in care delivery, however, physician leaders of the twenty-first century must be able to innovate new ways to capitalize on the transition of patients to consumers. As consumerism increases in health care and patients face more incentives and opportunities to engage in health behaviors or in seeking care, delivery systems have a role in optimizing those interactions in order to achieve the best outcomes.

## Conclusion

All leaders in the U.S. health care system face difficult challenges in the twenty-first century. Among these, physician leaders bring their expertise from clinical practice and direct patient care to seek improvement of delivery of care and advance organizational initiatives. The combination of the above-identified key forces results in the imperative to undertake no less than a complete transformation of the U.S. health care system. Likewise, this requires physician leaders that are not only prepared for transformation, but at the core have the tools and skill set to be transformational to the systems they lead. Health care facilities that collaborate across the continuum of care need strong and innovative leaders to develop and implement initiatives to control costs, improve quality, and transform the patient experience.

## Note

1 Comparison countries include Australia, Canada, Norway, the Netherlands, France, Germany, New Zealand, Sweden, Switzerland, and the United Kingdom.

## References

American Hospital Association. Committee on Performance Improvement. Jeanette Clough, Chairperson. Hospitals and Care Systems of the Future. Chicago: American Hospital Association. September 2011.

American Hospital Association (AHA). Annual Survey Information Technology Supplement, 2008–Present. National Center for Health Statistics (NCHS) National Ambulatory Care Survey (2008–2011) and National Electronic Health Record Survey (2012–present). 2022.

Association of American Medical Colleges. The Complexities of Physician Supply and Demand: Projections from 2019 to 2034. June 2021.

Barr, P. The Boomer Challenge. *Hospitals and Health Networks.* 2014;88(1):22–61.

Bodenheimer, T.S., Smith, Mark D. Primary Care: Proposed Solutions to the Physician Shortage without Training More Physicians. *Health Affairs.* 2013;32(11):1881–1886.

Boersma, P., Black, L.I., Ward, B.W. Prevalence of Multiple Chronic Conditions Among US Adults, 2018. *Preventing Chronic Disease.* 2020;17:200130.

Braveman, P.A., Kumanyika, S., Fielding, J., LaVeist, T., Borrell, L.N., Manderscheid, R., Troutman, A. Health Disparities and Health Equity: The Issue is Justice. *American Journal of Public Health.* 2011;101(S1):S149–S155.

Centers for Medicare and Medicaid Services. National Health Expenditure Projections 2021–2030: Forecast Summary. 2021. https://www.cms.gov/Research-Statistics-Data-and-Systems/Statistics-Trends-and-Reports/NationalHealthExpendData

Centers for Medicare and Medicaid Services. National Health Expenditure Projections 2021–2030: Forecast Summary. 2021. https://www.cms.gov/Research-Statistics-Data-and-Systems/Statistics-Trends-and-Reports/NationalHealthExpendData

Chetty, R., Stepner, M., Abraham, S., et al. The Association Between Income and Life Expectancy in the United States, 2001–2014. *JAMA.* 2016;315:1750–1766.

Claxton, G., Rae, M., Damico, A., Wager, E., Young, G., Whitmore, H. Health Benefits in 2022: Premiums Remain Steady, Many Employers Report Limited Provider Networks for Behavioral Health. *Health Affairs.* 2022;41(11):1670–1680.

Cooper, Z., Stiegman, O., Ndumele, C.D., Staiger, B., Skinner, J. Geographical Variation in Health Spending Across the US Among Privately Insured Individuals and Enrollees in Medicaid and Medicare. *JAMA Network Open.* 2022;5(7):e2222138.

Coughlin, S.S., Clary, C., Johnson, J.A., Berman, A., Heboyan, V., Benevides, T., Moore, J., George, V. Continuing Challenges in Rural Health in the United States. *Journal of Environmental Health Sciences.* 2019;5(2):90–92.

Davis, K., Stremikis, K., Squires, D., Schoen, C.. Mirror, Mirror on the Wall: How the Performance of the U.S. Health Care System Compares Internationally—2014 Update. The Commonwealth Fund. 2014.
Ely, D.M., Driscoll, A.K. Infant Mortality in the United States, 2018: Data from the Period Linked Birth/Infant Death File. National Vital Statistics Reports, vol. 69, no. 7. Hyattsville, MD: National Center for Health Statistics. 2020.
Hartman, M., Martin, B.M., Benson, J., Catlin, A. National Health Spending in 2011: Overall Growth Remains Low, but Some Payers and Services Show Signs of Acceleration. *Health Affairs*. 2013;32(1):87–99.
Health Affairs Forefront. The Medicare Value-Based Care Strategy: Alignment, Growth, and Equity. July 21, 2022.
Health Affairs Research Brief. Value-Based Payment as a Tool to Address Excess US Health Spending. December 1, 2022.
Health Research & Educational Trust. Rising above the Noise: Making the Case for Equity in Care. 2013. Accessed March 24, 2023. http://www.hpoe.org/Reports-HPOE/RisingAboveNoise_EOC_SlideDeck_Nov2013.pdf
Himmelstein, D.U., Thorne, D., Warren, E., Woolhandler, S. Medical Bankruptcy in the United States, 2007: Results of a National Study. *The American Journal of Medicine*. 2009;122(8): 741–746.
Jha, A.K., et al. Use of Electronic Health Records in U.S. Hospitals. *New England Journal of Medicine*. 2009;360:1628–1638.
Kaiser Family Foundation. Assessing the Effects of the Economy on the Recent Slowdown in Health Spending. 2013a. Accessed March 23, 2023. http://kff.org/health-costs/issue-brief/assessing-the-effects-of-the-economy-on-the-recent-slowdown-in-health-spending-2/
Kaiser Family Foundation. Summary of the Affordable Care Act. 2013b. Accessed March 24, 2023. http://kff.org/health-reform/fact-sheet/summary-of-the-affordable-care-act/
Kaiser Family Foundation and Health Research and Educational Trust. Employer Health Benefits: 2013 Summary of Findings. 2013c. Accessed June 16, 2023. https://www.kff.org/report-section/2013-summary-of-findings/
Kaiser Family Foundation. Disparities in Health and Health Care: Five Key Questions and Answers. 2023a. https://www.kff.org/

racial-equity-and-health-policy/issue-brief/disparities-in-health-and-health-care-5-key-question-and-answers/

Kaiser Family Foundation. The Facts on Medicare Spending and Financing. 2023b. Accessed March 23, 2023. http://kff.org/medicare/fact-sheet/medicare-spending-and-financing-fact-sheet/

Kaiser Family Foundation. Disparities in Health and Health Care: 5 Key Questions and Answers. 2023c. Accessed June 16, 2023. https://www.kff.org/racial-equity-and-health-policy/issue-brief/disparities-in-health-and-health-care-5-key-question-and-answers/

Karpman, M., Coughlin, T.A., Garfield, R. Declines in Uncompensated Care Costs for the Uninsured Under the ACA and Implications of Recent Growth in the Uninsured Rate. Kaiser Family Foundation. 2021. Accessed January 14, 2023. https://www.kff.org/medicaid/report/the-effects-of-medicaid-expansion-under-the-aca-updated-findings-from-a-literature-review/

Kellermann, A.L., Spencer S.J. What Will It Take to Achieve the As-Yet-Unfulfilled Promises of Health Information Technology. *Health Affairs*. 2013;32(1): 63–68.

Lee, A., Chu, R.C., Peters, C., Sommers, B.D. Health Coverage Changes Under the Affordable Care Act: End of 2021 Update. (Issue Brief No. HP-2022-17). Office of the Assistant Secretary for Planning and Evaluation, U.S. Department of Health and Human Services. April 2022.

Lee, R.J., Madan R.A., Kim, J., Posadas, E.M., Yu, E.Y. Disparities in Cancer Care and the Asian American Population. *The Oncologist*. 2021;26(6):453–460.

Miller, D.C., Gust, C., Dimick, J.B., Birkmeyer, N., Skinner, J., Birkmeyer, J.D. Large Variations in Medicare Payments for Surgery Highlight Savings Potential from Bundled Payment Programs. *Health Affairs*. 2011;30(11): 2107–2115.

OECD. *Health at a Glance 2021: OECD Indicators*, OECD Publishing, Paris, 2021.

Radley, D.C., Williams, R.D., Gunja M.Z., Baumgartner, J.C., Gumas E.D. Americans, No Matter the State They Live In, Die Younger Than People in Many Other Countries. To the Point (blog), Commonwealth Fund, Aug. 11, 2022.

Reschovsky, J.D., Ghosh, A., Stewart, K.A., Chollet, D.J. Durable Medical Requirement and Home Health among the Largest Contributors to Area Variations in Use of Medicare Services. *Health Affairs*. 2012;31(5): 956–964.

Schneider, E.C., Doty, M.M., Fields, K., *Mirror, Mirror 2021 — Reflecting Poorly: Health Care in the U.S. Compared to Other High-Income Countries*. Commonwealth Fund, August 2021. Schneider_Mirror_Mirror_2021.pdf (commonwealthfund.org)

Schreiber, M., Richards, A.C., Moody-Williams, J. The CMS National Quality Strategy: A Person-Centered Approach to Improving Quality. *CMS Blog*, June 6, 2022.

Song, Z., Kannan, S., Gambrel, R.J., et al. Physician Practice Pattern Variations in Common Clinical Scenarios Within 5 US Metropolitan Areas. *JAMA Health Forum*. 2022;3(1):e214698.

The Match, National Resident Matching Program (NRMP). 2023. http://www.nrmp.org/

The Miller Center. Cracking the Code on Health Care Costs: A Report by the State Health Care Cost Containment Commission. University of Virginia, 2014.

The National Association of State Budget Officers. Summary: NASBO State Expenditure Report. 2022. Accessed March 23, 2024. https://higherlogicdownload.s3.amazonaws.com/NASBO/9d2d2db1-c943-4f1b-b750-0fca152d64c2/UploadedImages/SER%20Archive/2022_State_Expenditure_Report_-_S.pdf

Ward, B.W., Schiller, J.S. Prevalence of Multiple Chronic Conditions among U.S. Adults: Estimates from the National Health Interview Survey, 2010. *Preventing Chronic Disease*. 2013;10:120203.

Wheeler, D.J. *Understanding Variation. The Key to Managing Chaos*. SPC Press, Knoxville, TN, 2000.

# Chapter 2

# Effectively Implementing Quality and Safety Improvement

## The Evidence

### *The Model for Improvement*

The Model for Improvement, developed by the Associates in Process Improvement, is perhaps the most basic and accessible framework for conducting improvement cycles. This model can be applied both horizontally and vertically throughout the organization and to nearly all improvement opportunities, from efforts to streamline workflows to initiatives to reduce surgical site infections to projects to reduce the number of no-show patients. It introduces three fundamental questions to be addressed by the improvement team: (1) What are we trying to accomplish? (2) How will we know that a change is an improvement? (3) What change can we make

DOI: 10.4324/9781003402831-2

that will result in improvement? These questions guide teams to establish measurable and time-specific aims for the project, define the patient population that will be impacted, and establish quantitative measures to monitor progress, and implement evidence-based change concepts (IHI 2014a). Once a team has identified answers to these guiding questions, the next step is to implement the Plan–Do–Study–Act (PDSA) cycles to test changes and watch for improvement.

Developed by Walter A. Shewhart in the 1920s, PDSA is a framework for planning and executing performance improvement efforts. PDSA provides the structure for most formally recognized performance improvement models, including Lean and Six Sigma. The PDSA cycle includes the steps listed in Figure 2.1 (Warren 2014).

The first step in any performance improvement project is to develop the aim statement or goal using the three questions in the Model for Improvement. Next, the project lead must recruit participants to join the improvement team (see Chapter 8 for more detail). Given the project's aim, the team then plans a change, observes the results, and acts upon what is learned, conducting a PDSA cycle or a small test of change (IHI 2014c). A project may require multiple PDSA cycles to arrive at an effective and sustainable improvement to the system. Once a successful intervention is established, it should be spread across the organization to increase efficiency and effectiveness on a larger scale (IHI 2014a).

PDSA is a very accessible tool for improvement teams at all levels of the organization. Teams or individuals can implement improvement cycles with or without a formal team charter. Organizations that support a culture of continuous improvement should also support PDSA cycles throughout the organization to improve processes and workflow in an ongoing basis.

| Plan–Do–Study–Act |
|---|
| **Plan** |
| ✓ Establish a goal. |
| ✓ Ask specific questions and develop hypotheses or predictions. |
| ✓ Plan the logistics of the cycle: what steps will be performed, who will be performing the functions, the timeline of implementation, deadline for completion, and location of the work. |
| **Do** |
| ✓ Train and educate staff. |
| ✓ Carry out the plan, preferably by starting out with a pilot or small-scale version. |
| ✓ During implementation, document unexpected observations/results and problems. |
| ✓ Initiate data analysis. |
| **Study/Check** |
| ✓ Assess and measure the effects of the intervention. |
| ✓ Compare the results of the process changes with your hypotheses/predictions. |
| ✓ Determine the level of achieved success as compared to the goal or objective. |
| ✓ Summarize lessons learned. |
| ✓ Determine what modifications need to be made to improve the process and determine next steps. |
| **Act** |
| ✓ Act on lessons learned. |
| ✓ Determine whether the plan can continue with modifications or if a new plan should be developed. |
| ✓ Make changes if needed. |
| ✓ Identify missing components in the process. |
| ✓ Carry out iterative PDSA cycles until the goal or objective is achieved. |

**Figure 2.1 Plan–Do–Study–Act. (Warren, K. Quality Improvement: Foundation, Processes, Tools, and Knowledge Transfer Techniques. In *The Healthcare Quality Book: Vision, Strategy, and Tools*, ed. Maulik S. Joshi et al., Leading Health Care Transformation, Health Administration Press, Chicago, IL, 2014, 83–107.)**

## Lean

Taiichi Ohno, cofounder of the Toyota Production System (TPS), originally developed Lean thinking as an improvement methodology applied to manufacturing (Graban 2011). The Lean Enterprise Institute offers the definition: "Lean is a set of concepts, principles and tools used to create and deliver the most value from the customers' perspectives while consuming the fewest resources and fully utilizing the knowledge and skills of the people performing the work" (Graban 2011). After extensive study of the TPS, it has been distilled into four essential principles, three of which describe work design and one describes the learning process for improvement:

1. **The content, sequence, time frame, and expected outcome of all work will be highly specified**. The more specified each step in a task is, the easier it is to identify discrepancies between the guidelines and actual behaviors. This enables a prompt response for problem-solving, by the worker and supervisor, through either process modification or additional worker training.
2. **Every customer–supplier connection must be standardized and direct by having an unambiguous yes-or-no way to send requests and receive responses**. This connection explicitly specifies which people are involved, what goods or services will be provided, the customer's request, and the expected time frame. By assigning direct connections between people, assistance and troubleshooting can be efficiently provided. Furthermore, accountability is strengthened when each person has a specific responsibility to another person.
3. **The pathway for every product and service must be simple and direct**. Contrary to the conventional method of sending the product or service to the next available person, this pathway requires that it is sent to a specific

person. If that person is not available, he or she will have a designated person to take his or her place, and so forth. This pathway also applies to workers' requests for help. This rule effectively tests the hypothesis that every worker in the pathway is needed, and any worker not in the pathway is not needed.

4. **Testing changes to create improvement must be made within the framework of the scientific method, under the guidance of a teacher, and at the lowest possible organization level**. This rule emphasizes that *how* changes are made is as important as what changes are made. It is not enough to be complacent with an observed improvement when it is made with seemingly random changes. Rather, the scientific method of testing a hypothesis—that is, a proposed change leading to an expected outcome—will explicitly identify the gap between the actual and expected outcome, if there is one. This, in turn, enables workers to make further modifications to their work processes, while deeply questioning assumptions about their work, until they get closer and closer to the expected outcome.

Although the above four principles emphasize rigidly structured steps, the underpinning of TPS is a flexible, highly experimentalist system that promotes learning and problem-solving at every level of the organization. This system has shown to be especially effective within an organization that has a nested, modular structure. This means that supervisors can enable workers to make design changes in one section of the organization without disrupting other sections. This is because each organizational section's ability to respond uniquely to its own problems remains intact. Therefore, different approaches to problem-solving in distinct sections can concurrently function within one umbrella organization (Spear and Bowen 1999).

The goal of applying this system's four essential principles is to reach an organizational ideal. This ideal explicitly constitutes that the product or service is defect free, can be supplied on demand in the requested version, delivered immediately, and produced without any unnecessary materials, labor, or other resources, and is produced in a safe work environment (Spear and Bowen 1999).

Due to the unprecedented effectiveness and success of the TPS, it has been applied to numerous other companies and industries, such as consumer products, aerospace, and health care, and evolved into the Lean framework.

When applying this framework to health care, the primary question to ask is: How can the health care system deliver the most value to patients and maximize the use of providers' skills and knowledge, all while using the least amount of needed resources? Lean is comprised of a tool set, a management system, a method for continuous improvement, and a philosophy of employee engagement. Lean tools and methods include A3 problem-solving, *kanban*, 5S, *kaizen*, error proofing, and visual management (Figure 2.2) (Graban 2011).

However, it is not sufficient to use a single tool or even a combination of tools to achieve the full benefits of Lean. The four principles described above form the backbone of the Lean system and require a substantial investment of time and effort. A common pitfall or shortcut among leaders is to mistake Lean tools as the Lean system itself (Spear and Bowen 1999). A physician leader must implement tools that specifically address the unique problems and needs of the health care organization. Furthermore, these tools must be implemented with the appropriate leadership and management mindset, one that guides employees toward understanding why improvement is needed and how Lean methods provide a path toward improvement (Graban 2011).

Lean works to create a shift from the top-down authoritative model, in which leaders issue commands to workers, to

| Lean Tool | Definition |
|---|---|
| A3 Report | A piece of paper, typically 11 x 17 inches, that standardizes and simplifies Follow-up and follows the PDCA cycle. The report is generally structured by: 1) Background, 2) Current Situation and Problem, 3) Goal, 4) Root Cause Analysis, 5) Action Items/ Implementation Plan, 6) Results, and 7) Follow Up. |
| Kanban | Japanese term meaning "signal," a method for managing inventory. |
| 5S | Method for organizing workplaces to reduce waste time and motion for employees, making problems more readily apparent. |
| Kaizen | Japanese term meaning "continuous improvement," focused on workplace improvement by employees. |
| Error Proofing | Method for designing or improving processes so errors are less likely to occur. |
| Visual Management | Method for making problems visible, providing for fast response and problem solving. |

**Figure 2.2 Lean tools. (Graban, Mark. Overview of Lean for Hospitals. In *Lean Hospitals: Improving Quality, Patient Safety, and Employee Satisfaction*, CRC Press, Boca Raton, Florida, 2011, 17–29.)**

one that has leaders actively listening to and asking for employees' opinions, engaging them in solving problems, and training them to drive improvement in their departments (Graban 2011).

In addition to the tools listed previously, Lean efforts focus on reducing waste, or *muda*, from care delivery or employees' workloads in order to improve efficiency. From the patient's perspective, waste encompasses activities that do not advance diagnosis, treatment, or discharge and includes unnecessary testing, waiting time, transportation, overproduction, and harmful medical errors (Graban 2011).

Lean thinking reinforces the idea that leaders should form a partnership with employees and nurture the intrinsic motivation to engage in continuous improvement. Employee engagement is maintained, in part, by ensuring that they are not subject to overwork (*muri*) and uneven workloads (*mura*) so as to avoid frustration and burnout. Therefore, a key difference between the Lean approach and traditional methods of increasing efficiency (e.g., cost cutting through budget reduction, layoffs) is that Lean improvement efforts must always strike a balance between efficiency and eliminating waste, while also respecting and engaging employees (Graban 2011).

## *Six Sigma*

Six Sigma, which denotes 3.4 defects per million, is a system to reduce variation and eliminate defects in key business processes by using statistical tools to analyze process flow and fluctuation. Six Sigma enables managers to predict outcomes of future processes and use statistical tools to understand the elements that influence those projections. The five steps of Six Sigma are outlined in Figure 2.3 (Warren 2014).

| Six Sigma DMAIC Model | |
|---|---|
| Define | Identify customers and specific key processes and characteristics that are important to them, their problems, current process elements, and associated output conditions. |
| Measure | Measure and collect data on key characteristics that influence processes. This is the most time-consuming step in the DMAIC model. |
| Analyze | Use statistical tools to analyze the collected data in order to analyze the variation in the process and how to minimize it. This analysis can also identify the root causes of defects or problems and whether the problem is a random event. |
| Improve | If the problem is not a random event, identify and test possible solutions to observe whether the changes are beneficial and how they affect other variables. Refine or select new changes as judged necessary. |
| Control | Control planning is required for sustained improvement. Quality control data must be collected in order to monitor processes and verify measurements regularly. This ensures that processes continue to run efficiently with no unexpected changes. |

**Figure 2.3 Six sigma: DMAIC. (Warren, K. Quality Improvement: Foundation, Processes, Tools, and Knowledge Transfer Techniques. In *The Healthcare Quality Book: Vision, Strategy, and Tools*, ed. Maulik S. Joshi et al., Chicago, IL: Health Administration Press, 2014, 83–107.)**

Similar to Lean, Six Sigma is commonly utilized by hospitals to improve operational efficiency related to patient safety and quality of care. Examples include initiatives to reduce variance of length of stay within a hospital, reduce wait times for appointments within a transplant center, and eliminate health care–associated infections (iSixSigma Magazine 2010). Lean and Six Sigma share similar concepts, allowing them to be blended in order to best address a hospital's mission to provide value for the customer—their patients. Individual training and certification are available for Six Sigma, including designations for yellow belt, green belt, and black belt.

## *International Standards Organization 9001*

The ISO 9001 is a set of quality management criteria that has been implemented in organizations in over 170 countries and can readily be applied to health care organizations (International Standards Organization). Its core components focus on controlled key functions, processes, and protocols as well as audits and measurements of key functions. The ISO 9001 standards, originally published in 1987, were most recently updated in 2015 and are comprised of the following seven principles and recommended actions (ISO Central Secretariat 2015):

1. **Customer focus**. Research and understand current and future customer needs and strive to exceed expectations. Ensure that organizational goals are linked to them. Measure customer satisfaction and use results to modify processes as necessary. Communicate customer needs and expectations throughout the organization. Every aspect of customer interaction provides an opportunity to create more value for the customer.

2. **Leadership**. Leaders provide unity of purpose and organizational direction. Establish conditions in which people are engaged in achieving the organization's quality objectives. Create and sustain shared values, fairness, and ethical models for behavior at all levels of the organization.
3. **Engagement of people**. People, at all levels of the organization, should understand the importance and contribution of their roles. Recognition, empowerment, and enhancement of competence facilitate the engagement of people in achieving the organization's quality objectives. They should be equipped to evaluate their performance against personal goals, empowered to accept ownership of problems and constraints in performance, as well as seek opportunities to improve their competence and knowledge. This is facilitated by the open discussion of problems and sharing of knowledge.
4. **Process approach**. Systematically define necessary activities for the desired outcome. Consistent and predictable results are achieved more effectively and efficiently when activities are understood and managed as interrelated processes that function as a coherent system. Establish authority, responsibility, and accountability for managing processes.
5. **Improvement**. It is essential for an organization to have ongoing focus on improvement in order to maintain current levels of performance, react to changes in internal and external conditions, and to create new opportunities. Promote establishment of improvement objectives at all levels of the organization. Track, review, and audit the planning, implementation, completion, and results of projects.
6. **Evidence-based decision-making**. Decisions based on the analysis and evaluation of data and information are more likely to produce desired results. Determine,

measure, and monitor key indicators to demonstrate the organization's performance. Understand cause-and-effect relationships and potential unintended consequences. Make decisions and take actions based on evidence, balanced with experience and intuition.

7. **Relationship management**. Determine relationships and prioritize management of interested parties including suppliers, partners, customers, employees, and society as a whole. Establish relationships that balance short-term goals with long-term considerations.

By achieving the ISO 9001 Standards, health care organizations can improve customer satisfaction, employee engagement and accountability, consistency and predictability of results, and their ability to review and challenge decisions. Furthermore, processes will become more efficient and better aligned with organizational strategic objectives, while allowing for flexibility and high responsiveness (Levine and Toffel 2008). ISO 9001 certification is increasingly being offered by accreditation bodies such as the Joint Commission, Det Norse Veritas (DNV) Healthcare, which is also known as National Integrated Accreditation for Healthcare Organizations (NIAHO) and Healthcare Facilities Accreditation Program (HFAP) (Lazarus and Chapman 2013).

## Case Study: Enhancing Vaccine Access

The following case study provides an example of an organization that identified an opportunity and need for improvement, built an improvement team, and executed improvement cycles to achieve the aim.

Jay W. Lee, MD, MPH, is chief medical officer at Share Our Selves Community Health Center in Orange County, California, serving 16,000 vulnerable patients in the sixth largest county in the United States. The health center is nationally recognized for providing quality, comprehensive safety net services and is one of 300 health centers in the nation to be designated a Healthcare for the Homeless provider. Their mission is to provide care and assistance to those in need and act as advocates for systemic change.

In early 2021, when COVID-19 vaccines became available, Dr. Lee and his team observed that there was inequitable distribution of vaccines in their immediate county. Initial access to vaccines was only provided to those that had access to technology to register and set up an appointment. Advocating to expand this, the collection of community health centers were all granted access to county supplies and they rapidly developed a model to distribute via large-scale community-based events in key zip codes. Dr. Lee and his team began by designing workflow for registration, screening for eligibility and potential side effects, administration, and post-vaccine monitoring. Given that clinics were set up in locations targeting disenfranchised populations, they were often held at centers such as local schools, and frequently over relatively short periods of time, such as four to six hours.

A leadership team was constructed to oversee vaccine distribution and drive improvement. To evaluate their processes, Dr. Lee and his team deployed rapid cycle quality improvement with PDSA interventions. The measurements for the initial cycle time were slower than expected, so observers were positioned at each key area to monitor processes and identify bottlenecks, in other words to seek opportunity for improvement. During distribution events, the leadership team huddled every hour to assess metrics including the volume of vaccines distributed and time studies for each area. They used these huddles to review data in real time and to continue PDSA interventions that were working and alter those that were not effective. As a result, cycle time was cut in half and vaccine distribution throughput increased to nearly

200 immunizations per hour. These were vaccines that otherwise would not have reached the hardest-hit zip codes in Orange County at a time when there was tremendous opportunity given the higher levels of vaccine acceptance in the communities served.

## Lessons Learned

Over the past few decades, emphasis on quality improvement has taken many forms. For many, this has led to a feeling that the industry jumps from one fad to another, never seeming to stick to one philosophy or method to drive improvement. Clinical leaders can glean many lessons from the experiences of the past implementation cycles in order to move forward with a more comprehensive, sustainable approach to improvement.

**Form follows function**. There are many frameworks, systems, and tools to guide quality improvement efforts, as noted previously. A physician leader's role is to lead the improvement team to define goals and objectives before selecting the system and tools to use. There is no "one size fits all" approach; improvement teams should abide by the philosophy "form follows function" in selecting a system and tools for improvement (Warren 2014).

**Knowledge transfer and spread**. Once an intervention proves successful at a unit or a department level, organizations should have systems in place to scale and spread the success across the organization. Without systems to effectively transfer insights and knowledge, organizations will experience stagnation, waste, inconsistent performance, and missed opportunities to improve performance (Warren 2014). The Institute for Healthcare Improvement's "A Framework for Spread: From Local Improvements to System-Wide Change" describes the spread of innovation as a "key factor in closing the gap between *best* practice and *common* practice" and identifies the following four questions to address when planning to spread an improvement (Massoud et al. 2006):

- How are decisions about the adoption of improvements made?
- What infrastructure enhancements will assist in achieving the spread aim?
- What transition issues need to be addressed?
- How will the spread of practices be transitioned to operational responsibilities?

The Health Research and Educational Trust, an affiliate of the American Hospital Association, has developed a spread assessment tool to identify how readily an initiative will achieve widespread adoption. The tool ranks initiatives across four factors: Environmental, innovation, target audience, and organizational, and produces a readiness score that helps predict initiatives that hold the most promise for widescale adoption (HRET 2010). Chapter 9 provides additional tools and information on spreading improvement.

**Create a culture of safety**. Patient safety should be the number one priority and the core of the patient experience. Work processes, culture, and teams must be redesigned in order to cultivate a nonpunitive environment in which employees are able to identify and report near misses or errors without fear of punishment. This may require new team communication methods, systems for reporting errors, and safer care processes. Without a culture of safety, it will be difficult to initiate, execute, and sustain improvements.

**Process design—human factors and high reliability**. Due to the complex nature of the U.S. health care system, improvement work cannot simply focus on staff "working harder." Nearly 80% of medical errors are attributed to system design, not individual incompetence. Therefore, improvement work should focus on redesigning processes and systems, through the methods identified previously, to make it easier for employees to "do the right thing" and harder for them to do the wrong thing. This can be achieved by human factors engineering, the design of facilities, and utilizing equipment and processes that promote safety and safeguard against human fallibility. Examples of human factors design include understanding human limitations and designing jobs with those in mind (e.g., avoiding reliance on memory by providing reminders), using constraints, forcing functions, user-centered design strategies, and simplifying and standardizing procedures when applicable.

**Engage leadership, frontline staff, patients, and families**. Leadership provides system-level expectations for improved quality and patient safety. However, a strategy's ultimate success is measured by how effectively it is executed. Excellent strategies often fail due to failure by senior leadership to entrust employees with authority and duty to make day-to-day decisions. As leaders guide direct actions, employees should feel empowered to actively drive those actions.

Patients and families are also powerful drivers of improvement. Patients and families should be engaged at the bedside as partners in care through strategies such as increased patient education and shared decision-making. Additionally, patients and families can contribute to quality and patient safety improvement initiatives by serving in advisory roles, participating in a patient/family advisory council, or sharing their experiences at board meetings to promote the importance of quality and safety.

**Rewards and recognition—celebrate the wins**. Establishing a culture of safety will take time before the aims are realized and many improvement initiatives are burdensome, disruptive, and time-consuming. Therefore, it is important to acknowledge the efforts of employees and how they contribute to the overall transformation of the organization.

Recognizing and rewarding short-term wins, including by feedback and recognition from leadership, is essential in sustaining a high level of urgency, momentum, and optimism among staff.

## Action Steps and Strategies to Lead

As a physician leader, you will need to lead improvement efforts, support and advise improvement teams, and foster the culture necessary to engender continuous improvement. Here are six action steps to lead:

1. **Become proficient in at least one improvement methodology**. As described previously, there are many methods, systems, and tools for quality improvement. Many organizations make significant investments in Lean or Six Sigma certification and have adopted an organization-wide improvement methodology. If your organization has a designated methodology, become proficient in that method. If not, lead your unit, department, or organization to adopt a methodology to promote continuous improvement.
2. **Create a culture of safety**. Begin by objectively assessing the current climate to identify opportunities for improvement. There are many surveys available to identify and address specific challenges, including the Agency for Healthcare Research and Quality's Patient Safety Culture Survey and the Safety Attitudes Questionnaire. As a leader, you contribute to creating a culture of safety through promoting transparency, accountability, and open communication. One example is encouraging employees to identify when mistakes and near misses occur.

3. **Become data driven**. Improvement opportunities should be identified based on data that show there is a gap related to quality or patient safety. Improvement projects should be developed and executed with a specific, data-driven aim in mind. Measurement and reporting are crucial components to demonstrating the value of an intervention, engaging employees, and facilitating spread. Whenever possible, leadership should present data as evidence to support their decisions.
4. **Empower frontline staff to lead**. Frontline employees, including nurses, physicians, physician therapists, and pharmacists, are well equipped to implement changes and sustain improvement as they are most familiar with the local environment and can identify problems in their daily work. Frontline employees who are engaged in the change process are more likely to take ownership over it, require less oversight, achieve greater success, and sustain any improvements. In order to effectively empower frontline staff to become involved in the change process, middle managers can model the way, inspire a shared vision, challenge current processes, encourage the heart, and enable staff to act.
5. **Provide resources to support improvement work**. As a physician leader, you provide the resources—financial, human, and time—that are necessary to support improvement projects. This can include funding for new materials or tools, allocating non-patient care time for improvement work meetings, and advocating on behalf of the teams in senior leadership meetings.
6. **Lead by example**. As a physician leader, you will be engaged in many projects and teams. You can teach and empower your employees to conduct improvement projects by demonstrating how to lead a quality improvement project. Likewise, by bringing your experience and

clinical background, you can demonstrate that the improvement can occur at all levels of the organization and across all settings. By modeling these skills and behaviors, you will encourage and empower others in the organization to improve quality and safety.

## References

A3 Thinking. 2008. Accessed January 15, 2023. http://a3thinking.com/faq.html

Berwick, D.M., Hackbarth, A.D. Eliminating Waste in U.S. Health Care. *JAMA*. 2012;307(14):1513–1516.

Blumenthal, D. Performance Improvement in Health Care—Seizing the Moment. *New England Journal of Medicine*. 2012;366(21):1953–1955.

Collins, J.C. *Good to Great: Why Some Companies Make the Leap. And Others Don't.* Random House, New York, 2001.

Gliner, M., Dorris, J., Aiyelawo, K., Morris, E., Hurdle-Rabb, D., Frazier, C. Patient Falls, Nurse Communication, and Nurse Hourly Rounding in Acute Care: Linking Patient Experience and Outcomes. *Journal of Public Health Management and Practice*. 2022;28(2):E467–E470.

Graban, M. Overview of Lean for Hospitals. In *Lean Hospitals: Improving Quality, Patient Safety, and Employee Satisfaction*, CRC Press, Boca Raton, FL, 2011, 17–29.

Griffin, F.A. Patient Safety and Medical Errors. In *The Healthcare Quality Book: Vision, Strategy, and Tools*, ed. Maulik S. Joshi et al. (3rd Ed). Health Administration Press, Chicago, IL, 2014, 269.

Health Research & Educational Trust. HRET Spread Assessment Tool. 2010. Accessed March 23, 2023. http://www.hret.org/dissemination/projects/hret_spread_assessment_tool.shtml

American Hospital Association. American Hospital Association and Health Research & Educational Trust. 2014.

Institute for Healthcare Improvement. Science of Improvement: How to Improve. 2014a. Accessed January 15, 2023. https://www.ihi.org/resources/Pages/HowtoImprove/ScienceofImprovementHowtoImprove.aspx

Institute for Healthcare Improvement. Science of Improvement: Selecting Changes. 2014b. Accessed January 15, 2023. https://www.ihi.org/resources/Pages/HowtoImprove/ScienceofImprovementSelectingChanges.aspx

Institute for Healthcare Improvement. Science of Improvement: Testing Changes. 2014c. Accessed January 15, 2023. https://www.ihi.org/resources/Pages/HowtoImprove/ScienceofImprovementTestingChanges.aspx

International Standards Organization. ISO 9000–Quality Management 2023. Accessed January 15, 2023. https://www.iso.org/iso-9001-quality-management.html

iSixSigma Magazine. Healing Healthcare. January/February 2010. Accessed March 23, 2023. http://www.isixsigma.com/industries/healthcare/5-tips-applying-six-sigma-three-top-hospitals/

ISO Central Secretariat. 2015. Accessed March 23, 2023. https://www.iso.org/files/live/sites/isoorg/files/store/en/PUB100080.pdf

Lazarus, I.R., Chapman, M.W. ISO-Style Healthcare: Designed to Keep Patients, Practitioners and Management Safe. *Becker's Hospital Review*. 2013. Accessed January 15, 2023. https://www.beckershospitalreview.com/hospital-management-administration/iso-style-healthcare-designed-to-keep-patients-practitioners-and-management-safe.html

Levine, D., Toffel, M.W., Quality Management and Job Quality: How the ISO 9001 Standard for Quality Management System Affects Employees and Employers. *Management Science*. 2008;56(6):978–996.

Massoud, M.R., Nielsen,G., Nolan, K., Schall, M.W., Sevin, C.A. *Framework for Spread: From Local Improvements to System-Wide Change*. IHI Innovation Series white paper. Institute for Healthcare Improvement, Cambridge, MA, 2006. Accessed January 15, 2023. https://www.ihi.org/resources/Pages/IHIWhitePapers/AFrameworkforSpreadWhitePaper.aspx

Ransom, S.B., Ransom, E.R. Implementing Quality as the Core Organizational Strategy. In *The Healthcare Quality Book: Vision, Strategy, and Tools*, ed. Maulik S. Joshi et al. (3rd Ed). Health Administration Press, Chicago, IL, 2014, 393.

Six Sigma Online: Aveta Business Institute. The DMAIC Model in Six Sigma. 2018. Accessed March 23, 2023. https://www.sixsigmaonline.org/wp-content/uploads/2018/06/SSO-Book-Complete-SS-BB.pdf

Spear, S., Bowen, H.K. Decoding the DNA of the Toyota Production System. *Harvard Business Review*. 1999;77(5):96–106.

Toussaint, J.S., Leonard, L.B. The Promise of Lean in Health Care. *Mayo Clinic Proceedings*. 2013;88(1): 74–82.

Warren, K. Quality Improvement: Foundation, Processes, Tools, and Knowledge Transfer Techniques. In *The Healthcare Quality Book: Vision, Strategy, and Tools*, ed. Maulik S. Joshi et al. (3rd Ed). Health Administration Press, Chicago, IL, 2014, 83–107.

# Chapter 3

# Building a Culture of Safety

## The Evidence

Schein defines culture as "a pattern of shared basic assumptions…which has worked well enough to be considered valid and therefore to be taught to new members as the correct way to perceive, think and feel" (Schein 2010). Culture often manifests by the behaviors of the organization's members, especially leadership. Culture is also understood through unspoken norms and dynamics such as commonly held values and norms. Often, these representations are in fact the more powerful elements of an organization's culture.

The importance of culture is aptly summarized in a quote attributed to management guru Peter Drucker: "Culture eats strategy for lunch." In other words, strategy and the accompanying tactics, work plans, and projects will never succeed in an organization with an incompatible culture. To translate to health care, all of the improvement work with frontline caregivers and providers, such as checklists, decision alerts, and care process redesign, will never succeed in an

DOI: 10.4324/9781003402831-3

organization with a culture that does not value safety, reliable system design, and a nonpunitive response to human error.

This notion of a nonpunitive response to error is considered a foundational element for a culture of safety. Dr. Lucian Leape, regarded as one of the founders of the modern patient safety movement, has stated, "The single greatest impediment to error prevention in medicine is that we punish people for making mistakes." The Institute of Medicine expounds on this concept in the report *Crossing the Quality Chasm*:

> The biggest challenge to moving toward a safer health system is changing the culture from one of blaming individuals for errors to one in which errors are treated not as personal failure, but as opportunities to improve the system and prevent harm.

Both quotes allude to the historical environment in health care organizations where the response to a safety event is to blame specific individuals for the occurrence of the event. Often this blame is accompanied by disciplinary action, punishment, or even termination.

In the short term, this may seem like an effective approach to punish "bad apples" and prevent an event from reoccurring. In reality, this approach is ultimately both unsatisfying and unhelpful. A model of blame and punishment fails to include an examination of the underlying system issues that contributed to an event. As a result, it is a poor prevention strategy. This model also fails to recognize the inherent fallibility of people and that perfection in human performance is an unrealistic expectation. In the absence of a perfectly designed system, human error is a realistic and common occurrence (Marx 2009).

This "names and blames" approach is contrasted with another extreme: No personal accountability for the occurrence of a safety event. Similar to the first approach, a blame-free culture also does not yield meaningful and lasting safety improvements. It does not acknowledge the role of risky or reckless individual human behavior and the contributory impact on safety events. In a culture of safety, there is still an assessment of individual behavior and accountability.

In an organization with a nonpunitive response to error, the approach is a balance between the two extremes of individual blame and blame-free responses to error. This is often articulated as the notion of a "just culture" that strikes a balance between total blame and no accountability in the evaluation of individual culpability in safety events. This deliberate approach to establishing individual culpability is a cornerstone of a safety culture.

James Reason is considered a founding thought leader of rigorous, human factor–based approaches to culpability management. His seminal work, *Managing the Risks of Organizational Accidents*, provides one of the first culpability decision trees developed to assess the role of individual behavior in safety events. According to James Reason:

> Just culture creates an atmosphere of trust in which people are encouraged to provide, and even rewarded for providing, essential safety-related information but in which they are clear about where the line must be drawn between acceptable and unacceptable behavior.
>
> *(1997)*

His work was initially used in the nuclear power industry to establish the culpability of individual actions in untoward events. This industry work provides much of the intellectual underpinnings and implementation lessons for the just culture approach within health care (Hobbs 2008).

From the time since Reason's initial publication, his work has been modified and expanded upon in a variety of proprietary and nonproprietary frameworks across many industries. Although the finer points and details may vary in different decision trees, there are common themes across all variations. As Marx has articulated, these frameworks prescribe an approach to culpability that is based on the intention or motivation of the individual's behavior. Marx states that human error should be met with consolation, at-risk behavior should be met with coaching, and reckless behavior should be met with punishment. The behavior should always be met with the same response, regardless of the outcome of the error (Marx 2009).

Just culture is one of the key components of a culture of safety. Other elements include the following:

- **Recognition of safety as a fundamental organization value**. For an organization to achieve a culture of safety, safety must be recognized as a core organizational value that is communicated and emphasized on a frequent and visible basis by the most senior leaders. Safety must be recognized as the foremost organizational concern and a value injected into decision-making from the front line to senior management. Paul O'Neill, former CEO of Alcoa, best recognized this primacy of safety within his organization by requiring personal notification of an employee accident within 24 hours of occurrence (Spear 2009). This set the tone within the organization regarding the importance and urgency of workplace safety. Leaders play a pivotal role in shaping their organizational culture and in establishing a culture of safety.
- **Encouragement and rewards for reporting safety events**. There may be a natural tendency for staff and leaders to hide safety events due to fear of repercussions. This reluctance may be even greater with regard to reporting "near miss" safety events that had the potential to cause patient harm. In an organization with a culture

of safety, these tendencies of reluctance to report should be actively discouraged and reversed. The hospital or health system must embody the characteristics of a learning organization and collect data and investigate all classes of safety events, including near misses. In order for this to be successful, there must be a concerted and deliberate effort to promote safety event reporting. The culture of safety must acknowledge and reward the value of reporting, especially self-reporting, of safety events and near misses. One way leaders can promote this is to shift the language to reward and celebrate "good catches" as opposed to "near misses." Leaders should celebrate the important role of humans in recognizing and recovering from potential safety hazards.

- **Establishment of a just culture and decision-making algorithm for assessing individual culpability in safety events**. In tandem with the encouragement of event reporting, organizations should have a formal process for establishing individual culpability in the context of safety events. This process should be nonpunitive, recognize the occurrence of human error, and establish increasing levels of accountability depending on the motivation and recklessness of the behavior. Such algorithms typically acknowledge the organization's contributory role in providing the correct policies, procedures, training, and work environment for staff to successfully carry out their duties. Though the presumption is often that these culpability algorithms and response processes are within the domain of the organization's safety team, they are in fact most appropriate for oversight and implementation within the human resources function and for use by operational leadership. A common mistake within hospitals and health systems is for a just culture approach/algorithm to be a safety function as opposed to a human resources initiative and organization-wide competency.

## *Transparency around Safety Events*

At an organizational level, there may be a tendency to avoid discussion of adverse events. This reticence among leadership to engage in candid dialog with staff about safety events discourages event reporting and inhibits collective organizational learning. A safety culture requires conversation and learning from safety events. Transparency should be appropriate, ensure patient confidentiality, and not unduly expose the organization to risk. Within these guardrails, it is possible to engender candor about an organization's failings and, most importantly, to collect and disseminate the lessons learned to prevent future safety events.

These domains of safety culture can be measured using survey tools. This assessment of an organization's safety culture can serve several purposes:

1. Provide a thorough assessment of the current state of safety culture with the capability to drill down to identify concerns in specific work areas.
2. Benchmark performance against other organizations.
3. Encourage leadership attention and the design of interventions to improve safety culture.
4. Assess intervention and leadership impact on safety culture.
5. Track and trend changes in organizational culture over time.

A variety of survey instruments exist for safety culture assessment. Two of the most popular are the Agency for Healthcare Research and Quality surveys on patient safety culture and the Safety Attitudes Questionnaire.

## *AHRQ Surveys on Patient Safety Culture (SOPS)*

AHRQ provides five surveys on patient safety culture tailored to hospitals, medical offices, nursing homes, community pharmacies, and ambulatory surgery centers. The surveys can be used to measure the culture of safety across the spectrum from the individual, work unit, and organization. This allows for the assessment of microcultures within an organization either by work unit or by employee role (e.g., staff vs. leadership; employed medical staff vs. nursing). Additionally, implementation of the survey itself supports increased awareness about patient safety as well as the opportunity overtime to evaluate trends and the impact of initiatives and interventions.

The initial SOPS program began in 2001, and has undergone several iterations, with the most recent SOPS Hospital Survey Version 2.0 released in 2019 (Figure 3.1). This includes

| Topics Covered by SOPS Hospital Survey 2.0 |
|---|
| **Composite Measures:** A composite measure is a grouping of two or more survey items that assess the same area of culture. The 10 composite measures and 32 survey items assessed in the SOPS Hospital Survey 2.0 are: |
| **Teamwork** (3 items) |
| **Staffing and Work Pace** (4 items) |
| **Organizational Learning - Continuous Improvement** (3 items) |
| **Response to Error** (4 items) |
| **Supervisor, Manager, or Clinical Leader Support for Patient Safety** (3 items) |
| **Communication About Error** (3 items) |
| **Communication Openness** (4 items) |
| **Reporting Patient Safety Events** (2 items) |
| **Hospital Management Support for Patient Safety** (3 items) |
| **Handoffs and Information Exchange** (3 items) |
| **Additional Measures:** In addition to the composite measures, single item measures included assess: |
| **Number of events reported** (1 item) |
| **Patient safety rating** (1 item) |
| **Background questions** (4 items) |

**Figure 3.1 Hospital survey on patient safety culture. (Agency for Healthcare Research and Quality, 2019.)**

ten composite measures with 32 survey items, while the medical office survey examines ten composite measures along with 38 survey items (Figure 3.2).

The survey tools, particularly the hospital survey, have been well validated and are widely used throughout the United States, allowing for benchmarking and comparison with other organizations. Another advantage is that the survey is freely available with a number of open access tools for survey implementation, recruitment, data entry, and analysis (AHRQ).

| Topics Covered by SOPS Medical Office Survey 2.0 |
|---|
| **Composite Measures:** A composite measure is a grouping of two or more survey items that assess the same area of culture. The 10 composite measures and 38 survey items assessed in the SOPS Medical Office Survey 2.0 are: |
| **Communication About Error** (4 items) |
| **Communication Openness** (4 items) |
| **Office Processes and Standardization** (4 items) |
| **Organizational Learning** (3 items) |
| **Overall Perceptions of Patient Safety and Quality** (4 items) |
| **Owner/ Managing Partner/ Leadership Support for Patient Safey** (4 items) |
| **Patient Care Tracking/ Follow-up** (4 items) |
| **Staff Training** (3 items) |
| **Teamwork** (4 items) |
| **Work Pressure and Pace** (4 items) |
| **Additional Measures:** In addition to the composite measures, single item measures included assess: |
| **List of Patient Safety and Quality Issues** (9 items) |
| **Information Exchange with Other Settings** (5 items) |
| **Screener Question Determining if Respondent is an Owner, Managing Partner, or in a Leadership Position** (1 item) |
| **Overall Ratings on Quality and Patient Safety** (6 items) |
| **Background questions** (3 items) |

**Figure 3.2 Medical office survey on patient safety culture. (Agency for Healthcare Research and Quality, 2019.)**

### *Safety Attitudes Questionnaire*

The SAQ is a survey developed by J. Bryan Sexton, Ph.D., and colleagues at the University of Texas at Austin. It was derived from the Flight Management Attitude Questionnaire, a human factor tool used to assess the culture in the cockpit in commercial aviation, allowing for comparisons between health care and other industries.

The SAQ consists of six individual surveys that are tailored to the work settings of the general inpatient floor, intensive care unit, labor and delivery, operating room, pharmacy, and ambulatory setting. Each survey instrument assesses six domains through 60 items answered on a five-point Likert scale and takes approximately 10 minutes to complete. These domains include the following:

1. Teamwork climate
2. Safety climate
3. Job satisfaction
4. Stress recognition
5. Perceptions of management
6. Working conditions

The SAQ is considered one of the best-studied tools to measure and assess patient safety culture. It has been validated and regarded as quick and easy to complete (Center for Healthcare Quality and Safety, 2006).

## Case Study: Improving Organizational Culture of Safety

The following case study illustrates the approach a hospital could take to review the culture of safety in their institution and strategic steps to take for improvement.

Community General Hospital has recently experienced a preventable safety event involving the death of a young patient. Upon event investigation, troubling trends were discovered regarding staff reluctance to speak up about possible errors in care, fear of retribution for event reporting, and an undue emphasis on staff efficiency, often at the expense of patient safety. Because of these findings, the hospital board had asked the management team to perform an assessment and create an improvement plan to address the organization's safety culture.

After review, the hospital leadership team chose to conduct an organization-wide safety culture assessment using the AHRQ hospital culture of safety survey. The goal was at least a 30% response rate from the hospital employees. The survey was conducted during a two-week period in June. In the weeks prior to the survey, the management actively promoted the survey in team meetings and implemented a publicity campaign, including information display on screen savers and visual display boards throughout the hospital. The chief medical officer (CMO) of the Community General Hospital emphasized the importance of physician voice and participation in the survey by sending the full medical staff an email conveying the context and goals. Additionally, the CMO worked with the chief of the medical staff to present to the Medical Executive Committee and obtain buy-in and support from key physician leaders, challenging division chiefs to promote among their colleagues. During the survey process, the response rates were reported to the leadership team on a daily basis. Frontline leaders and administrative leadership actively promoted the survey during routine work rounds.

At the conclusion of the survey period, the hospital had achieved a 34% response rate. Results were stratified and analyzed by unit and employee role, in addition to the organization level. The results were compared to external benchmarks provided by AHRQ. The analysis revealed an overall composite culture of safety score at the 40th percentile for the organization, compared to nationwide hospitals. Additional drill down on specific domains revealed opportunities around nonpunitive responses to error, feedback, and communication about error and frequency of events reported. In addition, the drill down revealed that there is a 10–15% difference between leadership perception and staff perception in any given domain. If the leader responses were to be excluded, the overall organization composite percentile score would decline below the 40th percentile.

Per the direction of the board, these results prompt the creation of a multipronged culture of safety action plan. Elements of this improvement plan include the following:

1. Revision of the hospital mission statement to explicitly message the primacy of safety and the establishment of both patient and associate safety as the first core value of the organization.
2. Under the leadership of human resources, the creation of a nonpunitive guide for establishing individual culpability in safety events. This nonpunitive guide is based on existing decision trees in the public domain and is customized for the organization. All leaders are trained on how to use the guide, and it is reflected in the human resources management policy and is communicated to all frontline staff.
3. To encourage greater transparency around safety events, leadership begins to talk about specific details of safety events, though removing patient-identifying details. Leaders adopt a narrative, story-telling style when discussing events so that the events are accessible and understood by the broadest possible audience in the organization. Each story is closed with lessons learned from the event and an emphasis on creating a platform for organizational change.

4. The initiation of a renewed emphasis on safety event reporting includes a public relations campaign to encourage safety event reporting that is refreshed at regular intervals and a goal of increasing reporting by 40% within a year with specific targets for leaders, public recognition of associates who self-report errors and near misses, and a quarterly organization-wide "life-saver" award.

The improvement plan is expected to be a journey lasting from months to years to embed within the organization's culture and leadership model. It is now a standing expectation of the board that the culture of safety will be assessed on an annual basis. In addition, leadership will develop an annual improvement plan on the results of the survey and the management incentive will now be tied to both the survey response rate and the overall composite performance with the goal of reaching the 75th percentile within four years.

## Lessons Learned

Although health care is unique, there are lessons to be learned from industries that have evolved to develop strong cultures of safety and accident avoidance. In these industries, including nuclear power and the U.S. aircraft carrier and submarine fleet, the culture of safety is considered foundational in their high-reliability performance.

A culture of safety must be proactively developed and actively managed by organizational leadership; a culture of safety will not evolve on its own. Actively managing culture first requires a basic assessment of the culture. This cultural inventory should be compared against the major components required within a culture of safety, including the primacy of patient and associate safety, the transparency and encouragement of reporting safety events, and a nonpunitive response toward error. Without these foundational cultural elements in place and practice every day, there will be limited return on the other "hard tactics" that focus on the practice and behavior by clinicians, physicians, and others at the frontline of patient care.

## Action Steps and Strategies to Lead

This chapter outlines some of the essential tactical steps toward measuring and managing culture. There is a fundamental role of leadership in safety culture:

1. **Assess your organization's culture**. Survey tools such as the AHRQ Hospital Survey of Patient Safety Culture and Safety Attitudes Questionnaire help leaders determine gaps in safety culture and identify opportunities for improvement.
2. **Actively manage workplace culture, including the culture of safety**. Leadership and culture are inextricably linked. Management guru Edgar Schein describes culture and leadership as two sides of the same coin. Schein provides a series of primary mechanisms that leaders can use to change, embed, and transmit culture (Schein 2010):
   a. What leaders pay attention to, measure, and control on a regular basis?
   b. How leaders react to critical incidents and organizational crises?
   c. How leaders allocate resources?
   d. Deliberate role modeling, teaching, and coaching?
   e. How leaders allocate rewards and status?
   f. How leaders recruit, select, promote, and excommunicate?

   In improving an organization's safety culture, it is not enough to simply adopt a nonpunitive algorithm and change a mission statement. Rigorous attention and examination by leaders are necessary to embed mechanisms and ensure consistency in approach and action toward establishing a culture of safety.

3. **Encourage and reward reporting of safety events**. Particularly, when the concepts of a safety culture are new, employees, fearing repercussions, will underreport safety events and near misses. The only way to identify system and process errors, however, is to report them. To support this, leaders must embody the characteristics of a learning organization including investigating the causes of all safety events and near misses.
4. **Utilize a nonpunitive policy and decision-making algorithm for assessing individual culpability in safety events**. Without a formal nonpunitive policy in place, organizations will not be able to achieve a safety culture. Leaders must develop and adhere to a formal process for establishing individual culpability in the context of serious safety events. Additionally, the algorithms developed should acknowledge the organization's role in providing the correct policies, procedure, training, and work environment for staff to succeed. This process should not be a quality and safety function, but rather a human resources function applied to the entire organization.

## References

Agency for Healthcare Research and Quality. Surveys on Patient Safety Culture. 2019. Accessed January 14, 2023. https://www.ahrq.gov/sops/surveys/index.html

Center for Healthcare Quality and Safety. Safety Attitudes and Safety Climate Questionnaire 2006. Accessed June 16, 2023. https://www.uth.edu/chqs/safety-survey

Hobbs, A.F. *Human Performance Culpability Evaluations*, University of Tennessee, Knoxville. 2008. www.efcog.org
Institute of Medicine (U.S.). Committee on Quality of Health Care in America. *Crossing the Quality Chasm: A New Health System for the 21st Century*, National Academies Press, Washington, D.C., 2001.
Marx, D.A. *Whack-A-Mole: The Price We Pay for Expecting Perfection*, Amanda Bray (ed.). By Your Side Studios, Plano, TX, 2009.
Reason, J.T. *Managing the Risks of Organizational Accidents*, Vol. 6. Ashgate, Aldershot, 1997.
Schein, E.H. *Organizational Culture and Leadership*, Vol. 2. John Wiley & Sons, New York, 2010.
Sexton, J.B., Helmreich, R.L., Neilands, T.B., Rowan, K., Vella, K., Boyden, J., et al. The Safety Attitudes Questionnaire: Physchometric Properties, Benchmarking Data, and Emerging Research. *BMC Health Services Research*. 2006;6(44):1–10.
Sorra, J., Gray, L., Streagle, S., et al. AHRQ Hospital Survey on Patient Safety Culture: User's Guide. (Prepared by Westat, under Contract No. HHSA290201300003C). AHRQ Publication No. 18-0036-EF (Replaces 04-0041, 15(16)-0049-EF). Agency for Healthcare Research and Quality, Rockville, MD, 2018.
Spear, S.J. *The High-Velocity Edge. How Market Leaders Leverage Operational Excellence to Beat the Competition*, McGraw-Hill, New York, 2009.

# Chapter 4

# Principles and Practices of High Reliability Organizations

## The Evidence

Much of the underlying concepts and literature regarding HROs originated in the book *Managing the Unexpected* by Karl Weick and Kathleen Sutcliffe (2007). In their landmark work, Weick and Sutcliffe identified industries that operate in difficult and unexpected conditions and yet have an extremely low level of accidents and injury to workers and customers. In these organizations, the possibility of failure can be overwhelming and catastrophic. Nonetheless, these organizations operate with exceptional records of safety and outcomes. Weick and Sutcliffe deemed this particular set of organizations to be "highly reliable." Examples of HROs include the U.S. submarine fleet, the U.S. aircraft carrier fleet, in-flight domestic commercial aviation, and the U.S. nuclear power industry.

Weick and Sutcliffe outlined the characteristics and operating systems of HROs and compared them to non-high


DOI: 10.4324/9781003402831-4

reliability industries and organizations. In this comparison, they identify five key principles that define the culture of management and leadership within HROs organizations:

1. Preoccupation with failure.
2. Reluctance to simplify.
3. Sensitivity to operations.
4. Commitment to resilience.
5. Deference to expertise.

Weick and Sutcliffe refer to these principles as components of a "mindful infrastructure." Another way to convey these ideas is to describe HROs as "always" organizations. These organizations are always mindful, always executing, always safe, and always anticipating the worst, which allows them to perform at an unusually high level despite the high-stake circumstances. Each of the five HRO principles yields important insights for leadership and operations across industries.

## *Preoccupation with Failure*

HROs treat any lapse or problem, no matter how small, as indicative of a potentially larger issue within an operating system. This manifests as a healthy paranoia that whatever could go wrong will go wrong. The preoccupation with failure is embedded within HRO culture and practiced from the front line to executive leadership. HRO leaders and employees pay great attention to detail, particularly small signals of error, and swarm these issues promptly before they propagate and lead to an error or incident. It is considered a management prerogative to proactively address the small blips within the system.

HROs operationalize this preoccupation with failure by encouraging event reporting and investigating near-miss incidents. For example, in an HRO, the discovery of a small, loose part on critical machinery would prompt an investigation of all similar parts throughout the plant and potentially a deeper investigation into the manufacture and installation process.

## Reluctance to Simplify

Humans are biologically capable of processing only a fixed amount of facts and information when understanding a situation or solving a problem. As a result, when organizations seek to explain an event or incident, it is a natural and almost an inevitable bias to consider only a limited set of facts and construct a logical explanation from the constrained set of what is known. This cognitive bias in the explanation of past events has been referred to as the narrative fallacy (Taleb 2010). The narrative fallacy occurs because it is appealing to find a simple story that provides order and structure for explaining events that appear random and unpredictable. Unfortunately, this bias limits true, in-depth understanding.

HROs understand this bias and the impact on situational awareness and incident investigation. They actively work against this natural tendency by refusing to simplify explanations of events. HROs consider as broad a set of information as possible from as diverse a group of sources as possible. HRO leaders attempt to preserve the diversity of opinion and perspective when synthesizing their explanations. This approach is a hallmark of high reliability and works against the natural human tendency toward narrative fallacy and simple explanations.

## Sensitivity to Operations

In any organization, the "real work" occurs on the front line. HROs are attuned to the daily situation and environment on the front line of operational work. HRO leaders are attentive, good listeners, and responsive to issues and problems at the operating level. This mode of operation may also be described as routine situational awareness.

Sensitivity to operations requires a process for easy, hassle-free communication of operational status from the front line to leadership. It also requires a leadership commitment to listening to these concerns and to working actively to eliminate the barriers and problems interfering with frontline work. This approach may also be branded as a form of servant leadership within the HRO.

## *Commitment to Resilience*

HROs recognize that problems will inevitably occur and that incidents may elude initial mechanisms for detection and control. HROs actively plan for these contingencies through implementing a system of redundancies at the levels of people, process, and technology. This commitment to resilience, persevering despite errors or failures, mobilizes the system rapidly and effectively to prevent an error from becoming more significant and leading to greater catastrophe. This ability to respond to an error is fundamental to HRO functioning. HRO leadership instills this culture through routine drills and even simulation. This leads to a priority on education and training for associates to ensure competency to respond to a crisis when it occurs.

## *Deference to Expertise*

HROs are flat organizations; that is, they lack the strict hierarchy that is present in many organizations. HROs encourage deference to the individual with the greatest experience or knowledge of a situation, regardless of their official title or position. HROs push decision-making down the chain of command in the organization and empower those at the front line, where often the greatest knowledge and understanding of a situation lies.

An example of this deference to expertise can be seen in the flight operations on a U.S. aircraft carrier. Within this HRO, any individual—regardless of rank or title—can halt operations for a safety concern that might jeopardize the crew, pilot, or aircraft. The organization places a premium on safety and does not allow hierarchy and rank to interfere with this priority.

To summarize with a quote from Karl Weick and Kathleen Sutcliffe:

> Unexpected events can get you into trouble unless you create a mindful infrastructure that continually tracks small failures, resists oversimplification, is sensitive to operations, maintains capabilities for resilience, and monitors shifting locations of expertise.
>
> *(Weick & Sutcliffe, 2007)*

Given these guiding principles, the next section focuses on the translation and operationalization of these principles to health care.

## Case Studies

The literature provides many examples of the real-world practice of high reliability principles within HROs. In contrast, for budding high reliability industries, including health care, there are fewer examples of published information on how to implement high reliability principles.

The following are sample tactics to lead to high reliability organizations, organized by each key principle. These examples are based on the authors' experiences and conversations with leaders in health care.

## *Preoccupation with Failure: Investigating Near Misses and Good Saves*

When a negative event occurs in the process of patient care, physician leaders have traditionally been trained to look for human errors by an individual, such as surgical technique or medical decision-making. Yet, system factors such as poor communication, inadequate staffing, distraction, equipment failure, inadequate environment, and many others can substantially increase the likelihood of error. Thus, identifying systems factors, those that involve the interrelationships between individuals, their tools, and the environment they work in is critical for physician leaders.

One approach to translating the high reliability principle of preoccupation with failure to health care is to invoke James Reason's "Swiss cheese model" of accident causation (Figure 4.1). This framework explains how although there

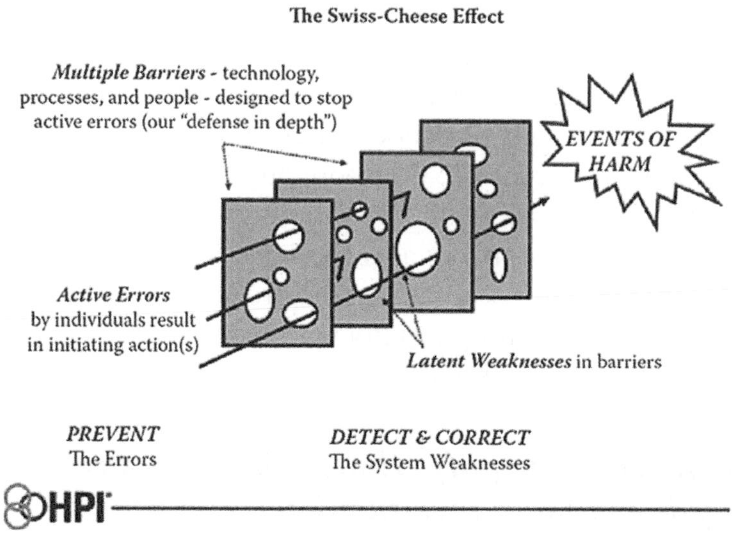


**Figure 4.1 The Swiss cheese effect. (Adapted from James Reason. *Managing the Risks of Organizational Accidents*, 1997.)**

may be many layers of defense between a hazard and potential safety event, represented as slices of Swiss cheese, an incident may still occur if the holes of the Swiss cheese have aligned to allow an error to propagate through the system. Despite the best intentions, all defenses have an opportunity to fail and adverse events occur when all defenses fail simultaneously.

In health care, our current model of safety event investigation is aligned with this approach to thinking. Events or errors are investigated only after harm has occurred. It is only then, after the fact and after an event has occurred, that the individual "holes" in the process are recognized and rectified.

In contrast, if a health care organization were to be preoccupied with failure, leaders would identify the individual holes in the safety systems before a safety event occurred. Once the flaws in the system are discovered, they should be proactively addressed to prevent errors. Operationally, the process of identifying the "holes" before a safety event is synonymous with the investigation of "near misses" and "good saves." A "near miss" or "good save" is a safety event that is thwarted by one last barrier of defense. Often, the defense is close to the front line of care. Instead of treating these "good catches" as lucky, a hospital or health system should regard these as small signals of deeper flaws in the system to be investigated and resolved. Consequently, a health care organization that aspires to be an HRO should not only just investigate their safety events but also routinely investigate a sample of near misses and good saves. This proactive approach of attentiveness to small signals helps to solve problems before they lead to significant harm.

## *Reluctance to Simplify: Thorough Root Cause Analysis and Event Investigation*

In a safety event investigation, it is important to resist the tendency to pronounce a simple or single cause of an event.

Although finding an easy or unifying answer is intellectually satisfying and allows work to progress, it may cause premature closure of the issue. A simple answer will likely not acknowledge the complexity of the intersection of people, process, and technology that contributes to an event.

To protect against this, hospitals and health systems are urged to adopt a standard and thorough approach to root cause analysis and event investigation. In particular, the complete approach should engage all relevant stakeholders, not just those that were proximal to the event. This approach will pull in groups that may initially feel their participation is irrelevant or not meaningful. Variety and richness of perspective, however, are critical to obtaining a thorough understanding of complex event occurrence.

The investigation team should identify multiple causation threads, each with its own event timeline, which contributed to and converged on the safety event. Establishing this expectation at the start of the event investigation will protect against the temptation to accept simple answers. It will also help to keep an open frame of mind among the investigation team, preserve the diversity of opinion, and enable a richness of perspective. Over time and with repetition of process and stakeholder involvement, this should promote the reluctance to simplify in many aspects of a health care organization's improvement process.

## *Sensitivity to Operations: Daily Organization Huddle*

An approach utilized by the U.S. aircraft carrier fleet to promote sensitivity to operations is the daily operational briefing. This briefing helps to promote organization-wide situational awareness at the beginning of each day. This tactic has been successfully adopted by a number of health care facilities and transformed into a daily safety huddle (Lee and Cosgrove 2014).

As is true across many industries, health care organizations often have overly structured, lengthy, and repetitive meetings. Because of the time required to complete a given meeting and the number of varied individuals required to attend, they are often not held frequently enough to accomplish rapid actions and regularly require significant lead time to schedule.

Meritus Health is a regional health system that serves more than 200,000 people in rural western Maryland. Meritus is an example of an organization that has adopted the practice of regular brief huddles, starting with senior leadership and working to every level of the system. The senior leadership team huddle for 15 minutes each morning to start the day, share situational awareness, review key metrics, and address pressing issues. The hospital also holds a daily safety huddle, attended by system leadership, and includes leads from each floor and service within the hospital, ancillary service, and administration. Each leader participating in the huddle is expected to briefly report on significant safety and quality events that occurred in the past 24 hours, anticipate any safety or quality issues that may arise in the next 24 hours, and provide follow-up to any issues that were identified in previous huddles. The huddle is largely a report out, not a problem-solving session. The leader of the huddle should help to manage the dialog, promote a robust cadence to the huddle, and encourage problem-solving at the conclusion of the huddle.

Implementing the daily huddle requires a thorough plan, practice, and a willingness to change and adapt to the daily organizational rhythm. One recommended practice is to establish a meeting-free zone from around 7:00 a.m. to 9:00 a.m. This provides time for leaders to round on their direct reports and collect the information needed for the huddle. It also signals the importance of this time within the organization to establish collective situational awareness. At Meritus, the huddle usually starts at around 8:45 a.m. and concludes within 15 to 20 minutes. Even in large organizations, this brief time frame is possible, although it does require practice and role modeling of report outs prior to implementation. Training videos of sample huddles can also be helpful.

Leaders at Meritus Health, including Chief Operating Officer Carrie Adams, Pharm.D., have noted that after implementation, support areas have found a platform to share critical supply shortages or unexpected downtimes that would greatly impact the clinical operations. Leaders of these areas now have a voice at the table, and delays in communication have been shortened. Utilizing this platform also allows real-time troubleshooting for mitigation strategies. The presence of physician leadership and engagement within the huddle framework is essential. At Meritus, huddles occur across all teams and extend into the community practice setting, led by dyad leadership with a practice or site manager and physician medical director. This allows global awareness of important issues, sharing organizational goals and successes, and reviewing and overcoming clinical barriers.

A final best practice is to bring frontline associates, board members, community members, and even patients and families to attend huddles on a periodic basis. This has a powerful effect in an organization to enable the individuals delivering care as well as the community to understand the collective situational awareness, dedication to improving quality and safety, and the responsiveness of the organization to issues directly impacting patient care. Because of the huddle, Meritus has found that problems that would ordinarily take several days to weeks to solve are now resolved in one to two days following the implementation of the daily huddle.

## *Commitment to Resilience: Simulation*

HROs almost universally conduct drills and practice for safety events and worst-case scenarios. In health care, this approach can be replicated with medical simulation. Simulation has already gained acceptance and application within health care. Although a component of it is geared toward procedural competency, simulation can also be utilized for training regarding adverse events, code situations, and rare occurrences. This persistent drilling helps to embed the commitment to resilience within the care delivery setting. It acknowledges that incidents will occur and emphasizes responsiveness and rapid containment of those occurrences.

In the context of high reliability, simulation does not need to be an expensive or capital-intensive undertaking. Low-fidelity simulation of particular events or codes can be an acceptable substitute to practice skills, thought processes, and resilience. Although it may not feel as authentic as a simulation lab, this is an easy way to deploy multiple training scenarios across an organization. It is also important to frame simulation in the broader context of an adult model of learning. Simulation is an educational approach for adults to embed skills in their routine work. As such, it should also be accompanied by an organizational commitment to actively developing their workforce, investing in their education, and maintaining competency.

In addition, it is important for physicians to participate in simulation exercises. They are key stakeholders in demonstrating and actualizing the commitment to resiliency. Strategies for the engagement of physicians are provided in Chapter 7. Suffice to say, the impact of simulation is limited without physician participation.

## *Deference to Expertise: Executive Rounding*

Flattening hierarchies within an organization is easier said than done. Within health care, significant power gradients exist between disciplines and roles. There are also disparities between administrators and frontline staff, physicians and nurses, and clinicians and non-clinicians. Eliminating these gradients requires awareness and attentive leadership. It also requires a basis of relationship building and familiarity with frontline staff. This can be actively promoted through intentional executive rounding.

The individual components of executive rounding can take many forms. They can focus on information gathering, influencing behavior, problem-solving, or a combination of all of these. Regardless of the emphasis, the foundational component in all executive rounding is relationship building with frontline employees. When rounding is done correctly, leaders and employees develop familiarity and comfort with each other. It enables a diminution of the power gradient between administration and the front line and can become the basis for more meaningful dialog and exchange in the future. Without these relationships in place and the cultural change that accompanies them, there will not be an organizational willingness to seek out guidance and help regardless of title or seniority.

## Lessons Learned

It is tempting to distill the process of becoming an HRO into a series of discrete tactics for implementation. However, simply focusing on discrete projects like simulation or daily huddles by themselves will fail to transform an organization into one of high reliability. At its core, an HRO requires a unique form of cultural mindfulness and associated leadership.

For a health care organization that aspires to become an HRO, the first commitment must come from leadership to embrace an approach of mindfulness and a cultural change in management. This commitment needs to be accompanied with articulating a "why" for the change commitment and conveying this to employees up and down the organization. On this journey, it is helpful to highlight and illustrate the practices of exemplars in high reliability, particularly outside of health care, in order to provide an aspirational goal for the organization.

The embodiment of this cultural and leadership mindset is key on the progression toward becoming an HRO. As Weick and Sutcliffe state:

> Change toward greater mindfulness often involves movement toward a more informed culture that is focused on reporting, justice, flexibility and learning.
>
> *(Weick & Sutcliffe, 2007)*

In the absence of this type of culture, the HRO principles and accompanying tactics will likely not succeed.

## Action Steps and Strategies to Lead

1. **Continuously monitor organizational culture**. Without proper preparation and fortitude, the journey toward high reliability for a health care organization can be daunting and at times seem impossible. The chances of success can be vastly improved by recognizing that an HRO has a unique cultural and leadership mindset that must be owned throughout the organization.
2. **Establish a compelling "why" for the high reliability journey**. Once a level of commitment has been made, the leadership team should establish a compelling "why" for their high reliability journey, accompanied with aspirational goals and examples of HROs.
3. **Educate the organization on the key components of high reliability**. After the leadership team has shared the "why" for the high reliability journey with the organization, there should be efforts to educate employees on the key principles of high reliability. Among these

include the value of nonpunitive reporting of errors or near misses. Additionally, going beyond rhetoric and actively demonstrating that it is acceptable to make errors, as long as they are learned from and drive improvement.

4. **Reduce variation in care delivery**. Variation in clinical processes and lack of standard work increases the likelihood of error and reduces reliability within an organization. Physician leaders should serve as educators to promote consistent, evidence-based content that drives standardized clinical knowledge and enhances readiness to practice.
5. **Generate and celebrate quick wins**. Once the organization understands the "why" and the "what" of high reliability, physician leaders can begin a rollout of discrete tactics, in particular the daily huddle, which can serve as a powerful initial and visible example of a new organizational process and rhythm of operating. This quick win should be followed with additional high reliability tactics and an ongoing commitment to leading and living HRO principles every day.

## References

Lee, T.H., Cosgrove, T. Engaging Doctors in the Health Care Revolution. *Harvard Business Review*. 2014;92(6):104–111.

Taleb, N.K. *The Black Swan: The Impact of the Highly Improbable*, Random House, New York, 2010.

Weick, K., Sutcliffe, K. *Managing the Unexpected: Resilient Performance in an Age of Uncertainty*, Jossey-Bass, San Francisco, CA, 2007.

Reason, James. *Managing the Risks of Organizational Accidents*, 1997. Ashgate London, UK.

# *Chapter 5*

# Key Quality, Safety, and Efficiency Measures

## The Evidence

Performance measurement allows organizations to meet both internal and external needs and demands including guiding team- or system-wide performance-improvement activities, demonstrating provider accountability, fulfilling public reporting requirements, and facilitating organizational evaluation and decision-making. As leaders in the field know, health care organizations are required to report on quality, cost, and patient satisfaction measures to fulfill a variety of external requirements. These evaluators then utilize hospitals' performance measurement data for accreditation, calculating reimbursement levels, and public reporting of outcomes to drive transparency and competition (Schmaltz et al. 2014).

Over the past decade, programs from both public (i.e., Medicare, Medicaid) and private (i.e., Blue Cross Blue Shield, United Healthcare) payers have shifted reimbursement policies to incentivize and reward high-quality care. Stakes are


DOI: 10.4324/9781003402831-5

high, and there are significant financial investments from all sides to produce advanced metrics that highlight and fundamentally improve care. For instance, the Centers for Medicare and Medicaid Services spent approximately $1.3 billion on development and support for quality measures during the decade between 2008 and 2018 (Wadhera et al. 2020). Meanwhile, the National Academy of Medicine suggests that many health systems spend up to $12 million per year and utilize 50 to 100 full-time employees solely on efforts for measurement and reporting (Blumenthal et al. 2015). To maximize reimbursement under these programs, organizations must not only provide high-quality care but also demonstrate that they have done so through providing accurate and timely data. To this end, physician leaders must be able to track and use data across a variety of metrics to demonstrate value to consumers and payers, and to guide internal improvement initiatives to remain competitive.

Substantial barriers to successful measurement and reporting include the sheer number of varied metrics, the frequency of changes, and the number of different programs across payers. In 2011, one study showed that across 500 distinct measures in use, only 20% of the measures were used in more than one program, and there was not a single measure common across all programs (NQF 2011). Thankfully, the decade of the 2010s brought some refinement and reduction in measures. While there were 905 measures utilized by CMS in 2015, that number had decreased to 686 by 2020 (CMS 2021). The Core Quality Measures Collaborative, convened by leaders at CMS, the National Quality Forum (NQF), and the National Physician Organizations, has sought to reduce the total number of measures by eliminating low-value metrics and to introduce these consistently across payers. The ultimate aim is to relate measure to patient health outcomes and to focus on those "measures that matter" (Conway 2015).

Some examples of programs that are driving the imperative for effective data management and analysis include the following:

- **Serious Reportable Events**: In 2002, the National Quality Forum published a list of 28 Serious Reportable Events, otherwise known as "never events," that were deemed to be clearly identifiable and preventable medical errors (NQF 2011). In 2008, the Centers for Medicare and Medicaid Services announced it would no longer reimburse facilities for the extra cost of treating these "never events" (CMS 2008). Moving forward, organizations that are unable to identify, track, and eliminate these "never events" will suffer financially.
- **Readmissions**: In October 2012, the Centers for Medicare and Medicaid Services instituted the Hospital Readmissions Reduction Program (HRRP). Under this program, hospitals with all-cause 30-day readmission rates for targeted conditions higher than the CMS-designated benchmark rate face financial penalties (CMS 2014). HRRP is a good example of a program that has evolved with measures gaining sophistication based upon early feedback. Hospitals were initially benchmarked against each other based upon patient mix including factors of age, sex, and comorbidity. However, that model did not account for health-related social needs. Thus, safety-net hospitals and others with higher socioeconomically disadvantaged populations initially received greater penalties (Joynt and Jha 2013). The 21st Century Cures Act of 2016 included identification of the proportion of Medicare patients dually eligible for Medicaid, which is a common proxy for low-income status, to compare hospital performance (Rogstad et al. 2022). Ultimately, facilities must implement comprehensive data systems to track readmissions, stratify data, and

use predictive modeling to effectively and efficiently reduce readmissions.

- **Merit-Based Incentive Payment System (MIPS)**: In an effort to reward clinicians and systems for value over volume, the Medicare Access and CHIP Reauthorization Act of 2015 (MACRA) sought to streamline multiple quality programs and offer bonus payments for eligible alternative payment models (APMs). Clinicians and groups are given a score based upon overall performance compared to CMS threshold benchmarks for quality, improvement activities, promoting interoperability, and cost. As of 2023, there are a total of 198 quality measures in the program, ranging from screening for social drivers of health to immunization and risk-standardized rates for heart failure admission. Ultimately, demonstration of high performance among metrics yields positive payment adjustment at the conclusion of the 12-month reporting cycle, while the lowest scoring groups will see up to a 9% reduction in payment (CMS 2023).

As programs such as these expand and reimbursement based on cost and quality outcomes becomes standard, organizations must be able to measure their performance across a number of dimensions to both meet external requirements and guide internal improvement projects.

## *Data for Performance Measurement: The Basics*

There are three fundamental purposes for conducting performance measurement, each of which is critical to ensuring a high-performing organization (Schmaltz et al. 2014):

1. Assessment of current performance.
2. Demonstration and verification of performance improvement.
3. Control of performance.

These three purposes for measurement complement and support the implementation of internal performance-improvement activities (Schmaltz et al. 2014). Organizations assess performance to identify the strengths and weaknesses of existing processes and to identify the target areas for intervention. Next, the impact of tested interventions is demonstrated by comparing post-intervention data to baseline data. Finally, ongoing measurement helps to sustain improved performance. Continuous data monitoring can provide early warnings and a correction system that highlights unintended changes in processes (Schmaltz et al. 2014). To succeed in the new era of value-based and consumer-driven health care, physician leaders must become proficient in utilizing performance measurements to implement ongoing improvement efforts across their organizations, from patient safety initiatives to projects to improve workflow and financial processes.

## Types and Dimensions of Measures

Historically, health care "quality" has been very difficult, if not impossible, to measure. A lack of metrics and reporting mechanisms has hindered the ability to collect and evaluate data to determine quality. Although challenges remain, over the past decade the availability of metrics, methods, and databases to collect, store, and evaluate quality data has vastly improved.

Avedis Donabedian, often referred to as the father of quality assurance, provided a basic framework of three dimensions of quality (Wyszewianski 2014):

1. **Structure**: It refers to the characteristics of care providers such as education, training, and professional certification and includes characteristics of care facilities such as adequacy of staffing, equipment, and overall organization.

2. **Process**: The quality of process varies across three aspects: (1) appropriateness—whether correct actions were taken; (2) skill—proficiency with which actions were carried out; and (3) timeliness of care.
3. **Outcomes**: It refers to indicators of health status such as whether a patient's pain has subsided, whether the patient has regained full function, cost of care, and measures of satisfaction.

Health care organizations can and should evaluate performance across each of these dimensions. Particularly, when implementing improvement initiatives, organizations should track both process and outcome measures to determine which processes may need to be modified to improve a given outcome.

When implementing improvement initiatives, teams should also consider balancing measures (IHI 2014b). Balancing measures help assess whether changes from an intervention designed to improve one part of the system inadvertently cause new problems in other parts of the system. For example, if a hospital is successful in reducing the amount of time that patients spend on a ventilator post-surgery, they should also note whether re-intubation rates have increased. In this example, the time spent on a ventilator is the outcome measure that is targeted for improvement and the rate of ventilation, a process measure, is the balancing measure. If time spent on a ventilator is decreasing yet the rate of re-intubation is increasing, this may indicate that the efforts to decrease time on a ventilator are leading to premature removal, resulting in re-intubation and additional episodes of ventilation and, thus, undermining the improvement. Another example relates to reducing the length of stay. Organizations working to reduce the length of stay should monitor readmissions as a balancing measure. If length of stay decreases but readmissions increase, this may indicate that patients are being discharged prematurely (IHI 2014b).

## Criteria and Standards

Once structure, process, and outcome measures have been established, criteria and standards are used to evaluate performance on each measure. *Criteria* are the specific attributes on which the assessment of quality is based. *Standards* are the quantitative level the criteria are required to meet in order to satisfy expectations about quality. For example, consider process measures related to discharge. The criterion for one such measure may be the percentage of individuals who receive a follow-up phone call from a nurse within 24 hours of discharge. The associated standard might be that at least 90% of individuals would have received a follow-up call within 24 hours post-discharge (Wyszewianski 2014). While the criteria define the metric, the standards define how success is determined or evaluated. Figure 5.1 provides additional examples of criteria and standards.

## Data Sources

There are many national sources of health care data. Organizations can use these databases to access data on structure, process, and outcome measures. The following

| Type of Measure | Focus of Assessment | Criterion | Standard |
|---|---|---|---|
| Structure | Information technology | Achievement of meaningful use standards for electronic health record | 100% of physicians' offices to achieve meaningful use requirements |
| Process | Patient discharge from hospital | Percentage of patients that receive a follow-up phone call within 48 hours of discharge | 95% of patients to receive a phone call within 48 hours of discharge |
| Outcome | Diabetic patients | Percent of patients with HbA1C levels within recommended range | 75% of patients within range |

**Figure 5.1 Examples of criteria and standards of measures.**

examples are nationally standardized survey instruments that measure quality of care:

- **Medicare Care Compare**: A CMS measurement and reporting tool that seeks to provide transparency to patients and support hospitals, groups, hospice, home health, nursing, and rehab and a host of other facilities in improving care. This reports overall star rating and patient survey results on a one to five scale, along with measures of quality including timeliness of care, complications and death, and payment and value (Barclay et al. 2022).
- **HEDIS**: The Healthcare Effectiveness Data and Information Set is a performance measurement tool developed by the National Committee for Quality Assurance to provide purchasers with information to compare performances of health care plans. HEDIS assesses more than 90 measures across six domains of care: Effectiveness of care, access/availability of care, experience of care, utilization and risk-adjusted utilization, measures reporting using electronic clinical data systems, and health plan descriptive information (NCQA "HEDIS & Quality Measurement"). Currently, more than 90% of health plans in the United States use HEDIS to measure performance. Due to the ubiquitous use of HEDIS and the highly specific design of these measures, it is an effective source of data for side-by-side comparison of organizations (NCQA).
- **NHSN**: The Centers for Disease Control's National Healthcare Safety Network is the most widely used health care–associated infection tracking system in the nation and is known as the Healthcare-Associated Infection (HAI) surveillance gold standard. It includes seven components: Patient safety, health care personnel safety, dialysis, outpatient procedures, neonatal, biovigilance, and long-term care facilities. NHSN provides support to

medical facilities, states, regions, and national data collection efforts by providing reporting tools to identify high rates of HAIs, monitor improvement efforts, and ultimately reduce infection rates. The NHSN website provides hospitals with information to enroll as well as opportunities to participate in state and national HAI collaboratives including CMS-operated HAI reporting programs (CDC 2023).

- **HCAHPS**: The Hospital Consumer Assessment of Healthcare Providers and Systems Survey is a standardized survey, initially deployed by CMS and AHRQ in 2008, that measures patients' experience of care. The survey asks discharged patients 29 questions about their hospital stay, with emphasis on communication with nurses and doctors, responsiveness of staff, cleanliness, discharge information, and communication about medications (Hospital Consumer Assessment of Healthcare Providers and Systems 2021). In many instances, HCAHPS scores correlate with quality and mortality outcomes, with studies showing hospitals in the top quartile of HCAHPS scores deliver better care for many services (Manary et al. 2013).

In addition to these national databases, organizations can track internal metrics that are relevant for the organization's specific priorities or initiatives. Chapter 6 describes strategies to access additional data sources. When choosing metrics, clinical leaders should prioritize a "critical few" measures that have the greatest impact on driving improvement. Leaders must be aware of data fatigue and ensure that every measure is tied to a report that is important to the organization. This helps to keep teams motivated and engaged in improvement projects and to manage the data burden.

Leaders should select measures that enable benchmarking against peers, competitors, and national standards. Benchmarking involves comparing metrics to other similar organizations to determine relative performance. Improvements in quality and safety are always positive, but organizations may be blind to additional opportunities for improvement if they do not benchmark their performance. For example, a facility may have great success in reducing its rate of early elective deliveries from 20% to 10%, a stunning 50% reduction. However, if the organization benchmarked its performance, it would realize that a rate of 10% still vastly exceeds the national benchmark of 2%. Benchmarking becomes increasingly important as transparency and competition increase in health care and comparative data becomes available to consumers and payers.

## *Metrics of the Future*

As the health care operating model and payment methodologies evolve, so will the metrics used to monitor health system performance. Metrics of the future will include continuum of care metrics, population health metrics, and patient-reported outcome metrics. These types of measures move beyond the amount and type of care delivered and attempt to more accurately evaluate effectiveness and efficiency from the view of the patient.

Continuum of care metrics will reflect quality and cost across multiple facilities. For example, the Medicare cost per beneficiary metric aggregates cost before, during, and after hospitalization. These metrics are a more accurate reflection of the total cost of care and help to identify strategies that truly reduce costs rather than simply shifting costs to another dimension of the system.

Population health metrics will also be important as entities such as accountable care organizations and patient-centered medical homes become responsible for the health outcomes of populations, not merely the medical services provided. Population health metrics will include measures of disease prevalence, the percentage of the population that receives treatment and preventive care consistent with recommended guidelines, and total cost of care metrics. Much investment will be required to develop and test such metrics, but some delivery systems and payers are already beginning to experiment in this area. An additional layer to this will be recognition of disadvantaged populations, and emphasizing specific improvement to drive more equitable care. Medicare and other payers have signaled interest in improving health care disparities, and thus measures that highlight and seek improvement of social determinants of health and other elements of health care inequity will be increasingly important. Chapter 11 addresses how physician leaders should approach improvement efforts centered around addressing disparities in care.

A final set of metrics for the future are patient-reported outcome metrics. As clinicians and delivery systems increasingly think in terms of value, an important component is defining what value is from the patient perspective. This will include those outcomes most relevant to patients, including both near-term and longer-term health. Definitions of "quality" will move beyond the use of HEDIS process measures and focus on what is most important to patients: Their health outcomes following treatment (Jacobs et al. 2023).

## Effective Strategies: Using Data to Drive Performance Improvement

Choosing metrics to monitor and evaluate quality is a first step. The second step is to use those metrics to drive improvement. To maximize the impact of measurement, three conditions must be met: (1) The measure construct must be sound, (2) the data analyses and interpretation must be scientifically credible, and (3) the data should be reported in a

| Benefits of Measuring Organizational Performance |
|---|
| Provides factual evidence of performance and improvement |
| Promotes ongoing organizational self-evaluation and improvement |
| Facilitates cost-benefit analysis |
| May help facilitate long-term relationships with various external stakeholders |
| May facilitate differentiation from competitors |
| May contribute to the awarding of business contracts |
| Fosters organizational survival |

**Figure 5.2 Benefits of measuring organizational performance. (Schmaltz, S., Hanold, L.S., Koss, R.G., Loeb, J.M. Statistical Tools for Quality Improvement. In *The Healthcare Quality Book: Vision, Strategy, and Tools*, ed. Joshi, Ransom, Nash, Ransom (3rd Ed). Health Administration Press, Chicago, IL, 2014, 135–173.)**

user-friendly, easy-to-understand format (Schmaltz et al. 2014). If all of these conditions are met, health care organizations can benefit from measurement in many ways (Figure 5.2).

## *Selecting Measures*

Selecting appropriate measures is foundational for improvement initiatives. Measures can be both adopted from external resources, as described previously, and developed internally to meet specific facility needs. Measures should be selected to meet the specific needs of the initiative goals. Figure 5.3 lists the critical characteristics of all appropriate performance measures (Schmaltz et al. 2014).

When selecting measures for an improvement project, physician leaders should consider the following:

- **What measures are currently in use?** An inventory should include mandatory measures that are already

| |
|---|
| **Relevant:** Measures should directly relate to organization's improvement goals and should align with the organization's overall mission, vision, values, and strategic goals and objectives. |
| **Reliable:** Measures should accurately and consistently identify the events they were designed to identify across multiple health care settings. |
| **Valid:** Measures should raise good questions about current processes, which also facilitate the identification of opportunities for improvement regarding the services provided and quality of achieved health care results. It's also important to assess how closely the intended use of a measure matches with the measure developer's intended use. |
| **Cost-effective:** The costs of any performance measurement versus the benefit must be considered in order to determine whether the measurement activities are worth the investment. |
| **Under the provider's control:** Performance measures should only collect data on processes or outcomes which the provider is able to influence. Otherwise, an opportunity for improvement identified through a measure cannot be intervened on by a provider or organization. |
| **Precisely defined and specified:** In order to ensure uniform application between measurement periods and comparability across organizations, performance measures and their data elements must be specified through precise, predefined, and standardized requirements. This will facilitate the reliable collection and calculation of data by various organizations. |
| **Interpretable:** The extent to which a user can understand the rationale and results of a measure's data and information. |
| **Risk adjusted or stratified:** The extent to which the influence of factors that differentiate comparison groups can be taken into account or controlled for. |

**Figure 5.3 Critical characteristics of performance measures. (Schmaltz, S., Hanold, L.S., Koss, R.G., Loeb, J.M. Statistical Tools for Quality Improvement. In *The Healthcare Quality Book: Vision, Strategy, and Tools*, ed. Joshi, Ransom, Nash, & Ransom (3rd Ed). Health Administration Press, Chicago, IL, 2014, 135–173.)**

reported (i.e., Joint Commission, NHSN, HCAHPS) and facility-specific measures that are being used internally to drive improvement or for other reasons.

- **Which measures align?** Depending on the purpose of the measurement activities, select measures that align with the particular requirements (e.g., those of CMS, NHSN, or the Joint Commission). Select measures that fulfill multiple requirements to streamline data collection processes and reduce data collection fatigue.

- **What are the greatest opportunities to improve processes and outcomes?** Are there areas or processes in which performance is inconsistent or not meeting standards? Do any of these adversely affect patient outcomes? Choose those process or outcome measures that are the best indicators of what is driving the targeted outcome.
- **What measures matter to your patients and team members?** Be sure to engage patients and team members in the process of selecting measures, where possible. This level of feedback may reveal unknown or surprising elements and measures that leadership may otherwise not be able to see. Further, such active engagement in the selection process will facilitate improved engagement in the subsequent steps toward improvement.

## Case Study: Reducing Unnecessary Testing

Meritus Health is a nonprofit community-based health system with a 327-bed hospital and an active medical staff of over 500 in rural Western Maryland. Like many health care organizations, Meritus Health faced the challenge of responding to rising health care costs in the setting of seeking to simultaneously improve quality. Meritus implemented a coordinated "Doing Wisely" initiative to reduce unnecessary testing by 10,000 tests over a 12-month period. This specific aim was one strategy that cascaded down as a part of the organization's overarching goals to have zero harm in the health system by 2030. The initiative to reduce unnecessary testing was viewed as an opportunity to improve care, limit harm, reduce costs, and decrease time constraints on staff ordering, performing, and following-up on testing.

The Meritus Health team used the Choosing Wisely recommendations as a starting point for discussions on reduction.

Choosing Wisely, launched in 2012 by the American Board of Internal Medicine (ABIM), drives specialty-specific and evidence-based recommendations for limiting unnecessary testing. For the Doing Wisely initiative, Meritus started with support and investment at the system-level senior leadership, and this distilled across multiple areas of care delivery. Task forces were established for each of the areas of focus, including daily and routine lab orders in ICU and medical/surgical units, day of discharge lab orders, preoperative lab testing, and imaging performed in the ED.

Each task force developed a strategic driver diagram to clarify opportunities for improvement and target change ideas and intervention strategies. Figure 5.4 shows a snapshot of a driver diagram used by the lab reduction taskforce. Each strategy was linked to a physician champion who was

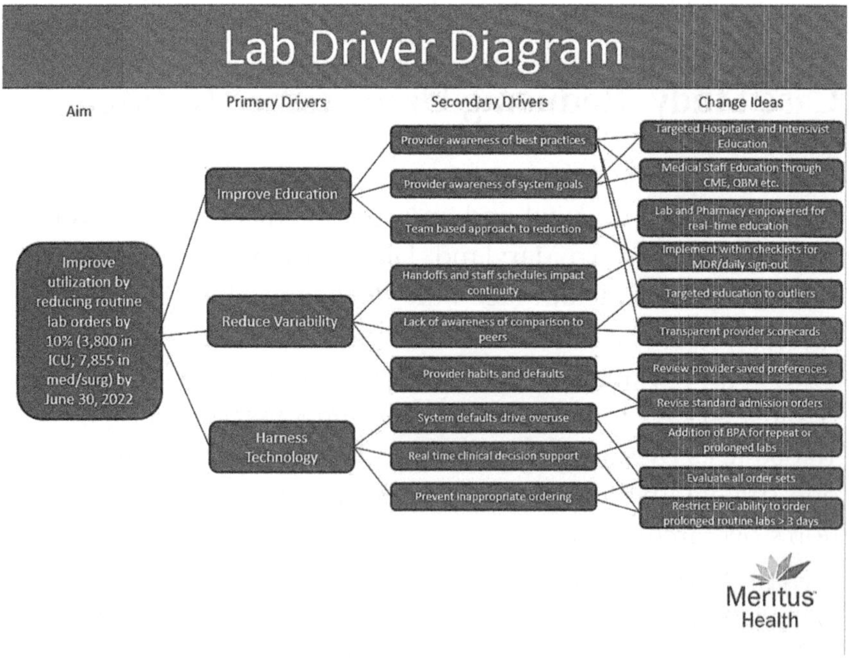


**Figure 5.4 Taskforce on decreasing lab utilization driver diagram. (Meritus Health, Hagerstown, MD.)**

accountable for review and progress alongside both oversight and tracking of data. Taskforces additionally included team members across the spectrum of care delivery, including physicians, nurses, quality-improvement specialists, radiology leadership, and at times even radiology and laboratory technicians, where needed. The task force meetings occurred in a brief huddle format weekly for the first three months, twice monthly for the next three months, and then once monthly for the remainder of the year-long project. Change ideas led to downstream interventions, including targeted education to attending physicians with regular updates on best practices, specific tests, and clinical communication.

In this initiative, Meritus Health shifted the reliance on change from the individual to the organization, establishing the target as a system-wide utilization goal. Data was updated and reviewed daily, allowing physicians to review their ordering tendencies drilled down to the level of the individual test, day, and service location. Physicians were able to see how often they ordered given tests, particularly in relation to their peers. Some of the common barriers to reducing unnecessary utilization include lack of provider education and awareness, fear of malpractice lawsuits, financial incentives that promote overutilization, and patient demand for tests and treatments. Prior to the start of the initiative, in some cases, there was limited data available on utilization patterns, which made it challenging to identify areas for improvement and measure impact. To address this, Meritus Health invested in new data analytics tools and worked to improve data collection processes.

Physician leaders can play a critical role in addressing barriers by promoting evidence-based practices and working to create a culture of appropriate utilization within their organizations. One strategy is to provide ongoing education and training to providers on appropriate use criteria, clinical guidelines, and the risks and benefits of different tests and treatments. This can help ensure that providers are making informed decisions that prioritize patient safety and quality of care. Another important strategy is to implement clinical decision support tools, which can help providers make more informed decisions by providing real-time guidance and feedback based on the patient's specific clinical situation. These tools can also help reduce the risk of unnecessary tests and treatments by flagging potential overutilization and suggesting alternative courses of action.

Ultimately, Meritus was able to reduce more than 30,000 unnecessary tests for fiscal year 2022, when compared with the previous year. This included a reduction of 21% in routine laboratory test orders in the ICU alone, and more than 2,000 fewer CT scans performed in the Emergency Department, without any balancing issues observed in patient outcomes. The initiative began in January of 2021, and Figure 5.5 depicts

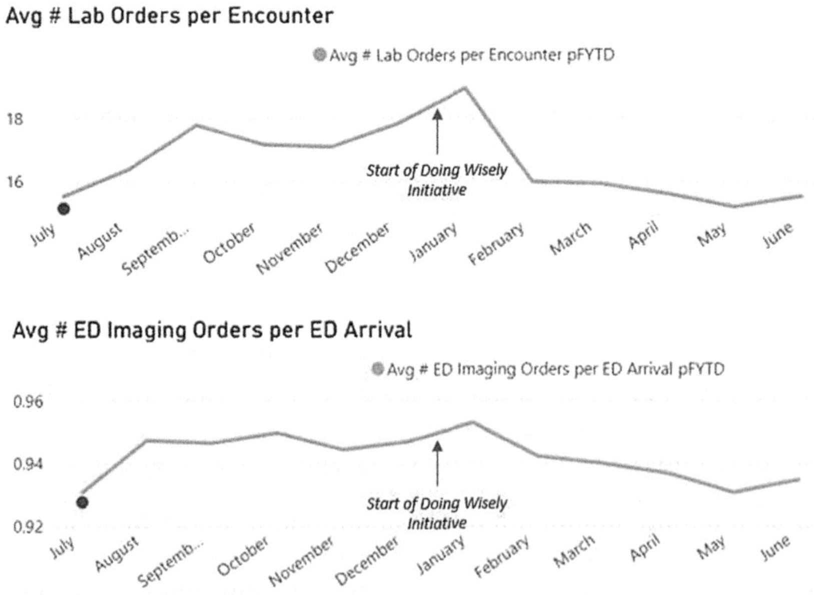


**Figure 5.5 Lab and imaging reduction trends at Meritus Health. (Meritus Health, Hagerstown, MD.)**

the trend and improvement for laboratory and imaging ordering in the acute care setting, including six months prior to the start. Keys for success were predicated upon leadership identifying a prominent issue impacting patient safety and quality and effectively communicating the need for improvement. From there, leadership articulated a clear aim and selected appropriate measures and strategies to meet targets. Physician leaders were critical in success, in particular in promotion of a culture emphasizing continuous quality improvement.

## Lessons Learned

When selecting measures, improvement teams should employ the strategy of "collecting the critical few" and should seek usefulness, not perfection, in measurement (Byrnes 2014). Measurement is a means to an end. Improvement is the primary goal and improvement teams should only collect data that identifies and corrects the process under scrutiny. To achieve this goal, every data element collected should link to a report. This ensures that teams are not collecting excessive, unused data (Byrnes 2014).

From a strategic perspective, physician leaders should begin moving beyond myriad measures and data sources and toward, at an organizational level, a few, specific measures that drive high performance. An important lesson from the past decade of quality measurement is the need to coordinate and simplify measurement to more effectively drive improvement and reduce the data burden. There is a great opportunity for innovation in this realm.

One example of an innovation in patient safety measurement is the implementation of a total harm measure. Currently the numerous, disparate, and unaligned sources of data and measures can lead to measurement fatigue, duplicative efforts, and an abundance of data that is not necessarily effective in driving organizational improvement. Some health systems such as the Cincinnati Children's Hospital are utilizing an aggregate system-level measure for all-cause harm. Ongoing monitoring and reporting of this measure have enabled the organization to progress toward the goal of eliminating harm. They organize these within four core dimensions of quality, including patient and employee safety, clinical excellence outcomes, access, flow and productivity, and patient and family experience (Cincinnati Children's). Although no national metric exists for all-cause harm, organizations can begin to aggregate and track data on hospital-acquired conditions in their facilities to show trends over time in pursuit of the goal of zero patients harmed.

Tracking total harm reinforces the imperative to drive all patient harm to zero, emphasizes the connections across multiple areas of harm, provides an opportunity to focus on organization-wide improvement strategies, and engages leadership and boards to drive quality and patient safety through accountability and transparency. Using a total patient harm metric simplifies the current state of quality measurement, one characterized by numerous convoluted measures, enables greater organization-wide engagement, more effectively drives rapid cycle improvement, and builds accountability through transparency.

## Action Steps and Strategies to Lead

1. **Integrate measurements for improvement into organizational culture**. Clinicians, administrators, and other staff in hospitals are busy providing patient care. Participation in data collection and improvement teams can feel like extra work and time away from patient care. Therefore, it is imperative for leaders to communicate the importance of performance-improvement efforts and the

relationship to patient care. Physician leaders have an essential role in creating a culture that is data-driven and focused on continuous improvement. Teams—from management to unit teams—should be equipped and empowered to design and implement their own improvement projects, complete with measures that reflect their projects (Ransom 2014).

2. **Choose a few key "big dot" measures to track at an organizational level**. Physician leaders can focus strategic improvement efforts through intentionally selecting the organization's "big dot" or top outcome measures. When an organization prioritizes things such as total harm, patient satisfaction, and quality of care measures, everyone is held accountable and acts accordingly to meet those goals (Martin et al. 2007). This is an important strategy for preventing both leaders and staff from being flooded with measures and data. Teams must know for which key measures they are responsible.
3. **Connect measurement to action**. All measures should have a purpose and should be connected to action, whether a reporting requirement, improvement initiative, or organizational priority. Connecting data and measurement to the mission of the organization and to an action helps the staff responsible for collecting the data to remain engaged. To this end, clinical leaders should also seek to engage frontline employees in determining which measures to collect and how to motivate others to participate in improvement projects. Those closest to patient care are often the best source of information about what metrics should be used, where and how to collect the data, and how to motivate others to participate in improvement efforts (American Hospital Association and Health Research & Educational Trust 2014).
4. **Monitor the data burden**. Physician leaders have a role in monitoring data burdens and ensuring that data

collection processes are efficient, effective, and purposeful. Given the proliferation of national, state, and local initiatives to improve quality and safety and the lack of coordination around metrics, data burden and fatigue are critical barriers to quality-improvement efforts. Leaders should seek ways to streamline and coordinate data collection and be comfortable identifying when collection of a given metric can be discontinued.

5. **Smart analysis: Balancing measures and benchmarking**. Physician leaders have a role to encourage and guide the selection and analysis of metrics that drive efficient and effective improvement initiatives. When choosing measures, teams should always consider balancing measures and sources for benchmarking the data. Employing these two strategies helps to ensure that the improvement efforts are linked to a larger context that informs the true impact of the initiative to maximize the effort and impact of these teams.

## References

American Hospital Association and Health Research & Educational Trust. Implementation Guide Part I: A How-To Guide for Improvement for the AHA/HRET HEN Partnership for Patients, 2014.

Barclay, M.E., Dixon-Woods, M., Lyratzopoulos, G. Concordance of Hospital Ranks and Category Ratings Using the Current Technical Specification of US Hospital Star Ratings and Reasonable Alternative Specifications. *JAMA Health Forum.* 2022;3(5):e221006.

Blumenthal, D., Malphrus, E., McGinnis, J.M. *Vital Signs: Core Metrics for Health and Health Care Progress*, National Academy of Sciences Press, Washington, DC, 2015.

Byrnes, J.J. Data collection. In *The Healthcare Quality Book: Vision, Strategy, and Tools*, ed. Maulik S. Joshi, Elizabeth R. Ransom, David B. Nash, Scott B. Ransom, (3rd Ed). Health Administration Press, Chicago, IL, 2014, 111–133.

Centers for Disease Control and Prevention. National Healthcare Safety Network (NHSN). 2023. Accessed February 14, 2023. https://www.cdc.gov/nhsn/index.html

Centers for Medicare & Medicaid Services. Letter to State Medicaid Directors. 2008. http://downloads.cms.gov/cmsgov/archived-downloads/SMDL/downloads/SMD073108.pdf

Centers for Medicare & Medicaid Services. Readmissions Reduction Program. 2014. Accessed March 23, 2023. http://cms.gov/Medicare/Medicare-Fee-for-Service-Payment/AcuteInpatientPPS/Readmissions-Reduction-Program.html/

Centers for Medicare & Medicaid Services (CMS). *National Impact Assessment of the Centers for Medicare & Medicaid Services (CMS) Quality Measures Report*, U.S. Department of Health and Human Services, Baltimore, MD, 2021.

Centers for Medicare & Medicaid Services (CMS). Quality Payment Program Calendar Year (CY) 2023 Physician Fee Schedule (PFS) Final Rule: Revisions to Payment Policies under the Medicare Physician Fee Schedule, Quality Payment Program and Other Revisions to Part B for CY 2023 (CMS-1770-P). 2023.

Cincinnati Children's. System Level Measures. 2023 Accessed June 16, 2023. https://www.cincinnatichildrens.org/about/quality-measures/system-level-measures

Conway, P.H. The Core Quality Measures Collaborative: A Rationale and Framework for Public-Private Quality Measure Alignment. *Health Affairs Forefront*. 2015. Accessed February 5, 2023. https://www.healthaffairs.org/do/10.1377/forefront.20150623.048730

Goldberg, F. Engaging the Board in Harm Reduction at a Rural New York State Hospital. Presented at the *Annual Meeting of the Symposium for Leaders in Healthcare Quality*. 2014.

Health Research & Educational Trust. Health Care Leader Action Guide to Effectively Using HCAHPS. 2012. www.hpoe.org

Hospital Consumer Assessment of Healthcare Providers and Systems. HCAHPS Fact Sheet. 2021. Accessed March 23, 2023. https://hcahpsonline.org/globalassets/hcahps/facts/hcahps_fact_sheet_march_2021.pdf

Institute of Healthcare Improvement. Measures. 2014a. Accessed March 23, 2023. www.ihi.org/resources/pages/measures/default.aspx

Institute of Healthcare Improvement. Science of Improvement: Establishing Measures. 2014b. Accessed March 23, 2023. http://www.ihi.org/resources/Pages/HowtoImprove/ScienceofImprovementEstablishingMeasures.aspx

Jacobs, D.B., Schreiber, M., Seshamani, M., Tsai, D., Fowler, E., Fleisher, L.A. Aligning Quality Measures Across CMS – The Universal Foundation. *New England Journal of Medicine*. 2023;388(9):776–779.

Joynt, K.E., Jha, A.K. Characteristics of Hospitals Receiving Penalties Under the Hospital Readmissions Reduction Program. *JAMA*. 2013;309(4):342–343.

Kaiser Health News. A Guide to Medicare's Readmissions Penalties and Data. 2014. Accessed March 24, 2023. http://kaiserhealthnews.org/news/a-guide-to-medicare-readmissions-penalties-and-data/

Manary, M.P., Boulding, W., Staelin, R., Glickman, S.W. The Patient Experience and Health Outcomes. *JAMA*. 2013;368(3):201–203.

Martin, L.A., Nelson, E.C., Lloyd, R.C., Nolan, T.W. *Whole System Measures*, IHI Innovation Series white paper. Institute for Healthcare Improvement, Cambridge, MA, 2007.

Medicare.gov. What is Hospital Compare? Centers for Medicare & Medicaid Services. Accessed March 23, 2023. http://www.medicare.gov/hospitalcompare/About/What-Is-HOS.html

National Center for Quality Assurance. HEDIS & Performance Measurement. Accessed February 14, 2023. http://www.ncqa.org/HEDISQualityMeasurement.aspx

National Quality Forum (NQF). Serious Reportable Events in Healthcare—2011 Update: A Consensus Report. NQF, Washington, DC, 2011.

National Quality Forum (NQF). How Measures Will Serve Our Future. Accessed March 23, 2023. http://www.qualityforum.org/Measuring_Performance/ABCs/How_Measures_Will_Serve_Our_Future.aspx

Nutting, P.A., Crabtree, B.F., Miller, W.L., Stange, K.C., Stewart, E., Jaén, C. Transforming Physician Practices to Patient-Centered Medical Homes: Lessons from the National Demonstration Project. *Health Affairs*. 2011;30(3):439–445.

Porter, M.E., What Is Value in Health Care? *New England Journal of Medicine*. 2010;363(26):2477–2481.

Ransom, S.B., Ransom, E. Implementing Quality as the Core Organizational Strategy. In *The Healthcare Quality Book: Vision, Strategy, and Tools*, ed. Maulik S. Joshi, Elizabeth R. Ransom, David B. Nash, Scott B. Ransom (3rd Ed). Health Administration Press, Chicago, IL, 2014, 393–421.

Rogstad, T.L., Gupta, S., Connolly, J., Shrank, W.H., Roberts, E.T. Social Risk Adjustment in the Hospital Readmissions Reduction Program: A Systematic Review and Implications for Policy. *Health Affairs*. 2022;41(9):1307–1315.

Schmaltz, S., Hanold, L.S., Koss, R.G., Loeb, J.M. Statistical Tools for Quality Improvement. In *The Healthcare Quality Book: Vision, Strategy, and Tools*, ed. Maulik S. Joshi, Elizabeth R. Ransom, David B. Nash, and Scott B. Ransom (3rd Ed). Health Administration Press, Chicago, IL, 2014, 135–173.

Wadhera, R.K., Figueroa, J.F., Joynt Maddox, K.E., Rosenbaum, L.S., Kazi, D.S., Yeh, R.W. Quality Measure Development and Associated Spending by the Centers for Medicare & Medicaid Services. *JAMA*. 2020;323:1614–1616.

Wyszewianski, L. Basic Concepts of Healthcare Quality. In *The Healthcare Quality Book: Vision, Strategy, and Tools*, ed. Maulik S. Joshi, Elizabeth R. Ransom, David B. Nash, Scott B. Ransom (3rd Ed). Health Administration Press, Chicago, IL, 2014.

# Chapter 6

# Using Data for Feedback and Improvement

## The Evidence

Individuals and organizations need access to accurate, timely data to drive improvement. External stakeholders, such as hospital accreditors, insurance companies, and governments, also collect and analyze data to develop new products and guide their decision-making. These external databases can also be used to guide improvement programs (see Chapter 5). Currently, hospitals have numerous, disjointed sources of data ranging from administrative databases to patient registries. Where technology has revolutionized most other sectors by collecting and driving actionable data, health care still awaits transformational connectivity and advancement from data analytics (Brennan 2020). The integration of EHRs across clinical environments over the past decade has opened vast potential for collection of massive amounts of data and the promise to leverage this for direct improvement initiatives. To date, this remains mostly unrealized.


DOI: 10.4324/9781003402831-6

Lacking a more global framework to assess data and benchmarking, hospitals and organizations in health care typically collect internal data across four key categories or domains:

1. Clinical quality (processes and outcomes).
2. Financial performance.
3. Patient, physician, and staff satisfaction.
4. Functional status/patient outcomes.

In order to maintain a balanced perspective of the overall process of care, most mature organizations will deploy teams to improve performance across all four domains (Byrnes 2014). Once an aim has been identified and an improvement team formed, the next step is to collect the data that will guide and drive improvement.

## Step 1: Data Collection: Objectives, Sources, and Methods

When beginning a quality-improvement project, clinical leaders should consider the following (Byrnes 2014):

1. Identify the purpose of the data measurement activity (e.g., monitoring at regular intervals, investigation over a limited period, and one-time study).
2. Identify the most appropriate data sources for the activity.
3. Identify the most important measures to collect.
4. Design a common-sense strategy that will ensure collection of complete, accurate, and timely information.

There are many sources of data, which vary in cost, feasibility, accessibility, and accuracy.

**Medical record review** is a form of retrospective data collection that is particularly useful in providing detail on links between interventions and outcomes by offering additional data and elements that are not often available in administrative databases. Many national quality-improvement database projects, including the Healthcare Effectiveness Data and Information Set (HEDIS), Joint Commission Core Measures, Leapfrog Hospital Survey, National Quality Forum's National Voluntary Consensus Standards for Hospital Care, and Patient-Reported Outcomes Measurement Information System (PROMIS) require retrospective medical record review for a substantial portion of the data elements included. Disadvantages of medical record review include the significant investments of both time and money required (Byrnes 2014).

**Prospective data collection** also relies on the review of medical records but is conducted during a patient's hospitalization as opposed to retroactively. Prospective data collection enables staff to observe trends in patients in real time and intervene accordingly. This method also provides the best insight into how the timely administration of certain therapies contributes to a difference in outcomes, especially when the time window is small. Similar to medical record review, the largest disadvantages of prospective data collection are the expense and time involved. Specifically, this method is often criticized as taking time away from patient care responsibilities. Therefore, if organizations utilize this method, they should consider hiring dedicated research assistants or data analysts to assist with data collection (Byrnes 2014).

**Administrative databases** include data elements such as enrollment or eligibility information, claims information, and information on managed care encounters. Examples include hospital billing systems, health plan claims databases, health information management or medical record systems, and registration systems. Administrative data often includes hospitals, laboratories, and prescription drug services. The advantages of administrative databases include cost (relatively inexpensive), accessibility (incorporate transaction systems already used in daily operations), standardization across administrative databases (simplifies internal comparison and external benchmarking), high volume of available indicators, and accuracy.

However, administrative databases have been developed for financial and administrative purposes rather than for quality improvement. Therefore, some argue that these databases contain inadequate detail, many errors, and "dirty data," meaning that the data makes no sense or appears to have come from another source, potentially compromising the accuracy of the data (Byrnes 2014).

**Health plan databases** are particularly good sources of data for those quality-improvement projects that have a focus on population health management or that focus across the continuum of care because they track all health care received by their enrollees, regardless of provider. This data is electronically available and relatively inexpensive to access. However, there are limitations including questions of accuracy, detail, and timeliness. Additionally, though these databases track events, procedures, and lab tests, they do not always contain detailed information on outcomes (Byrnes 2014).

**Patient registries** allow organizations to create specialty or condition-specific reports. Patient registries are advantageous due to the ability to collect data over time, ease of customization, and the ability to incorporate multiple data sources and collection methodologies. Though the ability to customize is a significant advantage of registries, the time and costs required for patient registry data collection must be weighed against the insight they would provide (Byrnes 2014).

**Patient surveys**, a favorite tool of quality-improvement professionals, are used to gauge the perceptions of patients in terms of quality of the services provided. Surveys should be administered at the point-of-service, thereby allowing patients to immediately comment on their experience. Survey forms should be concise and easy to read. Though patient surveys are relatively easy to develop, teams often underestimate the scientific complexity of their design. Poorly designed surveys can undermine the validity and reliability of results (Byrnes 2014). Accordingly, teams should consult an expert in survey design to ensure they are not inadvertently biasing the results.

When choosing a data source and collection method, clinical leaders must balance the investment of time and money with the value that the data will contribute to the improvement effort. Data collection strategies often combine both code- and chart-based sources to optimize strengths and cost-effectiveness while minimizing weaknesses (Byrnes 2014).

Before collection starts, clinical leaders should guide their teams to ask the following questions (American Hospital Association and Health Research & Educational Trust 2014):

a. Why collect the data?
b. What data elements and specific types of data will be collected? Is a sample of data sufficient or are all applicable data necessary?
c. What is the time frame for data collection? Is the measurement prospective, retrospective, or both? If prospective, is a baseline available?
d. Where do the data reside (e.g., clinical registries, clinical records, and administrative systems)? Are there any regulatory or confidentiality issues to address?
e. How will the data be collected and by whom? What data collection resources and tools will be needed? How will the data be coded, edited, and verified?

The Institute for Healthcare Improvement recommends using the following to guide the data collection process (IHI "Measures" 2014):

1. **Aim for usefulness, not perfection**. Measurement is only a means to an end; collect just enough data to determine whether changes are leading to improvement.
2. **Integrate measurement into a consistent routine**. Do not wait until the end of a project to collect patient outcome data. Instead, establish a protocol for who will collect which data and when.
3. **Use both qualitative and quantitative data**. Quantitative data is essential to demonstrate improvement, but qualitative data is often easier to access and can be highly informative. Qualitative data is helpful in determining the story behind the quantitative data, helping to inform more effective strategies for sustainability and spread.
4. **Use sampling**. When patient volume is high, using a sampling method enables teams to accurately track performance in a more manageable way. This is a more simplified way to understand how a larger system is performing, saving time and resources while still tracking performance.
5. **Plot data over time (see Step 2: Displaying the Data)**. Graphic displays of data over time are effective ways to illustrate trends and patterns. This allows teams to identify what changes resulted in an improvement and to monitor the process for changes.

Once the appropriate source of data and method for data collection have been identified, the next step is to display the data in a manner that is easy to comprehend and actionable.

## Step 2: Displaying the Data

Two important attributes in using data for improvement are transparency and real-time feedback. Thus, teams should display the most current data possible in a manner that is accessible, easy to understand, and actionable. Examples of effective ways to display data to drive improvement include physician profiles, dashboards, and customized run charts.

## Physician Profiling

Physician profiles have become more commonplace as greater emphasis is placed on delivering care that is high quality and low cost. These tools provide insight on physician practice patterns, utilization of services, and patient outcomes through analyzing provider-specific and practice-level data. Physician profiles facilitate objective assessment and evaluation of physicians' treatment patterns and can be compared with evidence-based best practice recommendations. Additionally, physician profiles facilitate comparison against peers at the local, state, and national levels. Profiles can be tracked over time to track levels of improvement, responsiveness to coaching, and overall trends for an organization.

Physician profiles can decrease practice variation through promoting adherence to evidence-based clinical protocols (Nash et al. 2014). Comparative data is a powerful motivator as physicians are highly driven, goal-oriented individuals who are motivated to improve their performance against their peers. Physician leaders should transparently share this data across their teams. It is reasonable to deidentify specific physician names upfront, and to simply acknowledge outliers and variation in practice. Over time, physician leaders should consider the value of full transparency and accountability that can be found in sharing physician profiles unblinded. The use of physician profiles also encourages physician development through the pursuit of credentialing, board certification, and organizational quality-improvement initiatives (Nash et al. 2014).

## *Dashboards*

Performance dashboards are an effective tool for driving performance improvement across all levels of the organization—from unit-based quality-improvement efforts to governance dashboards used to track high-level metrics. Dashboards enable teams to quantify and track progress toward a goal. Effective dashboards incorporate the following (Office of Inspector General):

- **Set ambitious targets**. Teams should set both target and stretch goals. Setting high goals helps drive improvement and keeps organizations from becoming complacent.
- **Avoid color coding to low expectations**. Many dashboard users track progress by updating goals as green (meeting target), yellow (progressing toward target), or red (in jeopardy of not meeting target). However, a dashboard that is colored all green should be examined closely. Meeting targets too early and readily may indicate that those goals were not challenging enough. Though color coding is a useful tool to track progress, it should not diminish the value and nuances of the dashboard.
- **Simple is better**. This mantra holds true for most displays of data. Keep both the format of the dashboard (e.g., number of measures, display) and the measures clear and concise. Track only the key drivers of success on the dashboard.
- **Align goals with activities of stakeholders**. To engage anyone in improvement initiatives, you must demonstrate value—how does this effort impact something they care about? Dashboard measures should emphasize how all stakeholders contribute to the outcome of the project.
- **Use benchmarks**. Using both internal and external benchmarks helps organizations recognize gaps or blind spots.

Though a process may be improving and showing "green," it may still lag behind competitors or other national benchmarks. Whenever possible, organizations should benchmark their data to understand their performance compared to others.

- **Monitor results**. To effectively drive improvement, teams must be reminded of the goal that they are working toward and see the progress. Dashboards should be revisited and shared with the team on a regular basis to monitor progress and make adjustments as necessary.

## *Run Charts*

One of the most effective ways to display data for a quality-improvement initiative is through a run chart. Though there are more complex statistical tools that may be utilized (e.g., control charts, statistical process controls), run charts are a relatively simple and accessible method that any team can adopt to track the progress of an improvement initiative.

Run charts display data over time and enable improvement teams to assess how well (or poorly) a process is performing, help determine when changes are truly improvements, and provide information about the value of specific changes or interventions. Improvement teams can create run charts to track both process and outcome measures related to the project's aim. To promote transparency, run charts can be posted in break rooms or even on the unit. At one hospital in Oregon, every unit has a bulletin board that displays the data, run chart, and intervention information related to the unit's current improvement project. For example, a unit working on falls tracked the process measure (completion of hourly rounds) and the outcome measure (total patient falls) using a run chart. The board includes information for patients on how to contribute to reducing falls (i.e., using the call light, using non-slip mats) in order to engage patients and family members in the efforts.

There are infinite ways to display data, but teams should choose a method that (1) aligns with the purpose of the project, (2) enables all stakeholders to access and understand the data, (3) promotes transparency and accountability, and (4) is continuously monitored to enable teams to change interventions as appropriate.

An example run chart is shown in Figure 6.1. This run chart tracks the weekly number of hours of phone calls made to lonely residents in a community served by Meritus Health. The run chart is annotated with interventions implemented at different times and shows the median increasing over time.

## Step 3: Analyzing the Data

One of the biggest challenges in improvement is distinguishing between common cause and special cause variation and determining whether a change is actually an improvement. Common cause variation is natural, due to chance, and has no assignable cause. Special cause variation, however, signals an unnatural pattern with an assignable cause. Within a stable process, common cause variation is normal.

As referenced above, there are many complex statistical tools that may be used; however, there are also more simplistic, guiding rules that should be understood and employed by all working on improvement initiatives.

The Institute for Healthcare Improvement has developed numerous modules and tools on using run charts for improvement and specifically to help determine if a change is really an improvement. These "run chart rules" help identify common cause versus special cause variation and help teams determine whether an intervention is actually driving an improvement (Perla et al. 2011).

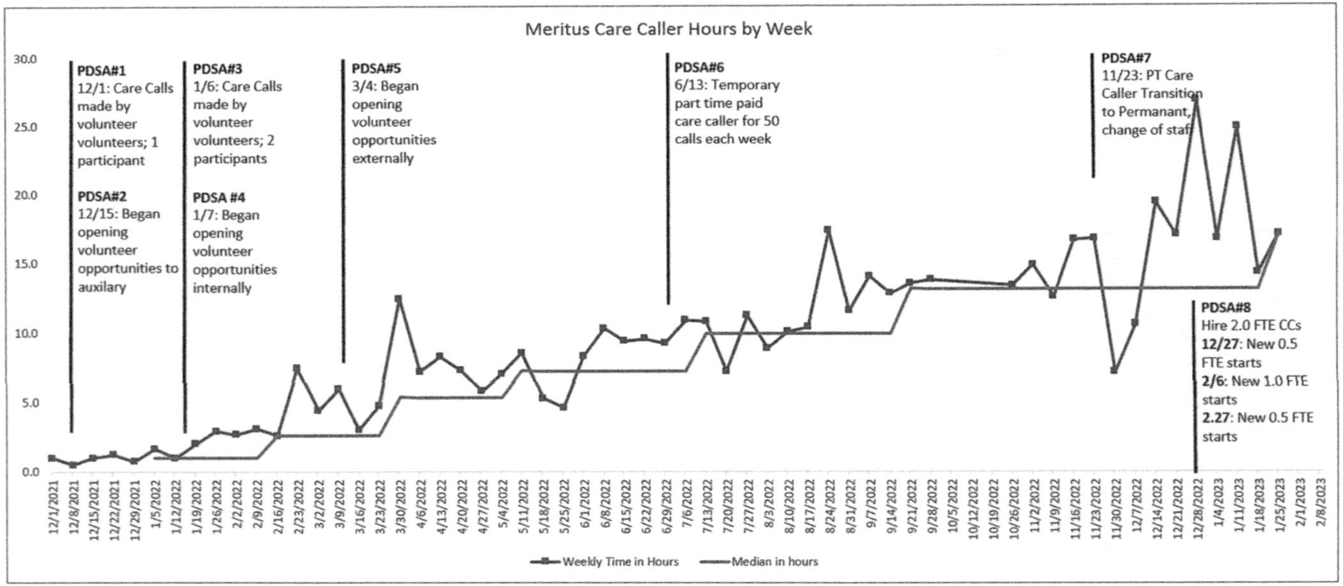


**Figure 6.1 Sample run chart demonstrating number of hours of calls per week trended over time, tracked with notation of PDSA interventions. Plan–Do–Study–Act. (Meritus Health, Hagerstown, MD.)**

The key elements of a run chart include the centerline, the median value of the run chart, the y-axis (i.e., the value of the measure), and the x-axis (i.e., time). Run charts can be broken into "runs," defined as one or more consecutive data points on the same side of the median (excluding those points on the median). Refer to these four run chart rules to determine if special case variation is present:

1. **A shift in the process**. Six or more consecutive points above or below the median indicate that there has been a shift in the process and that an intervention has made an impact.
2. **A trend**. Five or more consecutive points, all increasing or decreasing, indicate nonrandom variation.
3. **Too many or too few runs**. If a process is stable, there is a predictable number of runs. If an intervention is successful, the previous process will be disrupted and there will be fewer or more runs in the resulting data.
4. **An "astronomical" data point**. If a data point is significantly above or below the median, it is considered "astronomical" and indicates nonrandom variation. These should be investigated for special causes and addressed appropriately. This could be caused by having incorrect data or by some unusual event.

More details on these rules and methodology are available through the Institute for Healthcare Improvement (IHI QI Project Workbook 2019).

There are also many sources of information on statistical process control charts and additional tools for monitoring random versus nonrandom variation. As a physician leader, it is important to develop competencies in this area and guide teams to understand whether their changes are resulting in an improvement.

## Step 4: Implementing Improvement Cycles

The last step in the process of using data for improvement is to conduct improvement cycles, that is, to implement an intervention at first on a small scale and gradually to a larger group as an evidence base develops for its success. Chapter 2 provides details on improvement methodology including PDSA cycles, Lean, and Six Sigma. Whichever improvement method is chosen, all should be guided by ongoing data collection and analysis.

## Case Study: Improving and Enhancing Surgical Recovery

Anthony Petrick, M.D., is the chief quality officer for Inpatient Services at Geisinger Medical Center. Geisinger Health System, located in central Pennsylvania, was one of the early adopters of the electronic health record. At the time of implementation in the mid-1990s, system leaders recognized the opportunity to use EHR data to improve health outcomes. In 2017, leaders identified variation in surgical care, in particular with regard to outcomes across services and between providers. Seeking improvement, the ProvenRecovery® program was conceived as an evidence-based enhanced recovery initiative that hardwires best practices into the EHR, and then monitors protocol adherence and clinical outcomes. This program is specifically focused on the best perioperative care from the initial pre-surgical visit, through the operation, inpatient stay, and post-discharge care plan. Each area is monitored for adherence to the protocols as well as patient outcomes in a dashboard available to all providers and leadership.

Leaders recognized that significant time and effort are required to design best practice care pathways. However, evidence increasingly shows that monitoring adherence to pathways is what drives results. A recent study demonstrated that hospitals participating in the American College of Surgeons colorectal enhanced recovery program struggle to improve adherence. Over 80% of hospitals were unable to achieve meaningful improvement in care pathway opportunities. Adherence actually got worse in 28% of care elements (Shah et al. 2023). Geisinger understood that adherence to best practice protocols is necessary for successful outcomes. ProvenRecovery® dashboards were designed to pull data directly from the EHR, standardized between clinical programs, and developed to provide data in near real time with daily updates. Displays include quarterly and year-over-year trends allowing visualization of both snapshots and performance over time.

Adherence dashboards were built to measure key process indicators for each program. Figure 6.2 depicts data tracked from the EHR, showing key measures as well as outcomes as they progressed year-over-year through the initiative. Dashboards were standardized to reflect phases of care and targets were set at 70% adherence. The left dashboard in Figure 6.2 reflects the implementation of more than 40 clinical programs over seven years at Geisinger. A general trend toward improved adherence is clear, but adherence varies between programs and over time. Adherence was found to be primarily driven through order sets. Thus, unique order sets were designed for each program with best practices defaulted when possible. Operational efforts prioritized order set compliance resulting in greater than 90% adherence both pre- and post-operatively in the most recent year.

It is imperative that dashboards be intuitive, or providers will not use them. Color coding simplifies interpretation enabling providers to understand, immediately, whether goals are being met or an opportunity requires action. ProvenRecovery® dashboards allow users to dive deep into specific surgical programs, institutes, service lines, or even

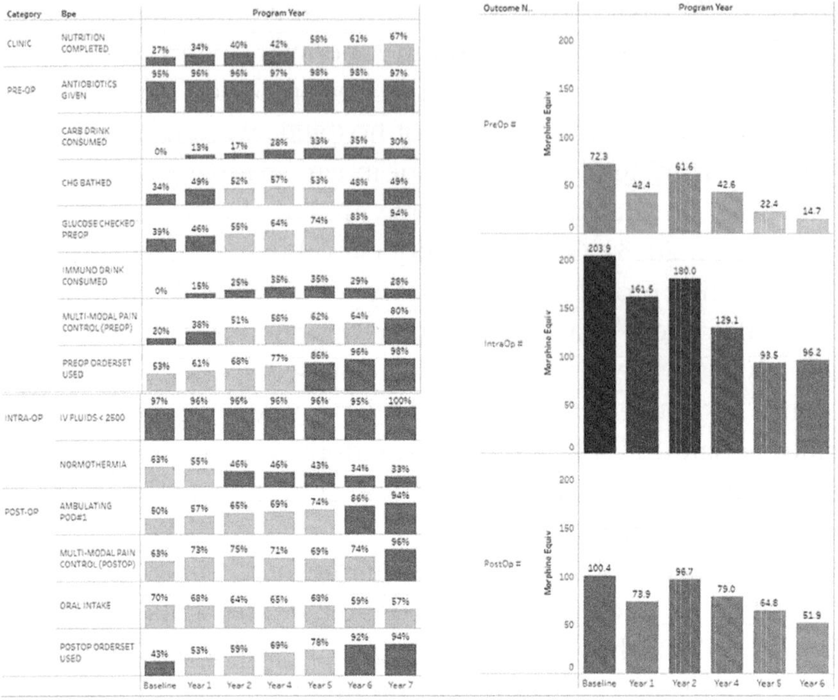


**Figure 6.2 Geisinger ProvenRecovery® enhanced recovery dashboard. (Geisinger Health, Danville, PA.)**

individual surgeons to learn how they compare to benchmarks and to their peers. The data is then used by providers and leadership to identify success and opportunities.

When designing the outcomes dashboard, Geisinger focused on quality (mortality, complications, readmissions, and length of stay) and cost of care, as depicted in Figure 6.3. The ProvenRecovery® dashboards report observed versus expected ratios (O:E) for these outcome measures. Again, year-over-year data demonstrated a general trend toward improved O:E for all clinical outcome measures. The cost of care throughout the initiative has improved as well.

ProvenRecovery® was launched as the opioid crisis was escalating and at a time when it became clear that opioid prescribing was a significant part of the opioid crisis.

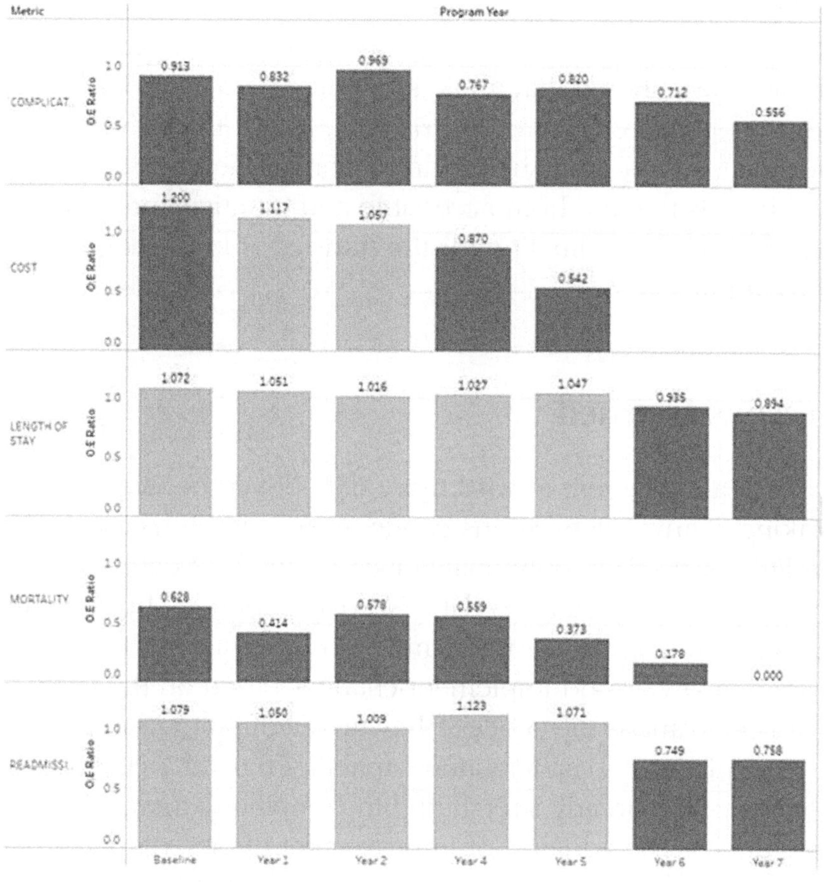


**Figure 6.3 Geisinger ProvenRecovery® clinical outcomes dashboard. (Geisinger Health, Danville, PA.)**

The effort to decrease opioids during and after surgery using multimodal pain medication regimens was tracked and showed large reductions in opioid use in all phases of care, and this is visualized on the right side of Figure 6.2. Morphine milligram equivalents (MME) that patients receive perioperatively has steadily decreased since the implementation of the program. More importantly, discharge opioid prescribing has been significantly reduced which limits the availability of prescription opioid for diversion in the community.

Data now seems ubiquitous in health care; however, we still struggle to use it effectively to improve patient care. Studies have shown that it takes 17 years for a best practice to become standard of care (Morris et al. 2011). Leaders at Geisinger have found success in utilizing adherence data in dashboards that are both accessible and intuitive and that this can compress the timeline for the transfer of knowledge into clinical practice.

## Lessons Learned

Despite a movement toward more data-driven decision-making, many organizations continue to make decisions based on little or no data, only qualitative or anecdotal data, or inaccurately characterized data. No data is perfect, but organizations and teams must find simple and useful ways to collect, display, analyze, and implement changes based on the data that is relevant to the process they are attempting to improve.

Organizational capacity and capability remain a challenge. Clinicians are already stretched thin completing their patient-care duties. The addition of improvement efforts, particularly those that require skills (i.e., data analytics) that have not been taught, is daunting. To combat this, physician leaders can support teams through training, designating specific staff time to these projects, or hiring data analysts or research assistants specifically to contribute to these teams.

Another challenge for improvement projects is sustainability, particularly sustaining data collection processes amid other competing demands. Given the many demands and opportunities for other improvement projects, teams must make decisions on when to scale back or end measurement in order to free up resources and attention to address new projects.

Processes should be monitored beyond the close of the improvement project to ensure that they are sustained and that any issues are addressed as they occur. However, once a process has become stable, monitoring does not need to continue indefinitely.

Finally, when implementing any project that involves data, especially data on individual performance, organizations should expect resistance, skepticism, and denial. For example, common critiques of physician profiling include the lack of consensus around what should be measured, where to pull the data, accuracy of the information, and how to compare data across organizations. Additionally, many physicians express skepticism claiming that clinical practice does not include "one size fits all" processes and that even generally accepted guidelines may not appropriately apply to their particular population of patients. When implementing new measurement tools or reports, it is important to include physicians in the discussion and development of the tools, acknowledge and address the shortcomings to the extent possible, but also recognize the value despite the shortcomings and emphasize those opportunities to drive improvement and provide safer, more high-quality patient care.

In all efforts to use data for improvement, physician leaders have a role in (1) demonstrating commitment and support for analytic capability, (2) finding easy, clear ways to display data, and (3) ensuring that data is transparent, current, and relevant.

## Action Steps and Strategies to Lead

1. **Support teams in developing plans for data collection, reporting, and analytics**. Finding and analyzing the relevant and accurate data involves commitment and resources. Physician leaders can help teams to develop feasible plans that add value and efficiency to their projects.
2. **Provide ongoing feedback through dialog and draw clear connections between the data and**

**recommendations (i.e., clinical guidelines) and what actions are necessary to improve the process**. Data is not useful if it is not reviewed on an ongoing basis to check for changes and opportunities. If clinicians do not understand the data or do not see it as valuable, then discontent, skepticism, and rebellion against the data and reports can undermine the project. As a physician leader, your role is to promote transparency, explain the data, including the strengths and caveats, and guide your colleagues to engage with the data in a productive way.

3. **Use graphical methods to display data**. Find simple, concise ways to display data that show the relationship between action and results. Physician leaders should find ways to make data accessible to all who are working on improvement projects. It should not require an advanced degree in statistics to understand the data required to implement an improvement project. Leaders should seek new and innovative ways to display data to drive improvement.
4. **Explain change and variation in terms of special cause versus common cause**. This is a core element of using data for improvement. Leaders must demonstrate an understanding of the difference in special versus common cause variation in order to effectively and efficiently drive improvement work. As a physician leader, if you explain changes in these terms, it becomes embedded in the organizational culture to think of processes in this way.

## References

American Hospital Association and Health Research & Educational Trust. Implementation Guide Part I: A How-To Guide for Improvement for the AHA/HRET HEN Partnership for Patients, 2014.

Brennan, N. The US Health Data Ecosystem in 2020—Brave New World or Same Old, Same Old? *JAMA Health Forum*. 2020;1(4):e200445.

Byrnes, J.J. Data Collection. In *The Healthcare Quality Book: Vision, Strategy, and Tools*, ed. Maulik S. Joshi, Elizabeth R. Ransom, David B. Nash, Scott B. Ransom (3rd Ed). Health Administration Press, Chicago, IL, 2014, 111–133.

Health Research & Educational Trust and Kaufman, Hall & Associates, Inc. Value-Based Contracting, 2013. www.hpoe.org

Institute for Healthcare Improvement. Science of Improvement: Establishing Measures. 2014. Accessed February 15, 2023. www.ihi.org/resources/Pages/HowtoImprove/ScienceofImprovementEstablishingMeasures.aspx

Institute for Healthcare Improvement. QI Project Workbook: A Resource for IHI's Quality Improvement Practicum. Run Chart Rules Reference Sheet. 2019. Accessed February 15, 2023. www.ihi.org/education/IHIOpenSchool/Courses/Documents/11_RunChartRulesReferenceSheet.pdf

Morris, Z.S., Wooding, S., Grant, J. The Answer is 17 years, What is the Question: Understanding Time Lags in Translational Research. *Journal of the Royal Society of Medicine*. 2011;104(12):510–520.

Nash, D.B., Jacoby, R., Berman, B. Physician, Provider Profiling. In *The Healthcare Quality Book: Vision, Strategy, and Tools*, ed. Maulik S. Joshi, Elizabeth R. Ransom, David B. Nash, Scott B. Ransom (3rd Ed). Health Administration Press, Chicago, IL, 2014, 175–192.

Office of Inspector General. Driving for Quality in Acute Care: A Board of Directors Dashboard. Government Industry Roundtable. Compliance Resources for Health Care Boards. Accessed February 15, 2023. https://oig.hhs.gov/compliance/compliance-resource-material/

Perla, R.J., Provost, L.P., Murray, S.K. The Run Chart: A Simple Analytical Tool for Learning from Variation in Healthcare Processes. *BMJ Quality & Safety*. 2011;20:46–51.

Schmaltz, S., Hanold, L.S., Koss, R.G., Loeb, J.M. Statistical Tools for Quality Improvement. In *The Healthcare Quality Book: Vision, Strategy, and Tools*, ed. Maulik S. Joshi, Elizabeth R. Ransom, David B. Nash, Scott B. Ransom (3rd Ed). Health Administration Press, Chicago, IL, 2014, 135–173.

Shah, T.A., Knapp, L., Cohen, M.E., Brethauer, S.A., Wick, E.C., Ko, C.Y., et al. Truth of Colorectal Enhanced Recovery Programs: Process Measure Compliance in 151 Hospitals. *Journal of the American College of Surgeons*. 2023;236(4):543–550.

Swed, F.S., Eisenhart, C. Tables for Teaching Randomness of Grouping in a Sequence of Alternatives. *The Annals of Mathematical Statistics*. 1943;14: 66–87.

# Chapter 7

# Physician Champions

## The Evidence

*"Were any physicians involved?"*

This is a question that every health care leader has likely heard at least once during his or her career, and it is a question with a lot of weight and implicit commentary. It is a statement that not only asks about the participation of a physician, but of the right kind of physician. The inquirer is not asking if a physician in administration was involved; he or she is asking if a currently practicing peer or clinical colleague participated in the design and implementation of the improvement initiative.

Another way to pose the question is: "Was there a physician champion involved?"

The restatement shows that physicians themselves recognize the importance of a specific physician in transformation activities. Physician champions are critical in facilitating improvement as they bring credibility and clinical experience. Physician culture tends to promote professional autonomy and independence. Further to this, physicians do often bring

DOI: 10.4324/9781003402831-7

unique perspectives on patient care and teamwork. Thus, the role of the physician voice in decision-making cannot be understated, and having engaged physician champions supporting and leading initiatives can make or break the success and spread of improvement.

It is also important to note that recent decades have brought increasing involvement of advanced practice professionals (APP), overarchingly nurse practitioners (NP), and physician associates (PAs) into direct clinical care. In 2010, there were approximately 106,000 nurse practitioners and 70,000 physician assistants practicing in the United States (AHRQ 2012). Just nine years later in 2019, that number had risen to 248,000 NPs and 115,500 PAs (Sarzynski and Barry 2019). In some cases, APPs function in clinical roles that share similar scope to those of physicians, and thus bring value in their perspectives and experience as well. While this chapter uses the term "physician" as champion, it is equally important to include and engage APPs in improvement work. There are many instances in which an APP can serve as an invaluable champion for improvement efforts, and likewise they will need to be involved in the processes of clinical transformation.

## Characteristics of Effective Champions

Physician leaders serving as change agents need several tools to influence physician behavior including strong evidence from scientific literature, performance metrics at the group and individual physician levels, and, perhaps most importantly, peer pressure and influence.

The key tactic in the strategy of peer influence is the engagement and development of a physician champion. Although a non-physician can provide the evidence and performance data, the receptivity of the message is heightened when it comes from a respected clinical peer. The role of a physician champion includes the following:

1. **Communicator**: Messaging is at the core of a physician champion's role. Communication includes effective dialog with peers one-on-one and in small group settings. It also includes the ability to communicate in large forums and in settings that are more formal.
2. **Advocate**: The physician champion should voice his or her individual perspective and also advocate for the consensus among clinical peers, particularly with regard to clinical matters. In some cases, the physician champion may be the only clinical representative on an improvement team. It is important for them to be able to speak about how decisions will impact clinical teams, direct care delivery, and ultimately patients.
3. **Role model**: A physician champion should be in the vanguard with respect to the adoption and the active promotion of new processes and new workflows. He or she should be an active role model whose visibility and communication about an initiative engenders a sense of trust and willingness to change among other physicians.
4. **Translator**: A physician champion serves as the bridge between an initiative and the physicians. The champion must effectively translate the need and basis for the initiative, the individual tactics that are required, and the relevant performance data into a format that is easily received and understood by physicians. This role of translator also extends between physicians and administration. The physician champion must be able to articulate clinical concepts to non-clinicians and similarly may need to translate administrative and business imperatives to clinicians.
5. **Test Driver**: New tests of change are typically carried out as small pilots to measure impact. Physician

champions are often the best suited to be a part of these initial test periods, and thus must be comfortable with change, flexibility, and innovation. When the tests of change lead to noted improvement, these champions can then speak from their position of experience to spread the initiative. When tests of change are unsuccessful, they must be able to rebound effectively. Physician champions can also be invaluable if they are able to be innovative and propose potential solutions to problems throughout the improvement process.

It is important to understand a physician champion's role in order to identify and select the right individual. A physician champion is a key opinion leader who is able to influence the behavior and practice of his or her physician colleagues. This does not necessarily require the physician to hold a formal title within an organization. Often, informal leaders without a designated institutional role can be the most effective champions for change. These champions are often widely admired and respected by their colleagues. They are individuals to whom peers turn for counsel and guidance. Use this as an informal gut check of a potential physician champion candidate—it is the physician that others tend to congregate around in the community, at events, as well as on the floors, units, and within the medical staff lounge. It is the physician that other physicians may want to care for them.

This quick visual of how physicians congregate or an informal dialogue with physicians about who they respect should help to readily identify potential candidates for a physician champion. Going deeper, the search for a physician champion should look for a few additional key characteristics:

1. Compassion to serve and improve patient care and well-being.
2. Enthusiasm and passion for the change initiative.

3. Advocacy of patient-centered care and outcome-based care.
4. Reception to coaching and feedback.
5. Strong communication skills in group and individual settings.
6. Willingness to grow, develop, and mature as a leader.

Once a physician champion candidate has been identified, the next step is to convince him or her to provide time and leadership, sometimes uncompensated, toward a clinical change project. It is important to connect to the candidate's "why" in order to identify the underlying passion and drive for the work he or she does. It is important to encourage the proposed champion to talk about his or her interests and concerns at both personal and professional levels. Active listening on behalf of the recruiter is essential to accurately gauge potential interest and secure the candidate's engagement. This also forms the basis in subsequent conversations to illustrate the intersection between the champion's "why" and the motivation for the change improvement program.

Active listening and connecting to underlying motivation to identify a potential champion are also motivational tools that the champion will use in his or her role. Tactics to influence behavior include the following:

1. **Active listening**. There may be an inherent bias by physicians to offer opinions and make decisions quickly and instinctively. The tendency arises from the model of clinical practice wherein a problem is presented in the form of a patient and a course of action must be prescribed quickly. This clinical framework can be adapted, however, and can alternatively be used to reinforce the notion of actively listening and understanding before making a decision. Active listening to clinical peers' concerns and comments is an important step toward

promoting engagement and building relationships that ultimately lead to more critical conversations around changing behavior. A dialog between a champion and an individual physician, or group, is not possible without this fundamental step of active listening.

2. **Connect to a physician's "why."** In the book *The Happiness Hypothesis*, author Jonathan Haidt articulates the need to appeal to both the emotional and rational sides of the brain to motivate change (Haidt 2006). For the physician champion, the emotional side involves connecting to some of the underlying intrinsic passion of a physician. This can be referred to as a physician's "why" or primary emotive motivation for their actions. This "why" is often connected to promoting the patient's best interest. It is important for a physician champion to identify this "why" in his or her colleagues and establish a link between this emotional motivation and the change initiative at hand. This often also involves tying the efforts for any initiative to expected improvement and positive impact on patient care. Additionally, those initiatives that increase efficiencies for physicians or their team members are likely to have greater buy in and can be messaged in line with decreasing work burden.
3. **Employing anecdotes and stories**. Stories and anecdotes are a powerful way to create a memorable basis for change. Narrative and storytelling are intrinsic within humans (Taleb 2010). These strategies are a key basis for socialization and are essential for the interpretation and distillation of complex information. Stories are a familiar format for the receipt, understanding, and internalization of information. Likewise, they are often the very heart of most physician's experience in patient care, that is, in the collecting of a patient history and the story of presenting illness. A physician champion should leverage stories in the form of cases of individual patients or personal

experiences to engender a familiar and enduring basis for change.

4. **Invoking evidence-based information**. The physician champion should have a ready base of literature and external evidence to support the need for a change. Although some of this evidence base may be strictly clinical, some of it may also be in the realm of health services research, including evidence related to organizational behavior, behavioral economics, incentives, and health care financing. In cases where published literature is scant or unavailable, it is helpful to obtain best practice information from external institutions. Qualitative benchmarking of practice against peers or best-in-class institutions can be an equally powerful substitute for peer-reviewed literature.
5. **Utilizing objective, personalized performance data**. In order to appeal to rational motivation for change, physician champions should utilize data and performance metrics. These measures can be process-oriented or outcome-oriented, aggregated at the level of the hospital or unit as well as community or clinic. These can then further be presented at the individual patient or physician level. Presenting individual physician-level data can be a powerful motivator for change. It is recommended to initially use blinded comparative data, except for in the review of an individual physician's performance. Each physician should receive his or her own unblended data. For an underperforming physician, a typical reaction includes denial, questioning, and dismissing the accuracy of the data and metrics. With validation and time, however, this resistance should gradually give way to acceptance and an increased intrinsic motivation for individual behavior transformation. Tethering data to real-world impact on patient care is essential to move beyond the perception of simply assigning grades to clinicians.

Physician leaders that identify peers as physician champions should seek to support their work wherever possible. This may be done by connecting champions to others that can help with their success, such as champions of past projects or individuals at other institutions. Physician leaders should also seek help with promotion and marketing, resource procurement, or production of visual aids, diagrams, run charts, etc. As time commitments for clinical work may be pressing, and particularly when physician champions are not directly compensated for leading initiatives, it is all the more imperative to make sure the work is not unduly onerous. At times, identification of co-champions for particularly important initiatives can enhance optics as well as divide the amount of work involved.

The role of a physician leader supporting a peer physician champion is to promote them to perform at the highest scope of their skillset. In many cases, this may require facilitating attainment of evidence, information, quality measures, and data. Empowering champions includes inviting their voice and perspective, sharing data, and placing them in the position to be a role model, communicate, and lead change. If physicians spend too much time sifting through spreadsheets and correlating data, this leaves much less time for them to do the important work of speaking, role modeling, and leading necessary change in clinical settings.

## Case Study: Identifying and Developing Champions

The following case study illustrates the application of these concepts around the physician champion role, responsibilities, and motivational tools for performance improvement.

At Community General Hospital, the leadership team has recently received nationally benchmarked data on length of stay in the intensive care unit. This risk-adjusted data indicates significant opportunity for improvement, prompting a decision to begin a quality improvement initiative dedicated to reducing ICU length of stay. The initiative will be led by the vice president of quality and safety.

This vice president has previously recognized the importance of physician practice and behavior change in improvement work. Accordingly, she begins a search for a physician champion. The vice president recognizes that there are several critical care groups practicing at their hospital and decides to identify at least two champions to balance the mix of practice and potential diversity of opinion.

As a first step, this vice president turns to several physician opinion leaders for guidance. These are individuals with informal leadership roles who represent a diversity of opinion and whose confidence and relationship the vice president has nurtured for several years. This informal "physician cabinet" results in the names of at least four critical care physicians who are well-respected members of the medical staff and have a passion for quality improvement and patient advocacy.

In conversation with the first physician champion candidate, the vice president begins a dialog around some of the physicians' concerns and areas of frustration from a quality and safety perspective related to critical care patients. The vice president spends most of the time actively listening, seeking to understand the physician perspective, and taking notes for future reference. The vice president concludes the brief conversation by saying she would like to process some of this feedback and follow up to see if the conversation might have a connection to some work under consideration for reducing ICU length of stay.

In a follow-up conversation with the physician, the vice president processes the initial physician feedback and explicitly connects it with the proposed project on ICU length of stay. The vice president shares a story of a recent patient that illustrates some of the opportunities for improvement and is purposeful in connecting the dialog to the physician's intrinsic motivation to provide high-quality care for patients. The vice president closes with an offer to the physician to leverage his passion and knowledge as a physician champion for the length of stay transformation initiative. The physician indicates that he is interested and would like additional details.

In their final conversation, the vice president follows up to ensure the candidate has an explicit understanding of the requirements for a physician champion. She emphasizes the key roles around advocacy, communicating with physicians in informal and group settings, role modeling, and serving as a bridge and translator between administration and practicing physicians. They also discuss key characteristics of a physician champion. The vice president assesses the candidate's enthusiasm for the work, responsiveness to coaching, capacity for growth, and communication and speaking abilities. In addition, information is provided to the candidate regarding the time commitment, potential schedule of meetings, and duration of the work.

After selecting and identifying the physician champions, the improvement project formally begins. During the project, the project leader encourages the physician champions to informally dialog with their peers and other clinical colleagues about the work. The champions also provide routine updates at the critical care department meeting to ensure transparency of the work and to solicit feedback from physician stakeholders. The physician champions provide stories and individual cases that illustrate defects in the care process and supply recently published literature and evidence reviews related to the process in question. Throughout the development process, the champions are encouraged to actively listen to feedback and are provided coaching on this technique from the vice president of medical affairs.

Once the review of results from an initial pilot is complete, the project group identifies individual physicians who are not following the new protocol and require individual coaching. The physician champions embrace the role and arrange for a series of informal "cup of coffee" talks in the medical staff lounge. The champions, who have been receiving coaching and guidance throughout the process, use a variety of motivational change techniques to connect and influence their colleagues, especially through using blinded comparison data on performance and evidence-based literature, and through connecting to the physicians' intrinsic passion for patient-centered care. Critical care physician peers provide additional reinforcement for the change. The champions themselves are also diligent about being visible in the ICU and role modeling the expected changes in practice before nurses, house staff, and their colleagues. All of these motivational tools are employed over a series of months, with a continuation of informal physician conversations. After a few months, the initiative is able to identify a sustained impact on the ICU length of stay. The project team continues to monitor the results, track and trend data, and meet on a less-frequent basis to ensure the sustainment of results.

## Lessons Learned

Across many industries, including health care, change initiatives often fail. This is anticipated and inevitable. Professor John Kotter has identified reasons for failure and the corresponding eight success factors for change (Kotter 2007). One of the essential elements is the notion of forming a powerful guiding coalition. Within health care transformation activities, a component of such coalition formation is the selection of an effective physician champion. A physician champion who can articulate the reasons for change and can influence peer behavior is essential in any change that will impact clinical care. The physician champion is often the core of the guiding coalition.

The importance of the physician champion in clinical process improvement has been increasingly recognized in the past several years. This is especially true with respect to the implementation of electronic medical records and advancement of telehealth (Shea and Belden 2015). Both of these technology initiatives have had a direct and, in many cases, irreversible impact upon physician workflow and practice. This experience with health care information technology and the critical importance of the physician champion can be applied to almost all health care change initiatives that require broad physician stakeholder support and engagement. The selection of a physician champion is now a "must" when contemplating an agenda of health care transformation.

## Action Steps and Strategies to Lead

1. **Identify key stakeholders to constitute a guiding coalition**. One of the first steps in working through a change is identifying key stakeholders to constitute a guiding coalition. In clinical transformation, physicians and APPs are an essential constituency to be acknowledged and influenced. The physician champion is a bridge role between the change team and administration, the community, and the broader medical staff to enact and sustain any successful process improvement.
2. **Seek guidance and counsel from other physicians**. In identifying and recruiting a physician champion, seek out guidance and counsel from other physicians. Ask colleagues to whom they turn for advice and whose

opinion is widely regarded. In assessing potential candidates, ensure they are not simply key opinion leaders, but individuals who have strong communication skills, a passion for patient-centered care, and an inherent willingness and ability to grow and develop.

3. **Actively guide and assist the physician champion**. Once you have identified a physician champion for your team, it is a leader's responsibility to actively guide and assist the physician champion. As a leader, you should demonstrate the behaviors of change for the physician champion to emulate. This role modeling should include active listening, connecting to the "why," utilizing storytelling, and relying on evidence-based data. These are not just tools in the physician champion repertoire; they are essential levers for any successful clinical leader.

The physician champion serves as an essential voice in clinical transformation and should be engaged as an extension of the prowess and impact of an organization's senior clinical leadership. As such, the selection and development of the physician champion should be done with prudence and deliberate, active coaching. This will ensure that the physician champion will measure up to the opportunity and potential of the role.

## References

AHRQ. *The Number of Nurse Practitioners and Physician Assistants Practicing Primary Care in the United States*, Accessed March 23, 2023. Agency for Healthcare Research and Quality, Rockville, MD, 2012. https://www.ahrq.gov/research/findings/factsheets/primary/pcwork2/index.html

Haidt, J. *The Happiness Hypothesis*, Basic Books, Philadelphia, 2006.

Kotter, J. Leading Change: Why Transformation Efforts Fail. *Harvard Business Review*. 2007. Reprint R0701J.

Sarzynski, E., Barry, H. Current Evidence and Controversies: Advanced Practice Providers in Healthcare. *The American Journal of Managed Care*. 2019;25(8):366–368.

Shea, C.M., Belden, C.M. What is the Extent of Research on the Characteristics, Behaviors, and Impacts of Health Information Technology Champions? A Scoping Review. *BMC Medical Informatics and Decision Making*. 2015;16(2), 1–17.

Taleb, N.N. *The Black Swan: The Impact of the Highly Improbable* (2nd Ed). Random House, New York, 2010.

# Chapter 8

# Leading Effective Teams: For Clinical Care and Performance Improvement

## The Evidence

Teams and teamwork are often hailed as solutions to many of the problems that ail the U.S. health care system. There is certainly much potential to improve quality, safety, efficiency, and patient experience through team-based care. Not all teams are created equal, however. Creating effective teams requires an informed and intentional approach.

A team is defined as involving two or more people who differentiate their roles, share common goals, interact with each other, and perform tasks that affect others (Taplin et al. 2013). Specifically, work teams accomplish tasks on an ongoing basis in a specific organizational setting (e.g., primary care team, surgical team, and emergency department team). Other types include parallel teams to address shared challenges,

DOI: 10.4324/9781003402831-8

project teams to focus on a one-time deliverable with a limited term, and management teams for oversight. This chapter includes strategies for physician leaders to create effective work teams (i.e., clinical care teams) and project teams (i.e., performance improvement teams with specific, measurable aims).

## *Clinical Care Teams*

Currently, much of U.S. health care is delivered in silos with physicians and practice staff isolated from one another. Practices are often designed around supporting physicians' routines, not around patient needs or preferences. As a result, practices struggle to meet the increasingly diverse needs of patients and, in many cases, patient satisfaction and outcomes suffer. As health care teams expand and integration improves, there is recognition that patient outcomes improve in concert (Pany et al. 2021).

National efforts such as accountable care organizations incentivize hospitals and practices to reorganize to be team based and to have processes and workflows that are dictated by patient, not provider, needs. Both local and national efforts are also increasingly emphasizing the role of patients and their family members as active and important members of care teams. In the broader scope of team development and feedback, physician leaders should be aware of and incorporate input from patients and families. See Chapter 10 for more on how effective leaders work with these groups.

Research shows that effective teams have the following characteristics: Strong leadership, a clear division of labor, adequate training for team members in their respective roles, and organizational policies that support the team structure. To build and maintain effective care delivery teams, organizations must invest in training, creation of protocols, adoption of rules related to decision-making and communication, and granting of designated, non-patient care time for team meetings (Bodenheimer 2007). Physician leaders have unique insights into the importance of these components and can be advocates for creating protocols and rules that effectively guide and streamline patient care work processes and allow all members of the team to maximize their contribution to patient care. Without organizational support and a culture that values teamwork, care will remain siloed and uncoordinated.

Two key mechanisms that leaders can use to enhance teams are: (1) Providing training and support (i.e., designated non-patient care time) for teamwork and (2) aligning incentives and interdependent functions of team members to achieve patient goals (Taplin et al. 2013). Support and training include creating an organizational culture that promotes teamwork, providing teamwork training for employees on specific skills, emphasizing hiring and promotion based on both team and technical clinical skills, prioritizing ongoing coaching, providing time for non-patient care, and ensuring that all team members are recognized and reimbursed for their time and contributions (Taplin et al. 2013). Aligning incentives also involves creating policies and reward and recognition systems that focus on patient outcomes. Leaders can create alignment by emphasizing and publicly recognizing the roles of all team members in achieving good patient outcomes. Increased understanding of the various roles of team members creates trust and respect, both of which are important to enabling high-functioning teams.

## *Performance Improvement Teams*

Performance improvement teams are project teams that are time limited and organized to achieve a specific improvement aim. A physician leader's first role in leading improvement teams is to recruit a multidisciplinary group of individuals to comprise the team. Performance improvement teams can vary in size and composition; both factors should be dictated by the needs of the project. Leaders should begin by reviewing the project's aim and considering which systems and departments contribute to the process under review (Health Research & Educational Trust 2013). The team should include representatives from all relevant disciplines, which may include nurses, physicians, APPs, administrators, patients, receptionists, environmental services, pharmacy, social workers, behavioral health, billing and finance, or others. The optimal size of an improvement team is five to eight individuals, but will vary based on the needs of the project. Improvement teams should include a patient or family member whenever possible. The Institute for Healthcare Improvement recommends that quality improvement teams include at least one individual with each of the following expertise: Clinical leadership, technical expertise, day-to-day leadership, and project sponsorship (Institute for Healthcare Improvement):

- *Physician leaders* have the authority to test and implement changes and can provide insight related to how proposed changes may inadvertently impact other parts of the system. They also provide insights into how proposed changes will impact clinical care.
- *Technical experts* provide the best insight into the specific process or subject at hand. For example, experts in performance improvement can guide teams in choosing measures and collecting and analyzing data. A project to improve discharge planning may include nurses as technical experts—those who deliver the discharge instructions—but also electronic health record technicians who may have intimate knowledge with regard to technical pieces of the discharge planning process.
- The *day-to-day leader* on the quality improvement team ensures the implementation of small tests of change, data

collection, and monitoring of results. This individual is the driver of the project and must work closely with the physician champion (see Chapter 4) to effectively engage clinicians and other frontline staff.

- Finally, every improvement team should have a *project sponsor*, someone with executive authority to provide resources, address barriers, and provide a link to senior management and the strategic aims of the organization. Project sponsors need not participate in the day-to-day activities of the project but should be regularly updated so they can effectively address barriers that arise.

## Strategies for Success

Implementation of science and research on effective teams is an emerging field. One program that has produced great success in changing organizational culture and building effective clinical care teams is Team Strategies and Tools to Enhance Performance and Patient Safety (TeamSTEPPS). The following case study highlights the key components of the TeamSTEPPS curriculum. Organizations can access tools online and enroll in the training program for more information.

### *Effective Strategy: TeamSTEPPS*

In 2006, the Department of Defense Patient Safety Program released TeamSTEPPS. The program incorporates more than 30 years of research on team development and performance across all industries and has been utilized extensively in health care (AHRQ 2019). Updated as TeamSTEPPS 2.0 in 2014, the program includes an evidence-based collection of tools, strategies, and training curriculum focused on establishing high-performing teams through the following:

- Producing highly effective medical teams that optimize the use of information, people, and resources to achieve the best clinical outcomes for patients.
- Increasing team awareness and clarifying team roles and responsibilities.
- Resolving conflicts and improving information sharing.
- Eliminating barriers to quality and safety.

The TeamSTEPPS curriculum includes five key principles: team structure, communication, leadership, situation monitoring, and mutual support. As depicted in Figure 8.1, the curriculum emphasizes the dynamic, two-way relationship between outcomes (performance, knowledge, attitudes) and

**Figure 8.1 TeamSTEPPS framework and competencies. (Agency for Healthcare Research & Quality, 2020).**

skills (leadership, communication, situation monitoring, and mutual support), encircled by the patient care team. The patient care team includes not only those directly responsible for providing medical care but also all of those on and off the medical staff (i.e., family members and caregivers) who are involved in the patient's care.

Physician leaders should be well versed in many of the communication and teamwork tools that are comprised within the TeamSTEPPS curriculum, and an overview of these are listed in Figure 8.2. More details and breakdown of strategies are available through online resources and the TeamSTEPPS pocket guide (AHRQ 2020). Beyond this, courses and workshops offer more advanced training for individual leaders or teams.

| |
|---|
| **Communication**<br>SBAR – Situation, Background, Assessment, Recommendation and Request<br>Call-Out<br>Check-Back<br>Handoff – I PASS THE BATON |
| **Leadership**<br>Tools: Team Events – Brief, Huddle, Debrief |
| **Situational Awareness**<br>Situational Monitoring (Individual Skill)<br>STEP – Status, Team, Environment, Progress<br>I'M SAFE Checklist – Illness, Medication, Stress, Alcohol and Drugs, Fatigue, Eating and Elimination<br>Situational Awareness (Individual Outcome)<br>Shared Mental Model (Team Outcome) |
| **Mutual Support**<br>Task assistance<br>Feedback – Timely, Respectful, Specific, Directed towards improvement, Considerate<br>Advocacy and Assertion<br>Two-Challenge Rule<br>Assertive Statements: CUS<br>DESC Script<br>Team Performance Observation Tool |

**Figure 8.2 TeamSTEPPS key principles. (Agency for Healthcare Research & Quality, 2014.)**

## *Effective Strategy: Understanding the Stages of Team Formation*

Physicians are inherently trained within environments in which team dynamics and composition of team members rapidly change. This is witnessed in the staggered shifts of emergency departments, the management of patients across multiple clinical units, and many other scenarios in which team member composition either frequently shifts or is otherwise unclear. For instance, take a single operating room staff that has a total of 80 different team members that could be working on any given day, including physicians, anesthesiologists, circulating nurses, and surgical technicians. The potential different composition of teams that could form on any given day is calculated at over two million different possible permutations. Despite the fact that physicians are familiar with such dynamic team environments, they and other members of health care teams are not traditionally trained to facilitate team formation and development.

The first step for physician leaders is identification and formation. This is sometimes referred to as "getting the right people on the bus" (Collins 2001). It is essential for performance improvement teams to clearly articulate the composition of its members, as well as each of their roles. Teams confront upfront challenges to success if they have ineffective or disengaged team members. Members can be ineffective if they do not possess the right skillset or do not understand their place in the team. Likewise, disengagement can occur if the nature of the team and its goals are not clear. Even if all of this is done well, physician leaders should recognize when the wrong person on the bus needs to be escorted off.

As noted above, team sizes can vary, and the larger a team is, the more challenging it can be to manage. Once all team members are known and identified, it is essential that each understand their role and expectations. Research in team development in the 1960s by Bruce Tuckman demonstrated that effectively all teams move through predictable stages as they work toward their goal (Tuckman 1965):

1. **Forming**: As teams come together, they typically will go through an initial stage of "forming." This is inherent in the identification of team members, clarification of group goals, as well as recognition of team member expectations. Teams typically display eagerness over a new initiative and will often stick to safer topics and conversations, seeking to avoid early conflict. Physician leaders should seek to be visible and take the lead during this stage, to provide the big picture, facilitate introductions, and communicate criteria for success.
2. **Storming**: Teams will nearly always encounter some element of conflict or resistance, even if this is typically non-confrontational. These may arise from competition between team members or differences of opinion. When such conflict arises, it can impede the team moving forward toward success, and this is referred to as "storming." Some teams can be stuck in storming indefinitely. When physician leaders recognize a team is in this stage, they should seek to encourage open dialogue and feedback, develop trust between team members, and resolve any issues.
3. **Norming**: As alignment of purpose and goal coincide, and commitment is solidified, successful teamwork takes off. In the norming stage, expectations and roles are well understood and teams begin to recognize and acknowledge individual and shared efforts. Physician leaders should seek to promote continued feedback and supportive engagement to drive toward performance.
4. **Performing**: Successful and high-performing teams are able to operate in a stage of consistent performance and production of consistent deliverables. At this point,

motivation and trust within the team is solid, and physician leaders should seek to focus on celebration of success and elimination of obstacles. Such high-performing teams require little intervention, and physician leaders should try to get as many teams to this stage as possible.

Physician leaders should be aware of these circumstances, and as they observe the dynamics of the teams they work with they will see these stages play out regularly. Tuckman's stages of team development provide a clear and straightforward framework that can be applied to any team, from inpatient rounding to performance improvement. Successful leaders can help to facilitate transition between the stages, and to seek to exist within the realm of "performing" for as long as possible.

## Case Study: Reduction of Central Line Associated Blood Stream Infections

The following case study provides an example of how an improvement team might be identified and formed and emphasizes the role of the physician leader in supporting such a team.

Kathy Weishaar, MD, is the chief medical officer at Frederick Health, a health system with 3,000 employees, over 450 active medical staff members and a 257-bed hospital serving over 250,000 people in central Maryland. In 2019, Frederick Health noticed an overall increase in harm events, and among these was a noted increase in central line associated blood stream infections (CLABSI). At the time, there was no formal process or systematic approach to respond to such events. While there was a history of well-intentioned efforts, these were not coordinated, not standardized, and generally lacked visibility. When a harm event occurred, an isolated response at the unit level may have followed, but results were rarely shared and there was little in the way of systemic and structured response to spread or sustain lessons learned.

In response to these circumstances, and to drive improvement, in 2019, system leadership at the organizational level set a measurable goal to reduce global harm events by 20% each year for five years. Ultimately, this meant that the initiative targeted an ideal to reach zero harm events by the conclusion of this period. For the overarching effort, all hospital harm events were parsed into groups that targeted specifics causes of harm, such as respiratory failure, aspiration pneumonia, catheter associated urinary tract infections (CAUTI), CLABSI, and others.

Frederick Health leadership sought to more meaningfully involve physicians within the improvement processes. Previously, for many crucial events, physicians were rarely involved in such initiatives. There was a desire for more crossover among all clinical roles involved in care and to raise overall awareness. Physician engagement was also seen as an opportunity to drive improvement, as opposed to nursing leaders operating in a silo. In total, 18 harm events were characterized, and from this ten harm team task forces were formed. Each taskforce focuses on a specific harm event and is led by a triad of a physician champion, nursing director, and clinical nurse specialist. Other ad hoc team members were regularly invited to participate as appropriate, including a performance improvement coordinator. The rationale for the triad leadership was that prior to this initiative, events were often viewed independently as either related to nursing issues, such as falls or pressure injuries, or physician issues, such as ventilator management. The team was tasked with reviewing all events, often meeting as frequently as weekly, and developing and implementing system changes in response to prevent additional events.

In 2022, leadership reviewed the structure of these taskforces and sought to increase transparency and accountability.

At that time, a revision to the taskforce structure was implemented to seek to make the process more sophisticated, increase coordination of activities, and drive improvement across a multitude of ongoing parallel tasks. Additionally, taskforces integrated A3 documentation for all ongoing work, and a snapshot of the Frederick team management process is depicted in Figure 8.3. Physician champions for each taskforce were involved in quarterly report outs to the overarching Quality Coordinating Council for the health system. This quality council includes system leadership, clinical leadership, and physician leadership, allowing heightened awareness of ongoing initiatives, accountability of the taskforces, and the ability for leads to request resources and support.

The role and value of the physician leader is clear, particularly when they are engaged as champions for the targeted area of harm. Frederick Health found that generally physician leaders are more easily able to translate the “why” of initiatives, to elicit change among colleagues, and even to garner attention and responsiveness from nurse leaders and other care team members. Barriers to success have occurred when there have been leadership changes or turnover within the teams. Further, the speed to move through steps of change was frequently slower than anticipated. In some cases, this was related to human factors such as training and changing practice patterns. In other instances, it was related to technological factors such as the time required to update documentation and orders within the EMR. Lastly, this initiative overlapped substantially with the COVID-19 pandemic, and this impacted staffing and added additional complexities to the care environment that challenged traditional harm events. Despite these barriers, Frederick Health’s team-based approach toward improvement saw success, in particular moving into FY23, with a noted reduction in CLABSI rate of nearly 50% anticipated from the previous fiscal year, as can be seen in Figure 8.4.

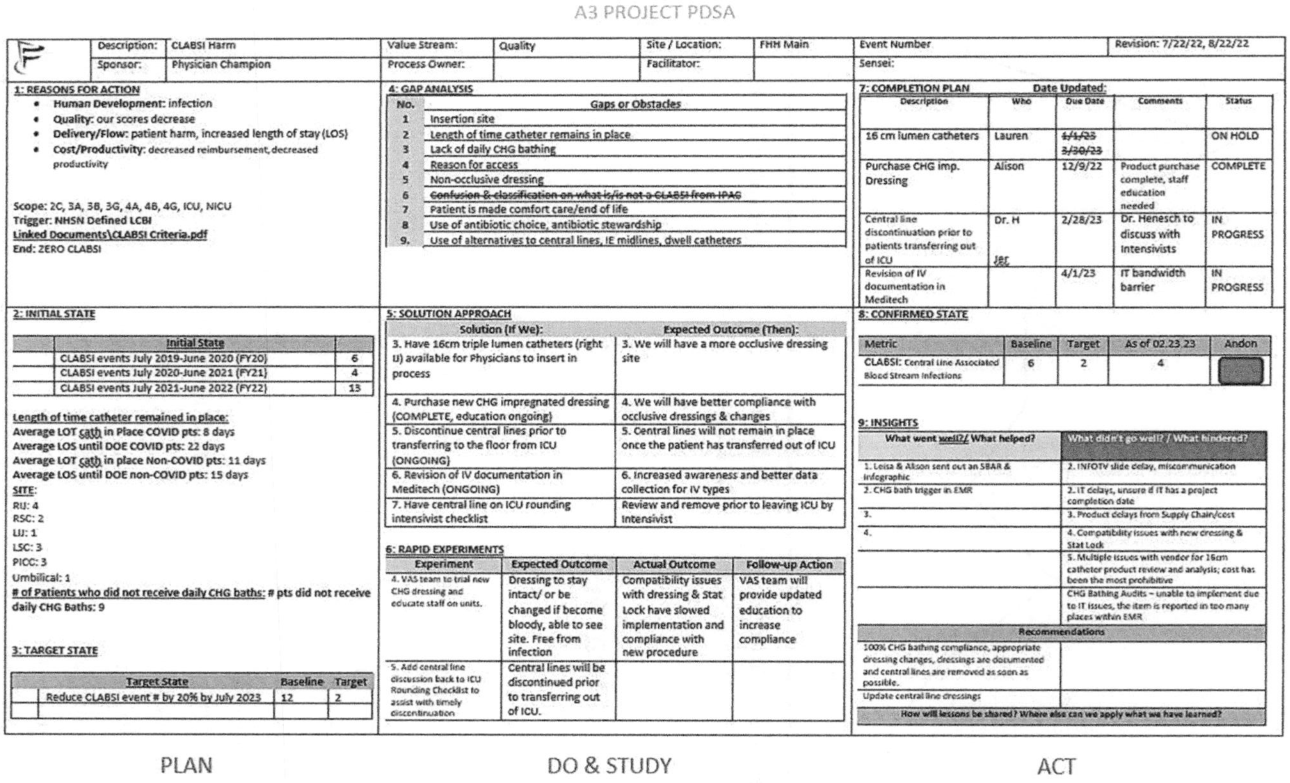

A3 PROJECT PDSA

| | | | | | | |
|---|---|---|---|---|---|---|
| Description: | CLABSI Harm | Value Stream: | Quality | Site / Location: | FHH Main | Event Number | Revision: 7/22/22, 8/22/22 |
| Sponsor: | Physician Champion | Process Owner: | | Facilitator: | | Sensei: | |

**1: REASONS FOR ACTION**

- **Human Development:** infection
- **Quality:** our scores decrease
- **Delivery/Flow:** patient harm, increased length of stay (LOS)
- **Cost/Productivity:** decreased reimbursement, decreased productivity

**Scope:** 2C, 3A, 3B, 3G, 4A, 4B, 4G, ICU, NICU
**Trigger:** NHSN Defined LCBI
**Linked Documents\CLABSI Criteria.pdf**
**End:** ZERO CLABSI

**2: INITIAL STATE**

| | Initial State | |
|---|---|---|
| | CLABSI events July 2019-June 2020 (FY20) | 6 |
| | CLABSI events July 2020-June 2021 (FY21) | 4 |
| | CLABSI events July 2021-June 2022 (FY22) | 13 |

**Length of time catheter remained in place:**
**Average LOT cath in Place COVID pts: 8 days**
**Average LOS until DOE COVID pts: 22 days**
**Average LOT cath in place Non-COVID pts: 11 days**
**Average LOS until DOE non-COVID pts: 15 days**
**SITE:**
RIJ: 4
RSC: 2
LIJ: 1
LSC: 3
PICC: 3
Umbilical: 1
**# of Patients who did not receive daily CHG baths: # pts did not receive daily CHG Baths: 9**

**3: TARGET STATE**

| | Target State | Baseline | Target |
|---|---|---|---|
| | Reduce CLABSI event # by 20% by July 2023 | 12 | 2 |
| | | | |

**4: GAP ANALYSIS**

| No. | Gaps or Obstacles |
|---|---|
| 1 | Insertion site |
| 2 | Length of time catheter remains in place |
| 3 | Lack of daily CHG bathing |
| 4 | Reason for access |
| 5 | Non-occlusive dressing |
| 6 | ~~Confusion & classification on what is/is not a CLABSI from IPAG~~ |
| 7 | Patient is made comfort care/end of life |
| 8 | Use of antibiotic choice, antibiotic stewardship |
| 9. | Use of alternatives to central lines, IE midlines, dwell catheters |

**5: SOLUTION APPROACH**

| Solution (If We): | Expected Outcome (Then): |
|---|---|
| 3. Have 16cm triple lumen catheters (right IJ) available for Physicians to insert in process | 3. We will have a more occlusive dressing site |
| 4. Purchase new CHG impregnated dressing (COMPLETE, education ongoing) | 4. We will have better compliance with occlusive dressings & changes |
| 5. Discontinue central lines prior to transferring to the floor from ICU (ONGOING) | 5. Central lines will not remain in place once the patient has transferred out of ICU |
| 6. Revision of IV documentation in Meditech (ONGOING) | 6. Increased awareness and better data collection for IV types |
| 7. Have central line on ICU rounding intensivist checklist | Review and remove prior to leaving ICU by Intensivist |

**6: RAPID EXPERIMENTS**

| Experiment | Expected Outcome | Actual Outcome | Follow-up Action |
|---|---|---|---|
| 4. VAS team to trial new CHG dressing and educate staff on units. | Dressing to stay intact/ or be changed if become bloody, able to see site. Free from infection | Compatibility issues with dressing & Stat Lock have slowed implementation and compliance with new procedure | VAS team will provide updated education to increase compliance |
| 5. Add central line discussion back to ICU Rounding Checklist to assist with timely discontinuation | Central lines will be discontinued prior to transferring out of ICU. | | |

**7: COMPLETION PLAN** Date Updated:

| Description | Who | Due Date | Comments | Status |
|---|---|---|---|---|
| 16 cm lumen catheters | Lauren | ~~1/1/23~~ ~~3/30/23~~ | | ON HOLD |
| Purchase CHG imp. Dressing | Alison | 12/9/22 | Product purchase complete, staff education needed | COMPLETE |
| Central line discontinuation prior to patients transferring out of ICU | Dr. H JEF | 2/28/23 | Dr. Henesch to discuss with intensivists | IN PROGRESS |
| Revision of IV documentation in Meditech | | 4/1/23 | IT bandwidth barrier | IN PROGRESS |

**8: CONFIRMED STATE**

| Metric | Baseline | Target | As of 02.23.23 | Andon |
|---|---|---|---|---|
| CLABSI: Central Line Associated Blood Stream Infections | 6 | 2 | 4 | |

**9: INSIGHTS**

| What went well?/ What helped? | What didn't go well? / What hindered? |
|---|---|
| 1. Leisa & Alison sent out an SBAR & infographic | 2. INFOTV slide delay, miscommunication |
| 2. CHG bath trigger in EMR | 2. IT delays, unsure if IT has a project completion date |
| 3. | 3. Product delays from Supply Chain/cost |
| 4. | 4. Compatibility issues with new dressing & Stat Lock |
| | 5. Multiple issues with vendor for 16cm catheter product review and analysis; cost has been the most prohibitive |
| | CHG Bathing Audits – unable to implement due to IT issues, the item is reported in too many places within EMR |

| Recommendations | |
|---|---|
| 100% CHG bathing compliance, appropriate dressing changes, dressings are documented and central lines are removed as soon as possible. | |
| Update central line dressings | |
| How will lessons be shared? Where else can we apply what we have learned? | |

PLAN DO & STUDY ACT

**Figure 8.3 Sample CLABSI taskforce A3 visualization tool. (Frederick Health, Frederick, MD).**

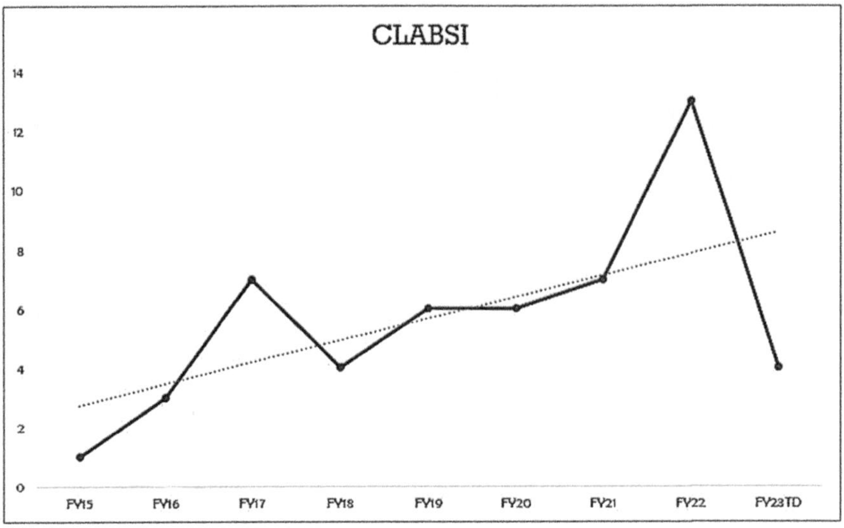


**Figure 8.4 Number of CLABSI harm events at Frederick Health FY15–FY23. (Frederick Health, Frederick, MD.)**

# Lessons Learned

Over the past decade, the increased focus on teams and team-based care has yielded many lessons learned. Key lessons for implementation include the following:

1. **Form drives function**. Teams—both for delivering clinical care and for driving improvement—must be built with the function or aim in mind. Emergency room teams will differ from primary care and surgical teams. Similarly, improvement teams to reduce hospital-acquired infections within a unit will differ from those working to reduce readmissions across a hospital system. Efforts to de-silo and coordinate care across the continuum will require new representation from home health to public health. Similarly, improvement efforts across the continuum of care—from unit-based interventions to

community-level interventions—will require different teams that include different perspectives (Health Research & Educational Trust 2013). The two key features of all teams, however, are that they should be interdisciplinary and engage a patient representative.

2. **Physician leaders and executive sponsors are keys to securing resources and removing obstacles**. As a physician leader, your primary role is to get the right people on the team and then advocate to senior leadership to secure the necessary resources (human, financial, and time) for the team to succeed. As a leader, your team should come to you with barriers and your energy should be focused on removing those barriers and not on micromanaging the day-to-day activities of the team.
3. **Culture change is essential**. Simply grouping individuals together and calling them a team is not sufficient. To truly promote both team-based care and a culture of continuous improvement, organizations must reorient to focus on the needs of the patient and not those of clinicians or administrators. Leadership plays a crucial role in initiating and supporting ongoing culture change by providing training in teamwork, engaging individuals throughout the organization in decisions that affect them, and modeling the behaviors associated with effective teamwork.

## Action Steps and Strategies to Lead

1. **Define the aims and objectives of the team first and then build the team accordingly**. For both clinical and improvement teams, the composition and size of the team should be dictated by the purpose or aim of the team. In both instances, teams should be multidisciplinary with individuals representing all key processes

affected by the team's work. Physician leaders should seek to have "the right people on the bus," first and foremost, and then promote team development toward the shared goal.

2. **Prioritize training and support for teamwork**. Leadership should provide both initial training in specific teamwork skills, such as TeamSTEPPS, as well as ongoing coaching to promote a culture that encourages and supports teamwork. Other forms of support can include, but are not limited to, designating non-patient care time for team meetings, reimbursing individuals for team activities, and developing communication plans and decision protocols that reinforce teamwork. Physician leaders should recognize where teams are in the stages of their development, and focus efforts early on teams that are coming together and forming.
3. **Engage patients and their families in both care and improvement teams**. Patients and family members provide important insights related to safety, quality, and efficiency. Teams should focus on and be built around the needs of the end user—the patient.

## References

Agency for Healthcare Research and Quality. TeamSTEPPS®: National Implementation. 2014. Accessed March 23, 2023. http://teamstepps.ahrq.gov/abouttoolsmaterials.htm

Agency for Healthcare Research and Quality. About TeamSTEPPS. 2019. Accessed January 27, 2023. https://www.ahrq.gov/teamstepps/about-teamstepps/index.html

Agency for Healthcare Research and Quality. Pocket Guide: TeamSTEPPS. January 2020. Accessed January 27, 2023. https://www.ahrq.gov/teamstepps/instructor/essentials/pocketguide.html

Bodenheimer, T. Building Teams in Primary Care: Lessons Learned. California Health Care Foundation. 2007. Accessed March 23, 2023. https://www.chcf.org/wp-content/uploads/2017/12/PDF-BuildingTeamsInPrimaryCareLessons.pdf

Collins, J. *Good to Great.* Random House Business Books, New York, NY, 2001.

Health Research & Educational Trust. *Leading Improvement Across the Continuum: Skills, Tools and Teams for Success.* Health Research & Educational Trust, Chicago, IL, 2013. www.hpoe.org

Institute for Healthcare Improvement. Science of Improvement: Forming the Team. 2003. Accessed January 27, 2023. http://www.ihi.org/resources/Pages/HowtoImprove/ScienceofImprovementFormingtheTeam.aspx

Pany, M.J., Chen, L., Sheridan, B., Huckman, R.S. Provider Teams Outperform Solo Providers in Managing Chronic Diseases and Could Improve the Value of Care. *Health Affairs.* 2021;40(3): 435–444.

Taplin, S., Foster, M., Shortell, S. Organizational Leadership for Building Effective Health Care Teams. *Annals of Internal Medicine.* 2013;11:279–281.

Tuckman, B.W., Developmental Sequence in Small Groups. *Psychological Bulletin.* 1965;63(6), 384–399.

# *Chapter 9*

# Spreading and Sustaining Improvement

## The Evidence

Spreading an improvement initiative within a hospital, health care system or organization is a complex and multidimensional process, with both technical and cultural factors influencing its success.

Technical factors include those that assure the improvement is worth spreading, such as the amount and quality of clinical evidence associated with improvement. When strong evidence exists for an intervention or treatment, external pressures often drive its implementation, such as required reporting or inclusion in value-based purchasing. Another important technical factor is the relevance of the improvement to the patient population within the given unit or department. A technical factor is the number of change elements. To promote adoption, the number of change elements should be limited and as simple as possible. Moving from initial adoption to sustainability, it is essential to be aware of the number

 DOI: 10.4324/9781003402831-9

of elements as well as the complexity and frequency of changes requested of team members.

Cultural factors are equally as important as technical factors in successfully promoting spread. In addition to awareness and a sense of urgency, there should be a sense of ownership for the improvement by those that are directly involved in the processes and systems associated with it. Support by organizational leadership as well as unit or department leadership is a foundational component for all improvement efforts. There must be effective communication between the improvement team and those accountable for executing the processes or systems under scrutiny. Lastly, there must be accountability for not only the design of systems, but also the behavioral choices to obtain and sustain the improvement. Once teams are involved in successful improvement efforts, the cultural components serve as a platform for other successful improvement interventions.

In the late 1990s, a team at the Institute for Healthcare Improvement was charged with the aim to "develop, test and implement a system for accelerating improvement by spreading change ideas between and within organizations." The result was the well-known and often-cited "Framework for Spread" (Massoud et al. 2006). In 2006, the Institute for Healthcare Improvement (IHI) expounded upon this framework in a white paper that has become the basis for toolkits developed by numerous researchers, government agencies including the Agency for Healthcare Research and Quality and many health care delivery organizations. The three key components of the IHI framework are preparing for spread; establishing an aim for spread; and developing, executing, and refining a spread plan.

## *Preparing for Spread*

Despite the promising results of a new initiative, history has demonstrated that even the best innovations rarely spread organically. Accordingly, health care leaders must devote significant resources and commitment to supporting the dissemination of "best practices" to ensure they become common practices.

A first step in preparing for spread is to assess organizational readiness, including identifying potential barriers and facilitators of spread. The Health Research and Educational Trust, an affiliate of the American Hospital Association, developed a spread assessment tool to assess the feasibility and likelihood of widespread adoption for a given initiative. This assessment tool evaluates the initiative across four factors and related questions:

Environmental factors:

- Will the innovation make/save money?
- Will the innovation meet current regulation?
- Is the innovation more or less of a priority than other currently promoted innovations?

Innovation factors:

- Is the innovation easy and simple to implement in the clinical setting?
- What will the impact of the innovation be on quality measures?
- Are the data collection methods to measure impact well defined and easy to implement?

Organizational factors:

- Are leaders in the organization strongly supportive of spread efforts?
- Are needed resources available?
- Does the organization have a culture that embraces continuous improvement?

Target audience factors:

- How many staff roles and individuals are needed to approve the innovation?
- Do most needed stakeholders believe that the innovation will improve their job satisfaction?
- Will the innovation provide financial benefits to the target audience?

Insights derived from using the spread assessment tool responses may also inform the development of the spread plan (HRET 2010).

In addition to using the HRET Spread Assessment Tool, clinical leaders should consider whether the initiative aligns with broader strategic priorities including state or national requirements for reimbursement, reporting, or performance-based incentives. If so, the organization may have greater incentives to incorporate the innovation as a strategic priority and commit resources to its spread (Erb et al. 2015).

Clinical leaders play a pivotal role in initiating a spread plan and actively facilitating its implementation (Massoud et al. 2006). First, leaders can effectively "set the agenda" by communicating that the improvement is a key strategic initiative. In some cases, it may be useful to communicate the initiative's alignment with existing incentive programs (Rogers 2010). This communication can take place in leadership and staff meetings and information can be provided on the organization's website and in publications. Leaders should also emphasize the importance of committing not only funding but also staff time to support the initiative's spread. Since this staff time will most likely be in addition to the staff's regular duties, communicating this up front will facilitate transparency (Massoud et al. 2006).

## Establishing an Aim for Spread

The next step for spread is to establish an aim. The aim is essentially the "who, what, and where" of spread. The following should be addressed in order to clarify the purpose of spread efforts:

- Target population.
- Specific desired goals.
- Specific improvement processes/protocols that will be undertaken by the target population.
- Quantifiable and measurable targets for spread.
- Time frame of spread effort.

## Developing a Spread Plan

Once the aim is established, the organization must create a plan to address "how" spread will be achieved. The leadership team should develop a logical plan based on their knowledge of the organization's infrastructure and decision-making processes. For example, for nested organizations, in which one unit is directly related to other units within the centralized organizational structure, successive waves of spread among organizational units is often most effective.

Leadership should also consider whether decisions are made in a centralized, top-down manner or if decisions are largely based on consensus. This will affect the timeline of the initiative and reasonable expectations for spread efforts. Furthermore, teams should attempt to anticipate challenges and barriers in transitioning to a new system. For example, lack of staff knowledge on how to use an electronic health record would hinder progress in providing customized electronic reports during patient handoffs between nurses (IHI 2006).

Frequent and consistent communication is essential for maintaining organization-wide awareness of performance improvement initiatives. Early in the planning process for spread, a communication plan should be developed in order to update leaders and staff about the spread initiative's progress in a deliberate, organized, and systematic manner. The communication plan is the roadmap for relaying prioritized messages and information to stakeholders and ensures that communications are purposeful and ongoing, thereby promoting an environment of transparency and accountability. The communication plan can take the form of a written document and be developed by performance improvement team members, as well as staff members with marketing, communications, or public relations expertise. The plan should identify objectives of the planned communication, stakeholders that need to or should be informed, modes of communication that will be used, timing and frequency of information release, and individuals responsible for developing and disseminating the various communications. Figure 9.1 provides examples of existing communication tools, along with their intended audience, frequency of usage, and respective content developers (HRET 2014a).

In addition to the communication plan development and implementation, it is recommended to have the "how to" technical knowledge of the intervention communicated through interaction between colleagues. To start this, consider utilizing pilot unit staff or "early adopters," to communicate the "why, what, and how," along with the results and benefits of the intervention being spread (HRET 2014b).

Over the past decade, many organizations have implemented spread initiatives internally, and many notable health care stakeholders have funded and supported initiatives to spread best practices within and across states. One emblematic example is the AHRQ-funded initiative to eliminate

| Communication Tool | Intended Audience | Frequency | Content Developer |
|---|---|---|---|
| Medical Staff Bulletin | Physicians | Quarterly | Medical Staff Services |
| General Medical Staff Meetings | Physicians | Quarterly | Chief of Staff and COO |
| Medical Staff Department Meetings | Physicians | Monthly | Medical Staff Services |
| Patient/Family Educational Materials | Patients and family members | Ongoing – in displays, waiting rooms | Patient Care Committee |
| Patient – Family Council | Patient and family council members | Monthly | Chairman |
| Nursing Newsletter | Nursing staff | Bi-monthly | CNO |
| Nurse "Huddles" | Nursing staff | Change of shift | CNO |
| Department Leadership Meetings | Hospital leadership (VPs, Directors, Managers) | Monthly | COO |
| Medical Center Newsletter | Employees | Monthly | Communications Department |
| Intranet Bulletin Board | Physicians Employees | Continuous | HR and COO |
| Staff Meetings | Department employees | Variable | Department Director |
| Organization Website | Community, Employees, Physicians | Continuous | PR Department |
| Community Newspaper | Community | Daily | PR Department – press releases |
| Board Meetings | Board members | Monthly | CEO, COO |
| Poster Displays/Easels | All | Ongoing – in entry and waiting rooms | PR Department (submit request) |

**Figure 9.1 Examples of existing communication tools. (Health Research & Educational Trust and Cynosure Health. Implementation Guide Part II: Advanced Topics., 2014b.)**

central line-associated bloodstream infections, the Comprehensive Unit-based Safety Program. The project began with the Intensive Unit Safety Reporting System, developed by the Johns Hopkins University Quality and Safety Group. Given its initial success, *CUSP* was subsequently adapted and implemented in more than 100 ICUs in Michigan. This statewide safety initiative to prevent CLABSI was known as the Keystone Project. In three months, the intervention achieved a 66% reduction in CLABSI rates across the participating units (Pronovost et al. 2006).

Because of this statewide success, AHRQ funded *CUSP*: Stop BSI efforts to spread the interventions on a national scale. To date, the over 1,000 hospitals participating in *CUSP* have documented a 40% reduction in CLABSI. This translates to an estimated prevention of over 2,000 infections, 500 mortalities, and a cost avoidance of over $34 million in health care expenditures (Sawyer et al. 2010).

*CUSP*: Stop CLABSI combined both technical and cultural knowledge to facilitate change. The approach includes recommendations related to using a catheter insertion bundle and other evidence-based interventions to prevent infection, all while focusing on improving communication and safety culture. The approach has had widespread success in reducing health care-associated infections while improving safety culture because of its adaptability and focus on crosscutting strategies to eliminate harm.

## Effective Strategies for Executing and Monitoring Spread

Given the success of initiatives such as on the *CUSP*: Stop BSI, the following are recommended as best practices for facilitating spread.

1. **Obtain clear and demonstrated support from senior leadership**. For spread initiatives to be successful, the organization's leadership must be willing to commit to

aligning the initiative with organizational strategic priorities, supporting the effort by removing organizational and system barriers, and supplying the required resources. Leaders must buy in and be committed to the initiative and understand how it relates to other organizational priorities. Without a clear link to high-level goals, it is likely the initiative will be abandoned when new priorities arise.

2. **Carefully select units for spread and designate a "spread organizer."** Identify clusters of units with similar needs, processes, or priorities. These can form a first group for spread where the initial intervention will be most applicable. It is also important to identify both official and unofficial leaders within those units who will be allies and champions for the initiative.
3. **Don't start with a resistor or in a chaotic unit**. In the initial stages, it is best to begin with advocates and units that are willing to adopt the change, rather than those units that may have the greatest need but may also be the most resistant. Once the initiative gains momentum, data, and evidence that demonstrates its success, it will be easier to convince the more resistant units to change.
4. **Designate nurse champions to promote innovations and spread improvements**. Just as it is important to engage physician champions in order to work effectively with physicians, it is also important to find nurse champions. As day-to-day caregivers, nurses have a first-hand understanding of patient needs. They are in a good position to tailor spread efforts based on the existing infrastructure and processes of a unit.
5. **Involve physicians**. Given their inherently high standards, natural propensity for competition, and eye for detail, physicians are important and effective team members for spreading improvement within and across

departments. As in all clinical improvement initiatives, clinicians should be involved in all stages of spread to ensure their crucial engagement and support.

6. **Build consensus among staff by showing your data**. As the initiative spreads to additional units, the amount of data, evidence, and momentum for it will build. This enables the spread team to begin approaching people within units that are more ambivalent about the spread effort. Data is a powerful motivator for change.
7. **Ensure ongoing communications**. Designated spread organizers can be important points of contact to facilitate mutual exchange of information. More widely, however, the employees throughout the organization should be kept abreast of the progress of the spread initiative. Frequent communication to all stakeholder groups is imperative for success, and improvements in quality, safety, and efficiency should be recognized and celebrated. Recognizing these success stories helps keep staff engaged and motivated.

## Sustaining Improvement

Moving through the steps of quality improvement may lead to a positive change, and as detailed above, effective leaders will drive the spread and adoption throughout the larger organization. However, adept physician leaders must be attentive to the need to support the sustainability of improvement as well. They must be proactive in ensuring that team members are fully engaged in the change, that new team members have appropriate orientation, that workflows and processes are ingrained, and above all that long-term accountability is present. Leaders that neglect these steps will quickly find that they will confront the same problems repeatedly.

Backslides in improvement can lead to reversion to back to previous behaviors. This is much akin to the classic story of the Dutch boy who attempts to plug successive holes draining water in a dike. Simply plugging a finger in the hole for a period and then moving on will inevitably lead to the return of the leak.

To complement the roadmap for spreading improvement, the IHI has also developed a framework for health care organizations to sustain improvements in safety, effectiveness, and efficiency of patient care (Scoville et al. 2016). In this model, the key is to emphasize the day-to-day work of frontline leaders and managers. This work should be structured and consistent under a high-performance management system with clear standard tasks and responsibilities for managers at all levels of the organization.

Building upon the science of quality improvement and the Plan–Do–Study–Act (PDSA) approach covered earlier in Chapter 2, the IHI depicts how leaders can take successful improvements and transition these into a cycle of quality control (Scoville 2017).

Institute for Healthcare Improvement's six Essential Practices for Sustainability (Scoville 2017):

1. **Standardization**: Once an initiative has demonstrated success, the improved design must be standardized. This includes documentation of clear and specific standards for the workflow or procedure to be performed. These should be shared with leaders at all levels involved with the work. The goal is for all staff and leaders to have clarity in what is to be done and how to do it. Checklists are one example of standardized clinical work.
2. **Accountability**: Processes that have been standardized require regular monitoring to ensure that the standard work is being performed accurately and consistently. One mechanism to ensure standard work is to audit daily compliance. However, high-functioning organizations are

increasingly using team-based huddles to drive individual and team accountability. In addition, frontline managers must be accountable for the work expected for their teams.

3. **Visual Management**: Moving beyond talking about improvement, driving culture of sustainability includes intentional display of clear data, important information, and key quality measures at the team level. This shows commitment and transparency and serves to inform as well as drive accountability. Review of these dashboards at the team level, such as in brief morning huddles, can increase awareness and engagement. Involving team members in the development and input for the boards can take these a step further.
4. **Problem-Solving**: Frontline staff, as well as managers, should be empowered to seek to solve problems and find resolution to issues as they arise in daily work. If staff do not perceive the ability to do so, then problems can fester and those closest to the issue are not involved in providing expert input. Such a culture of problem-solving includes clear methods for frontline staff to develop improvement skills. It also involves the need for clear lines of communication between frontline staff and managers. Daily huddles can be an ideal opportunity to share barriers and issues.
5. **Escalation**: When quality control issues are identified, physician leaders must ensure that there are safe and rapid pathways for team members to escalate problems. A chain of appropriate escalation, which includes review and resolution at the lowest possible level allows movement back into the quality control cycle or triggers an analysis of the process and return to consideration of change ideas.
6. **Integration**: Integration requires effective communication across the levels of management and professional

> staff as well as consistency of purpose across all departments and teams. This requires physician leaders to clearly articulate and advance organizational mission statements and values. Likewise, it requires a formal system in which organizational goals are coordinated alongside improvement initiatives, team development, planning, and team member engagement. Once these are established, they can routinely be shared and reinforced through visual management dashboards as well as team huddles.
>
> *(Scoville 2017)*

To move from spread to sustainability for any improvement initiative, physician leaders can use the following simple steps as a starting point for this framework (Mate and Rakover 2016):

1. **Choose a Pilot Within the Organization**: Start small with a pilot project ideally assigned to an already-high-performing team or clinical area. Physician leaders should use the tools and skills outlined in Chapter 7 to identify local clinical champions for the initiative, and then those identified in Chapter 8 to implement the improvement team.
2. **Start with the Immediate Supervisor at the Point of Care**: Physician leaders must be adept at recognizing when to lead and when to inspire others to do so. From the very start, frontline managers should be involved in innovating processes that will impact the work of their teams. They will be essential in the monitoring of standard work, identification of issues, and escalation. They should be accountable for the improvement initiative, and likewise accountable for any necessary sustainability.

3. **Use Early Wins to Build Momentum**: Physician leaders should set out simple and clear initiatives and use simple and clear data to demonstrate change. Sharing this data in huddles, as well as stories from team members or patients, can create easy and early wins. Leaders should seek to avoid complex and frequent changes and waiting too long to celebrate success.
4. **Motivate Frontline Clinical Managers by Tackling What Irks Them**: When frontline leaders and their team have skin in the game, they will be much more likely to be engaged to tackle improvement as well as sustain over the long term. Physician leaders that seek to listen to problems faced in the front lines can gain the twofold benefit of gaining trust in their listening and also being responsive to concerns as they are raised. Ultimately, if staff members do not care about the outcomes, or if the change makes their work more difficulty, sustainability will be certainly challenging.

## Case Study: On the CUSP: Stop CAUTI

Barb Edson was the former vice president of Clinical Quality at Health Research and Educational Trust and previously directed the AHRQ-funded *On the CUSP: Stop CAUTI* project, a national initiative to eliminate catheter-associated urinary tract infections. The following interview describes experiences from her previous leadership role in achieving spread:

*Q*: What was your approach for assessing readiness for spread?

*A*: Observing trends provides a quantitative perspective of an organization's readiness, while survey tools and culture assessments provide an in-depth qualitative perspective of organizational readiness. To assess specific units' readiness for spread, utilizing bloodstream infection rates and a tool to identify common barriers for improvement help identify greatest need and willingness for spread, respectively.

For hospital/unit data trends, publicly reported data can be used to assess and compare rates with other hospitals/units. For the national *CUSP* project, we deployed a readiness survey that specifically gauged hospitals' technical level of preparedness in avoiding bloodstream infections (BSI). For instance, the survey asked whether a department implemented a cart to keep line supplies in or whether they used chlorhexidine to clean the site. However, the readiness assessment did not include questions on culture aspects such as whether the cart was used, and if not, why? Were staff members explicitly assigned and held accountable for maintaining the cart? These elements of culture turned out to be very important in a unit's readiness to implement the initiative.

Assessing the culture of an organization can be as powerful as it is challenging. We know that various levels of an organization have different perspectives on culture and safety. For example, senior leaders may view safety more positively than those who are delivering care. We also know that culture can be vastly different from one unit to another within an organization. For these reasons, assessing culture can be very challenging.

In our *On the CUSP: Stop CAUTI* work, the faculty at the University of Michigan developed the CAUTI Guide to Patient Safety Tool through qualitative interviews with over 400 individuals in 43 hospitals. The tool asks questions about important key success factors, such as champions, resistance, and leadership support.

*Q*: As a clinical leader, what leadership strategies and tools would you advise others to leverage in order to achieve spread?

*A*: Start small and seek out opportunities while avoiding initial resistors. Next, identify leaders that can be your point of contact within units. Utilize coaching skills to assist the team with improvements. Lastly, be vigilant and continuously monitor the progress of spread.

First, analyze your order of spread. Always start very small and look at similar units. In regard to seeking out opportunities, it is sometimes not necessarily better to start with the problem but with an advocate. The first person I would approach was somebody who *wanted* to work with me and champion my efforts. That was more important than going first to departments that clearly had opportunities for improvement. In the beginning, it is also important to not start in a chaotic unit, such as the emergency department, where there are too many unknowns and too many variables.

Personally, I had a difficult time starting the spread work, so I identified someone who could lead from a direct provider perspective (i.e., an unofficial leader). I talked with staff to figure out who the good leaders were. The best way to figure this out is to find out who staff go to when there is a clinical challenge. In other words, whose opinion do they seek? Keep in mind, this leader may be a charge nurse, bedside nurse, or doctor. Regardless of the role, interpersonal and communication skills are key. They don't have to be in official leadership roles as long as they possess the characteristics of a leader and are able to mentor the team members.

After identifying a leader, forming an effective team is crucially important in order to achieve spread. The team should include people involved in every phase of the project. They should also have the characteristics and attributes of high-performing teams, which include clear roles, a shared vision, strong leadership and a sense of trust, and the ability to communicate, provide regular feedback, and create ways to work together.

Regarding monitoring the spread process, I refer to the data in the units where the process was spread. If the data is showing trends that are within the control limits that were set, then we transition to a monitoring plan. The plan delineates who will monitor the data, how often it will be monitored, the control limits, and what actions will be taken if the data is no longer within the control limits. In spread, monitoring for process variation is a key success factor. There will be many times when a process may need to be varied slightly because the unit that the process was spread to was different in some way.

*Q*: What are some important characteristics/functions of an intervention bundle that facilitate the success of its spread?

*A*: Integrating technical aims with cultural aims, along with effectively telling the story of "why" these aims are important. Limiting the number of change elements and making them as concise and simplistic as possible. These functions will assist the staff in adoption and facilitate spread.

The *On the CUSP: Stop BSI* project had two aims. The cultural component was to improve safety culture. The technical component was to reduce the infection rate to less than 1 infection per 1,000 line days. Although many units achieved zero, we were emphasizing the importance of improvement rather than perfection.

In providing a case on why the intervention is important, showing data and rates is not enough. This requires changing the norm, showing evidence, and talking about the "why." This involves stories that make personal connections, such as who has been adversely harmed due to the current state of operations. Additionally, it involves demonstrating that improvement and successes are attainable and that patient harm is not inevitable.

*Q*: Can you describe a time you faced opposition from another clinical leader and were able to persuade them through data?

*A*: Even after going through all the steps outlined above, you will typically find someone who doesn't want to do the intervention. This is where the use of coaching, monitoring, and meaningful influence is important.

For example, while working to spread the Surgical Care Improvement Project measures, I was collaborating with a quality improvement professional that was unable to get a department of surgery chair on board with implementation. In response, she first sought the support and participation from other department chairs. She was able to recruit a general surgeon as an advocate, who then piloted the measures, shared evidence, and tweaked and refined them. This took place over a six- to eight-month timeline. After more sub-specialty surgeons piloted the intervention and built consensus across the organization, it became evident that the department chair, who was in opposition to the SCIP measures, was out of compliance. The data finally convinced him of the need to improve, especially in comparison to his peers. He reached out to the quality improvement professional to seek assistance to implement the measures.

This situation underscores the importance of involving physicians in the process. Personal high standards, paired with natural competition in their environment that facilitates social motivation, work in combination to influence clinicians to implement these interventions to see true results.

*Q*: What are roles of leadership and staff in transitioning spread efforts into routine operational responsibilities?

*A*: Time and time again, people try to implement a top-down approach, but this is not often effective. The better method is a top-down framework and bottom-up implementation. Specifically, the hospital leader should support the intervention, through organizational alignment, removal of system barriers, and resource support. However, the direct care providers are very important players on the team. After the intervention is proposed, these leaders drive the improvement work. Nurses, pharmacists, and other clinical staff who are involved in the daily clinical work have the most opportunities to test and modify the intervention until it effectively works within a given setting.

From a leadership standpoint, involve successful people who do the day-to-day clinical work and encourage them to lead and support the spread efforts. A team of committed nurses would be a more effective implementation team than individuals in leadership positions who were removed from patient care. A leader can contribute by listening to his or her staff, aligning the organizational priorities, and removing the organizational barriers.

## Lessons Learned

Regardless of the quality improvement challenge at hand, from reducing hospital-acquired infections to preventing patient falls, spreading and sustaining improvement is a major challenge. The following are important to address, as they are often poorly addressed before, during, and after the implementation of an intervention (Pronovost et al. 2006):

1. **Convincing people that there is a problem**. It is often difficult to convince clinical teams to change if they do

not perceive there to be a problem. Important challenges for spread teams are to (1) demonstrate the need for improvement and (2) demonstrate why this particular problem should take priority over other pressing challenges. Possible strategies include using data, using patient stories to emotionally engage the team, prompting clinicians to define what they want to improve, and showing that there is a "relative advantage" in implementing the intervention.

2. **Convincing people that the chosen solution is the right one**. More often than not, an improvement intervention will be "essentially contested." That is, even if everyone agreed on the need for good quality, there will likely be disagreement on what defines "good quality" and how to achieve it. Lack of sufficient or consistent evidence for an intervention may lead to resistance from clinicians and other staff. Therefore, it is essential to ensure acceptability by hosting facilitated discussion forums to explore, discuss, and debate the evidence. A "program theory" may provide a helpful framework in which improvement efforts are broken down into actionable activities and the spread team demonstrates causal links between these activities and desired outcomes. This theory will clarify why an intervention is likely to work and better define the focus and strategic direction of the initiative.
3. **Excess ambitions and "projectness."** Conversely, it is also common for an improvement initiative to be met with a high and potentially unsustainable level of enthusiasm. This may lead to a subsequent exhaustion of available resources. The scale of resources required to support improvement initiatives is often underestimated, which can quickly cause difficulties in improvement efforts, especially if the lack of the resources is not diagnosed in a timely manner. Therefore, careful assessment of resources should be conducted at the outset of the project.

Additionally, metrics and measurable objectives should be developed for the post-implementation period and routinely monitored to track progress and identify areas for future development and refinement. This will provide continuous feedback necessary for reevaluation. To continue the momentum of an initiative, organizers should emphasize that the initiative will evolve over time. Otherwise, if an initiative successfully spreads, it may become so standardized that continuous improvement may encounter the barrier of stagnation. In continuous improvement, learning and advancement of new knowledge is not a one-time event, but a culture and ongoing process of continuous improvement (Bristol and Joshi 2014).

## Action Steps and Strategies to Lead

The clinical leader should take the following steps in order to achieve spread (Sawyer et al. 2010):

1. **Find opinion leaders and champions**. These individuals can include not only nurses and physicians but also nurse assistants, pharmacists, non-clinical staff members, and any other stakeholders in the process. Begin identifying champions through discussions with staff on who they look to for advice and expertise. Once identified, assess whether these potential leaders would be willing to advocate for and commit to spread efforts.
2. **Consider the implementation/dissemination model**. Leaders should determine how best to reach and engage the target population for spread efforts. This should include considerations of the hospital's structure, whether infrastructure enhancements could accelerate the adoption of improvements, transition issues and knowledge gaps, and standard operational processes. Then, the

physician leader can adopt an appropriate model that will accommodate all of these aspects.

3. **Use data to demonstrate the effectiveness of the implemented practice**. Data shows whether the intervention is effectively achieving its technical aim. If the intervention is working, it also provides a powerful catalyst for other units to achieve the same improvements.
4. **Use stories to engage other leaders and explain the "why" for spread**. In combination with data, which provides the rationale for spreading an intervention, leaders will be compelled by the human aspect of the intervention's potential impact. Understanding that the intervention could save the life of a relative or friend or substantially improve their quality of life will further motivate them to get on board.
5. **Track spread adoption though data**. Measurement is an important part of tracking improvement. Two different kinds of measures that should be used are measures that demonstrate the extent of spread, as well as the outcome of the implemented changes. Furthermore, the rate of spread should be monitored. Self-reporting to a designated data coordinator is a feasible way of collecting and managing data.

*(IHI 2006)*

## References

Bristol, S., Joshi, M.S. Transforming the Healthcare System for Improved Quality. In *The Healthcare Quality Book: Vision, Strategy, and Tools*, ed. Maulik S. Joshi et al. Health Administration Press, Chicago, IL, 2014, 541.

Burke, R.E., Marang-van de Mheen, P.J. Sustaining Quality Improvement Efforts: Emerging Principles and Practice. *BMJ Quality & Safety*. 2021;30:848–852.

Erb, N.D., Joshi, M.S., Perlin, J. Faster by a Power of Ten: A PLAN for Accelerating National Improvement. *American Journal of Managed Care*. 2015;21(2):e99–e102.

Health Research & Educational Trust and Cynosure Health. Implementation Guide Part I: A How-To Guide for Improvement for the AHA/HRET HEN Partnership for Patients. 2014a.

Health Research & Educational Trust and Cynosure Health. Implementation Guide Part II: Advanced Topics. 2014b.

Institute for Healthcare Improvement. Improvement Standards: Shifting to a Higher Standard. 2014. Accessed March 23, 2023. http://www.ihi.org/resources/Pages/ImprovementStories/ShiftingtoaHigherStandard.aspx

Interview with Barbara Edson. Leadership and Spreading Improvement on the CUSP: Stop BSI Project. October 31, 2014.

Massoud, M.R., Nielsen, G.A., Nolan, K., Schall, M.W., Sevin, C. *A Framework for Spread: From Local Improvements to System-Wide Change*. IHI Innovation Series white paper. Healthcare Improvement, Cambridge, MA, 2006.

Mate, K., Rakover, J. 4 Steps to Sustaining Improvement in Health Care. *Harvard Business Review*. 2016 Accessed January 26, 2023.https://hbr.org/2016/11/4-steps-to-sustaining-improvement-in-health-care

On the CUSP: Stop HAI. About: Barbara S. Edson. http://www.onthecuspstophai.org/about-us/key-personnel/barb-edson-rn-mba-mha/

Pronovost, P., Needham, D., Berenholtz, S., Sinopoli, S., Chu, H., Cosgrove, S., et al. An Intervention to Decrease Catheter-Related Bloodstream Infections in the ICU. *New England Journal of Medicine*. 2006;355(26):2725–2732.

Rogers, Everett M. *Diffusion of Innovations*. Simon and Schuster, New York, NY. 2010.

Sawyer, M., Weeks, K., Goeschel, C.A., Thompson, D.A., Berenholtz, S.M., Marsteller, J.A., Lubomski, L.H., et al. Using Evidence, Rigorous Measurement, and Collaboration to Eliminate Central Catheter-Associated Bloodstream Infections. *Critical Care Medicine*. 2010;38:S292–S298.

Scoville, R., Little, K., Rakover, J., Luther, K., Mate, K. *Sustaining Improvement*. IHI White Paper. Institute for Healthcare

Improvement, Cambridge, MA, 2016. Accessed January 30th, 2023. https://www.ihi.org/resources/Pages/IHIWhitePapers/Sustaining-Improvement.aspx

Scoville, R. 6 Essential Practices for Sustainable Improvement. *Institute for Healthcare Improvement.* 2017. Accessed January 30th, 2023. https://www.ihi.org/communities/blogs/six-essential-practices-for-sustainable-improvement

# Chapter 10

# Engaging Patients and Families in Safety and Quality

## The Evidence

A growing body of evidence supports the practice of patient and family engagement (PFE) at both the direct care level and at the organizational level as an effective strategy to improve outcomes in patient safety, quality, and patient satisfaction (Carman et al. 2013; Epstein and Street 2008; Coulter and Ellins 2007; and Charmel and Frampton 2008). A report from the Health Research and Educational Trust summarizes the ways in which PFE can positively impact health care facilities (HRET 2013):

1. Contributes to better clinical outcomes (Weingart et al. 2011).
2. Reduces institutional and individual costs of care (Hibbard et al. 2013 and Institute of Medicine 2012).


DOI: 10.4324/9781003402831-10

3. Increases adherence to recommended treatment regimens, which can lead to fewer complications and readmissions (McCarly 2009).
4. Improves patient satisfaction with care coordination and other patient experience measures that impact hospital reimbursement rates (Sorra et al. 2012 and Weingart et al. 2011).

Engaging patients and families as active partners in care improves the experience of care, promotes patient activation, and leads to improved outcomes—all goals that health care organizations should strive for as places of healing. There are also additional financial motivations for PFE. Reimbursement is increasingly tied to measures of patient satisfaction, experience, and outcomes. PFE can have an obvious impact on improving satisfaction and experience, and can impact health outcomes as well. For example, PFE is an effective strategy to collect diverse perspectives on organizational efforts, generate feedback on new initiatives, identify potential unknown opportunities for improvement, and much more.

Research suggests that patients who are more actively involved in their care experience better outcomes. The measure of "patient activation," which refers to a patient's knowledge, skills, ability, and willingness to manage his or her own health and care, is predictive of both outcomes and cost (Hibbard et al. 2013). Studies have shown that patients with the lowest patient activation scores (i.e., those with the least skills and confidence to actively engage in their own health care) incurred costs up to 21% higher than those with the highest activation levels (Hibbard et al. 2013). Engaging patients and families in care to increase activation levels shows promise as a strategy to achieve all three dimensions of the Triple Aim: Better care, better health, and lower costs.

Patient engagement can take many forms: At the direct care level, in organizational design and governance, and in policymaking in the larger community. One framework to consider is a continuum of patient engagement across these settings segmented by "how much information flows between patient and provider, how active a role the patient has in care decisions and how involved the patient or patient organization becomes in health organization decisions and in policy making" (Carman et al. 2013). This continuum provides a framework to strategize and prioritize initiatives to build more patient- and family-centered health care facilities. For example, at the direct care level, the lowest level of engagement, "consultation," involves patients simply receiving information about a diagnosis. At the highest level of engagement, "partnership and shared leadership," the same opportunity would be approached through encouraging treatment decisions made based on patients' preferences, medical evidence, and clinical judgment.

In the same way that the COVID-19 pandemic accelerated the progress of telemedicine, so too did it enhance the pathways by which patients connect with health care organizations. The shift to virtual platforms for meetings enhanced opportunities for patients and families to connect and serve in feedback and advisory roles to health systems. While social and economic disparities do continue to provide roadblocks to participation for some, for others digital connectivity overcomes known transportation barriers.

The following sections describe the key strategies organizations should implement to increase patient and family engagement.

## Effective Strategies for Patient and Family Engagement

### *Strategies at the Direct Care Level*

When patients and families are active participants in their care, patient satisfaction, adherence to treatment and medication regimens, and care outcomes improve. Patient engagement at the direct care level includes "integrating patients' values, experiences, and perspectives in relation to prevention, diagnosis, and treatment" (Carman et al. 2013). Organizations and health care teams should create environments that enable and encourage patients and their families to become active members of the care team. Examples of "must do" strategies at the direct care level include the following:

- Providing patients and their identified family members immediate and unrestricted access to their medical records.
- Developing and enhancing online personal health records.
- Allowing patients the ability to update their own records and illness history.
- Supporting bidirectional mechanisms for patients to interact with their care team in meaningful ways outside of traditional office visits and acute care.
- Using patient teach-back, having patients repeat back what the provider has explained to ensure effective communication.
- Ensuring patient-centered bedside change-of-shift reports.
- Involving patients and families in multidisciplinary rounds.
- Using patient- and family-activated rapid response.
- Transitioning policies on "visiting" to be inclusive, welcoming, and patient-driven to include individuals identified by the patient to be "partners in care."

One important policy emphasized by the Institute for Patient- and Family-Centered Care (IPFCC) that encourages greater engagement not only from patients but also from their family members and caregivers is to revise visiting policies to move from "families as visitors to families as members of the care team." Evidence shows that the presence and participation of families as partners in care leads to cost savings, improved patient experience, and reduced readmissions (IPFCC). The evidence is so compelling, in fact, that the Joint Commission has recommended that patients bring a family member or trusted friend with them to the hospital as a safety strategy (McGreevey 2006).

To promote this practice, hospital visiting guidelines should consider the importance of language and proactively invite patients to decide which family members and important friends should participate in their recovery. The definition of "family" should not be dictated by the facility, staff, or traditional conceptions. Instead, hospital staff should ask the patients to define their family and other "partners in care" and determine how they will be involved in care and decision-making.

The IPFCC has developed a brief that includes recommendations for health care leaders with respect to changing hospital visiting policies and practices:

- Ensure that senior executives provide leadership and support to change restrictive visiting policies and practices.
- Involve patient and family advisors in revising visiting policies and practices as well as in orienting, training, and supporting hospital staff for change in practice.
- Use the language of partnership, support, and mutual respect. Avoid terms like "visit," "visitors," and "visitation." Use words such as "welcome," "encourage," or "invite" instead of "allow," "permit," or "authorize."
- Develop systems and processes to determine which family and friends the patient designates as "partners in care" and how they will be involved in care.

## *Strategies to Engage Patients in Organizational Design and Governance*

Beyond the direct care experience, health care organizations can engage patients and families in organizational design, quality improvement initiatives, and governance structures in order to more completely and proactively integrate the patient perspective into the organization's operating model (Figure 10.1). The key to PFE at the organizational level is to intentionally, consistently, and meaningfully engage patients and families as advisors through inclusion on ad hoc, short-term projects; enduring patient and family advisory councils (PFACs);

| Policies and Procedures | Personnel |
|---|---|
| Policies in place related to key patient, family-engagement efforts | Commitment to patient and family engagement in position descriptions |
| Mechanisms for employees patients and families to report concerns about failures to engage patients or families | Patient engagement embedded in new employee orientation and other staff and physician training with patients and family as faculty |
| Processes for acknowledging and correcting engagement failures | Support for patient and family engagement evaluated in employee reviews |
| Defined ways to review and improve patient and family engagement processes over time | Incentives linked to meeting patient and family engagement goals |
| **Meetings and Committees** | **Data Systems** |
| Routine inclusion of patients and families as advisors | Patient experience data collected and reviewed |
| Agendas with topics directly related to patient and family engagement | Evaluation data collected about patient engagement efforts and training |
| Minutes to reflect substantive discussion of patient and family engagement | Monitoring targeted outcomes for improvement linked to engagement initiatives |

**Figure 10.1 Integrating a vision for patient- and family-centered care. (Health Research & Educational Trust. A Leadership Resource for Patient and Family Engagement Strategies. 2013. www.hpoe.org)**

and quality and safety committees and the board of trustees. Strategies include the following:

- Building PFACs.
- Inviting patients to serve on boards or other committees.
- Engaging patients in the design and execution of quality improvement projects.
- Engaging patients to assist with staff hiring and training.
- Integrating a vision for patient- and family-centered care throughout all policies and procedures, personnel decisions, meetings and committee structure, and data systems.

## Working with Patients/Family Advisors

The Agency for Healthcare Research and Quality has published a series of toolkits that outline strategies for engaging patients and families. The number one strategy identified is to work with patients and families as advisors. Study by the American Institutes for Research (AIR) has shown that systems that engage patient advisors demonstrate better health outcomes, including reductions in preventable readmissions and increased patient experience scores (American Institutes for Research 2017). Health care organizations and leaders of these systems must be intentional and thoughtful about recruiting and engaging patient/family advisors and maximizing their contributions. The AHRQ toolkit identifies the following steps in engaging patient and family advisors:

1. Identify a staff liaison.
2. Identify opportunities for working with patient and family advisors.
3. Prepare hospital leadership, clinicians, and staff to work with advisors.

4. Recruit, select, and train patient and family advisors.
5. Implement and coordinate advisor activities.

In addition to working with individual patient family advisors (PFAs), organizations can also form PFACs to provide ongoing mechanisms for interaction with PFAs. PFACs are freestanding committees that serve as an advisory resource to the organization. PFACs provide patients with a venue to offer input into policy and program development at the hospital, express challenges or concerns, and provide new ideas and a patient perspective. Hospitals benefit from new insights that may improve care processes and develop stronger relationships with their patients and the larger community. Studies have shown that organizations that support PFACs have increased employee satisfaction and improved financial performance (AHRQ).

PFACs are not simply venues for patients to bring personal grievances to be addressed and resolved. Rather, PFACs provide opportunities to use stories and experiences, both negative and positive, as catalysts for change. Particularly in light of the need for rapid and transformational change at every level in health care, PFACs can serve to generate feedback and recommendations in real time as changes are implemented.

The American Hospital Association's Physician Alliance developed a start-up map and strategy guide in 2022 as a blueprint for developing a PFAC:

Step: 1 **Determine Size**: Smaller groups encourage greater discussion and engagement while larger groups promote greater diversity of experience. Successful PFACs have been between 12 and 25 advisors. Ultimately, the composition of the membership should promote diversity of perspective and background. An ideal PFAC demonstrates representation of the backgrounds and demographics of the patient population that the organization serves. Large organizations or those with substantial variation in services offered can consider forming a network of advisory councils.

Step: 2 **PFAC Structure**: The PFAC should serve as more than just a sounding board or opportunity for community members to air grievances. One step to legitimize the council is to treat it like other formal committees within the organization. Establish a definitive structure, membership, and mission statement or charge for the group. Consider bylaws, terms, officers, and reimbursement for participants. These will be especially important to differentiate PFACs in larger organizations that utilize a network of councils. The structure of the PFAC should include a dedicated staff and resources to respond to items identified in meetings.

Step: 3 The AHA blueprint suggests the following to be considered in the initial PFAC strategic planning sessions (AHA 2022):

- *How will the PFAC accomplish its work?*
- *How does the PFAC charge align with the organizational strategies?*
- *What education and resources should be developed for guiding the PFAC on organizational efforts?*
- *How will PFAC activities be connected to the larger organization?*
- *How will the PFAC be engaged in ongoing projects?*

Ultimately, the structure of the PFAC should be reflective of the institution's purpose and goals for engaging patients.

Step: 4 **Advisor Recruitment and Retention**: Organizations must consider an active recruitment strategy, particularly to accomplish the goal of maintaining representative membership and a diverse viewpoint. Initially, physician leaders can engage providers and clinical site leadership to recommend advisors. When patients or families independently voice concerns about some service or experience, alongside responding to the issue, consider inviting them to join a PFAC. More active recruitment includes intentional social media and online posting, advisor recruitment fairs, and community events. Purposeful recruitment also includes how and when meetings are to be held, with consideration for advisor work schedules or transportation issues. Thus, meetings should be held at more convenient times for advisors, and virtual options for participation should be offered.

Step: 5 **Orientation**: When new advisors join the council, they should receive an orientation to the group and the role. This orientation can include information about the organization, the council, its members, roles and responsibilities, expectations, and strategies to be an effective council member. Additionally, some orientation on the basics of health care quality and patient safety may be helpful. For example, an explanation of basic improvement methodology, the organization's structure and methodology for improvement, safety or quality priorities within the institution, and common acronyms, terms, and medical jargon may be helpful to address. Current PFAC members and advisors should help to offer feedback on orientation, and be a part of the onboarding for new members.

Step: 6 **Determine Staff Support Members**: For a PFAC to be successful, it should truly be composed primarily of patients and family members. That said, a limited staff involvement of at most three or four members can help to meaningfully facilitate discussions, promote clinical context, and create a more direct connection to the bedside. Staff members should be engaged and have the ability to attend regularly. Selection should be placed for those noted to be active listeners. Informal leaders from across the organization should be involved as well as members that provide direct patient care.

Step: 7 **Goals and Ongoing Engagement**: The AHA blueprint outlines the importance of establishing measurable goals to drive performance (AHA 2022):

- Set annual goals and report on progress and completion.
- Communicate PFAC goals and accomplishments across the organization.
- Provide ongoing education to staff on the value of the PFAC.
- Measure impact and share feedback and results with the PFAC.
- Ensure follow-up when PFAC input is requested.

Step: 8 **Create a Culture**: Organizational leadership at every level must support a culture of patient-centered care and incorporation of goals of the PFAC. This means that the organization takes recommendations seriously and demonstrates responsiveness to PFAC feedback. Likewise, advisors are invited to participate in other clinical meetings, community events, and join in for quality improvement or clinical care rounds.

There are many ways to engage patients, from individual care encounters and through board committees to improving safety. The following case studies provide examples of organizations that are highly committed to PFE.

## Case Study: Developing a Patient and Family Advisory Council

Barbara Jacobs, chief nursing officer at Luminis Health Anne Arundel Medical Center, helped lead the long-term development of a comprehensive PFAC. The process began in 2010, with the motto "Nothing about me, without me" adopted early by the PFAC as a guide for all efforts. The overall framework consists of a central leadership council and multiple sub-councils, with each council comprising of appropriate clinical staff and advisors. Patient family advisors have participated in over 60 committees and initiatives across the community and health system, and their participation is an integral part of operations.

To increase engagement and reduce transportation barriers, since the outset of the program advisors have been offered the ability to participate by conference call or through virtual means. Flexibility with various opportunities on how to connect has been found to be integral in encouraging greater participation.

The goals of the PFAC include:

- Designation of a hospital employee with dedicated time to help in the administration and guidance of the council. Significant time must be given to the selection and onboarding of new advisors and in the matching of advisor skills and interests to the requested work. In addition, it is important that the advisors and hospital staff have an identified liaison for this work.
- Regular participation by senior clinical and administrative leadership in council meetings. It is essential that senior leadership models the relationship with advisors and that the advisors feel like their work is valued.
- Leadership expectation that advisors will be valued members of many committees and work groups.
- Demonstrated appreciation of the contributions of the advisors in multiple ways such as in leadership reports, in social media, and in special recognition events attended by hospital leadership such as an annual dinner. The importance of leadership acknowledgement of this work cannot be overemphasized as this encourages the growth and momentum of the advisors.

Advisors contribute to the orientation of new employees, training for medical residents, shaping the electronic patient portal, developing appropriate policy, and many quality committees and initiatives. An advisor is a part of the hospital daily operations safety call. In addition, the leadership of the PFAC sit on the Board Quality Committee and they give the reports of the advisor work to this group. PFAs participated heavily in the development of training material and in person training sessions for nurses in performing bedside shift report. The work of the IPFCC has been a continuing source of reference and guidance as well as the Beryl Institute and Planetree. When Anne Arundel Medical Center was selected in 2017 to participate as a pioneer system working with the Institute for Healthcare Improvement (IHI) and the John A. Hartford Foundation on the development of the framework for age-friendly care, patient advisors were identified as core members of the team. They traveled with staff to national and regional meetings and were actively a part of the innovative work being done.

To date, more than 95 advisors have been involved in donating hundreds of hours of time annually. Patient satisfaction scores have risen, and the involvement of the PFAC is among initiatives credited for this improvement. Lastly, the organization has received overall positive responses from those members that serve in these capacities, and has additionally benefited from the unique insight and perspective they provide.

## Lessons Learned

A narrow focus on patient satisfaction and patient experience metrics is far too limited to truly partner with patients and families. Likewise, simply providing a forum or pathway for patients to vocalize concerns is no longer sufficient. PFE extends beyond individual care encounters; it is a concept that must be embraced and integrated throughout leadership and governance decision-making processes. Patient experience, satisfaction, or engagement should not be a siloed activity, but rather one that is integrated across all initiatives and departments in the organization.

Results from initial efforts by hospitals to effectively and meaningfully engage patients have been mixed. While some institutions have had great success, others have struggled to overcome barriers. The following lessons represent key learnings from past efforts in PFE that should be noted and translated to improve the effectiveness of future interventions.

## *Beyond the Bedside*

PFE extends beyond the medical encounter. Historically, organizations have focused on increasing patient satisfaction scores related to the experience of care (i.e., noise levels, proximity of parking, and overall aesthetics of the facilities). Gradually, patient satisfaction measures have expanded to include measures of patient engagement in the care process. These patient engagement initiatives include hourly rounding to incorporating the patient and family, teach-back, effective discharge planning, shared decision-making, and less restricted visitation policies. All of these are important and notable priorities to improve activation and engagement; however, most of these policies focus on the one-on-one interactions between patients, families, and clinicians when the patients present themselves for treatment. At this point, it is often too late to modify the design of the facility (i.e., signage, dietary offerings, care processes) or the patient safety and quality protocols that may significantly impact that patient's stay.

Recognizing this shortfall and the need to move beyond the direct care interactions, the national focus has now shifted again to emphasize partnering with patients and families to proactively build patient- and family-centered care facilities. Increasingly, hospitals and health systems are even extending beyond the walls of the facility to engage patient and family advisors in community-based initiatives and in advocacy and policymaking.

## *Engage Patients as Partners*

Patients and families must be engaged as equal partners in the care process. The concept of patient- and family-centered care is built on the covenants of respect and dignity, information sharing, participation, and collaboration (Johnson et al. 2008). Particularly when patients and family members serve in advisory roles, they should be regarded as equal partners and not as special guests or one-time participants who are quickly dismissed or forgotten. To truly build patient- and family-centered organizations, the patient perspective must be systematically integrated throughout decision-making processes.

## *Provide Meaningful Opportunities for Patients and Families to Contribute*

Individuals who commit to serving in an advisory role aspire to contribute in a significant and meaningful way. Often, organizations build PFACs or invite PFAs to serve in advisory roles but lack the infrastructure or capacity to maximize the input of these advisors. As a result, councils or individuals feel underutilized or ignored. Many PFAs have expressed frustration with working on projects such as "selecting the paint color for the maternity ward" or "reviewing building plans after they are already drawn and approved." They do not feel that these efforts are meaningful or contribute to creating safe spaces for patients to heal. Leadership must demonstrate an ongoing commitment to engage patients in new and meaningful initiatives early and often and should periodically report to the advisors on how patient feedback has been incorporated into decision-making.

### *Patient and Family Engagement as a Strategy to Eliminate Harm*

PFE should not be a siloed initiative; it should be a cross-cutting strategy to improve care, including patient experience, safety, and quality. In particular, PFE should be recognized and utilized as a key strategy to eliminate harm in facilities. As demonstrated in the case studies and examples provided in this chapter, PFAs can be effective advisors and advocates to improve safety and quality. PFAs can serve to improve quality and safety in many capacities: Through formal PFACs, as members of standing quality and safety committees, or through participation in board meetings.

## Barriers to Engagement

Despite the substantial evidence that supports PFE, many leaders and organizations continue to cite significant barriers to engaging patients and families. A guide from the Health Research and Educational Trust outlines potential barriers (Figure 10.2) at the provider, organizational, and patient levels.

As a physician leader, one important role is to effectively communicate the evidence that supports the implementation

**Provider Barriers:**

- Perception that involving/engaging patients takes more time
- Limited availability to recognize decision aid opportunities and follow through
- Weak interpersonal skills (communication skills as well as strategies for appropriately involving patient/family members) of care team members
- Uncertainty about what bedside reporting should entail
- Uncertainty about how to involve the patient appropriately

**Organizational Barriers:**

- Patient privacy/HIPPA concerns
- Risk management concerns
- Liability issues that may arise from sharing data with patients and multiple providers
- Competing priorities for scarce resources in a system that does not consider patient and family engagement to be a top priority
- Lack of resources to set up advisory councils
- Foreign language/cultural barriers
- Lack of senior leadership understanding of and involvement with patient and family engagement issues
- Limited financial support/resources
- Insufficient training of clinical providers about how to engage with patients
- Limited availability and high cost of patient engagement technology and clinical information systems
- Time it takes to set up and implement advisory programs
- Disagreements about when patients should be provided with access to certain data

**Patient and Family Barriers:**

- Unwillingness of patients to participate in care activities
- Reluctance of patients and family to share personal, sensitive information
- Intimidation felt by patients in the traditional patient/provider relationship

**Figure 10.2 Potential barriers to patient and family engagement. (Health Research & Educational Trust. A Leadership Resource for Patient and Family Engagement Strategies. 2013. www.hpoe.org.)**

of PFE initiatives in order to persuade and motivate the organization to adopt these policies. Figure 10.3 includes a checklist for leaders related to integrating PFE throughout the organization.

| 1. Develop a Clear Vision for Patient Engagement | 2. Assess Strengths and Gaps in Your PFE Efforts |
|---|---|
| 1. Ensure your organization has a clear definition of patient and family engagement. | 1. Elicit feedback from your senior leadership team, staff, patients, and families about various patient engagement efforts. |
| 2. Discuss patient and family engagement with your senior leadership team so that they understand it matters to you and the organization. | 2. Use one or more formal patient engagement assessments to identify strengths and gaps. |
| 3. Elicit input from your board, your staff, and representative patients about what your organization will look like if you are successfully engaging patients and families. | 3. Inventory policies, processes, position descriptions, and training programs to determine whether patient and family engagement is appropriately included. |
| 4. Make improving patient and family engagement an organizational goal. | 4. Discuss findings and conclusions with leadership, staff, and patients to create awareness and lay the groundwork for improvement efforts. |
| 5. Allocate time in meetings with senior leadership, staff, and the board to hear and tell stories about engagement successes and shortcomings. | |

| 3. Implement Your Plan to Strengthen PFE Efforts | 4. Monitor Your Progress in Improving PFE |
|---|---|
| 1. Assess options for strengthening patient and family engagement at your hospital. | 1. Select measures that will allow you to see whether processes and outcomes are changing. |
| 2. Prioritize initiatives based on needs, opportunities, and input from key stakeholders. | 2. Ensure systems are in place to collect, analyze, and share data on an ongoing basis. |
| 3. Equip and empower your staff to support the engagement strategies you are implementing. | 3. Compile results in a format that is easy to understand and monitor. |
| 4. Anticipate barriers and proactively intervene to overcome them. | 4. Share results with staff, senior leadership, the board, community, and the public. |

**Figure 10.3 Checklist for leading patient and family engagement. (Health Research & Educational Trust. A Leadership Resource for Patient and Family Engagement Strategies. 2013. www.hpoe.org.)**

## Action Steps and Strategies to Lead

1. **Determine your organization's current state of patient and family engagement using an assessment tool**. All improvement initiatives should begin with an assessment of the problem; PFE is no different. There are several tools available to help determine your organization's current state and priorities for improvement. For example: Strategies for Leadership: Patient- and Family-Centered Care—a hospital self-assessment inventory; Patient- and Family-Centered Care—an organizational self-assessment tool or a checklist for attitudes about patients and families as advisors.
2. **Develop a clear vision of how your organization will engage patients and families**. Efforts to increase PFE should not be isolated initiatives but rather should be integrated throughout the organization's culture and work systems. Beginning with the organization's mission, leadership should develop and communicate a comprehensive vision for what patient- and family-centered care means at their facility. Leaders have a key role in communicating and role modeling this vision for partnering with patients and family members.
3. **Demonstrate commitment through providing resources and infrastructure to support patient- and family-centered care**. Many of the barriers to PFE relate to time and limited resources. PFE is often seen as one more initiative that takes away from patient care. Leaders must not only communicate the evidence for PFE and publicly commit to these initiatives but also must support that commitment through providing the resources and infrastructure necessary to support these practices. This includes intentional commitment to development of a PFAC or a network of PFACs, and engaging advisors across organizational efforts.

# References

AHRQ. Working with Patient and Families as Advisors. Implementation Handbook. 2017 Accessed March 23, 2023. https://www.ahrq.gov/sites/default/files/wysiwyg/professionals/systems/hospital/engagingfamilies/strategy1/Strat1_Implement_Hndbook_508_v2.pdf

American Institutes for Research. PfP Strategic Vision Roadmap for Person and Family Engagement. 2017. Accessed February 4, 2023. https://www.aha.org/sites/default/files/hiin/pfp-strategic-vision-roadmap.pdf

Carman, K.L., Dardess, P., Maurer, M., Sofaer, S., Adams, K., Bechtel, C., Sweeney, J. Patient and Family Engagement: A Framework for Understanding the Elements and Developing Interventions and Policies. *Health Affairs*. 2013;32(2):223–231.

Charmel, P.A., Frampton, S.B. Building the Business Case for Patient-Centered Care. *Healthcare Financial Management*. 2008;62(3):80–85.

Coulter, A., Ellins, J. Effectiveness of Strategies for Informing, Educating, and Involving Patients. *BMJ*. 2007;335(7609):24–27.

Epstein, R., Street, R. *Patient-Centered Care for the 21st Century: Physicians' Roles, Health Systems and Patients' Preferences*. ABIM Foundation, Philadelphia, PA, 2008.

Health Research & Educational Trust. A Leadership Resource for Patient and Family Engagement Strategies. 2013. www.hpoe.org

Hibbard, J.H., Greene, J., Overton, V. Patients with Lower Activation Associated with Higher Costs: Delivery Systems Should Know their Patients' "Scores". *Health Affairs*. 2013;32(2):216–222.

Institute for Patient- and Family-Centered Care. Changing Hospital "Visiting" Policies and Practices: Supporting Family Presence and Participation. 2010 http://www.ipfcc.org/visit-ing.pdf

Institute of Medicine. *Demanding Value from Our Health Care: Motivating Patient Action to Reduce Waste in Health Care*. National Academies Press, Washington, D.C., 2012.

Johnson, B., Abraham, J. Conway, L. Simmons, S. Edgman-Levitan, P. Sodomka, J., et al. *Partnering with Patients and Families to Design a Patient- and Family-Centered Health Care System: Recommendations and Promising Practices*. Institute for Patient- and Family-Centered Care, Bethesda, MD, 2008.

McCarly, P. Patient Empowerment and Motivational Interviewing: Engaging Patients to Self-manage their Own Care. *Nephrology Nursing Journal*. 2009;36(4):409–414.

McGreevey, M. *Patients as Partners: How to Involve Patients and Families in Their Own Care*. Joint Commission Resources, Inc., Oakbrook Terrace, IL, 2006.

Sorra, J., Khanna, K., Dyer, N., Mardon, R., Famolaro, T. Exploring Relationships Between Patient Safety Culture and Patients' Assessments of Hospital Care. *Journal of Patient Satisfaction*. 2012;8(3):1–9.

Weingart, S.N., Zhu, J., Chiapetta, L., Stuver, S.O., Schneider, E.C., Epstein, A.M., et al. Hospitalized Patients' Participation and its Impact on Quality of Care and Patient Safety. *International Journal for Quality in Health Care*. 2011;23(3):269–277.

American Hospital Association Physician Alliance. Patient and Family Advisory Councils Blueprint: A Start-Up Map and Strategy Guide. January 2022. Accessed June 16, 2023. https://www.aha.org/system/files/media/file/2022/01/alliance-pfac-blueprint-2022.pdf

# Chapter 11

# Health Equity and Addressing Disparities

## The Evidence

Racial and ethnic bias has been an issue within the borders of the Unites States for centuries. It is natural that such biases based on an individual's skin color, country of origin, or language spoken could likewise impact the medical care sought by these same demographic groups. In 2003, the Institute of Medicine published a landmark report that highlighted the inequities in care underserved minorities receive in the United States. This report, *Unequal Treatment*, provided a detailed look at the sources of racial and ethnic biases in health care at system, patient, and clinical levels. It further provided interventions that should be taken to address rampant health inequities that have disproportionally impacted underserved minorities (Institute of Medicine 2003). Since then, health equity in health care has become an increasingly relevant issue, with a significantly heighted degree of importance rightfully placed on mending these cracks in the system.

DOI: 10.4324/9781003402831-11

Health care disparities and inequities are not routinely recognized or transparent within traditional clinical settings. This can be as simple as the fact that lack of transportation limits the number of individuals within groups who even have access to such traditional care. Further, health care research and data does not typically emphasize marginalized or minority populations. Studies show that over 90% of all clinical trial participants in the United States are non-Hispanic whites of European ancestry, more often male (Ma et al. 2021). Thus, fewer than 2% of more than 10,000 cancer clinical trials were found to be focused on racial or ethnic minorities. One prominent example: While Black Americans are significantly more likely to suffer from respiratory ailments, only 1.9% of all studies on such diseases included any minority subjects (Scientific American 2018). These circumstances create disparities for who has access to care, what patient data is measured, and how treatments are considered effective.

Inequities in health outcomes are driven by the social determinants of health. Examples of such social determinants that play a role in the poorer health outcomes for these demographic groups include socioeconomic status, geographic location, education level, and access to health care services, among others. The ramifications of these social determinants of health are of no fault to the individual patients who suffer from them. Rather, they are engrained in many places into the very fabric of our society. It is the responsibility of physician leaders and health systems to seek to mitigate these disparities through strategic, innovative initiatives targeting the root of the issue. Such implications can even be found within disparities in salary between varying demographics, which directly translates to a varying ability to access or pay for necessary medical treatment.

In the last decade, there have been attempts by payors to address health equity in models of reimbursement. In an effort to facilitate heightened awareness and intentionality to the practice of equitable medicine, payors are increasingly providing financial incentives to drive meaningful change and improvement. In 2010, it was found that Medicaid fee-for-service payment rates were nearly 30% lower than Medicare rates (Mann & Striar 2022). Compounding this, it was determined that commercial payor rates were 30% higher than Medicare rates. Hispanic/Latino and black/African American populations account for a disproportionate share of Medicaid and Medicare's total beneficiary population. Thus, the U.S. health care system fundamentally exists with under-represented minority groups primarily covered by programs reimbursing physicians at lower rates. Systematic overhaul of reimbursement will continue to be an issue until it is appropriately addressed in a manner in which equitable care is truly incentivized. In recent years, Medicare has started to integrate measures of equity and diversity within its reports and has signaled that these will increasingly be measured within the definition of value and quality care delivery.

For the past two decades, the Agency for Healthcare Research and Quality (AHRQ) has published an annual National Healthcare Quality and Disparities Report. This report provides a snapshot of the quality of care, health outcomes, and health disparities impacting differing racial and sociodemographic groups within the United States (National Healthcare Quality 2022). Additionally, Health and Human Services (HHS) includes the Office of Minority Health (OMH), which, among other resources, maintains a compendium of federal datasets that address health disparities. For physician leaders and health systems seeking to evaluate the care in which they provide, this report can serve as a valuable source for benchmark data and measures pertinent to health equity.

Some of the disparities highlighted in the most recent National Healthcare Quality and Disparities Report include the following:

- The 2020 U.S. Census estimates that 12.8% of the population lives in poverty. Poverty is a state in which a person or household lacks sufficient financial resources to afford basic needs, such as food, shelter, or clothing. Poverty also hinders people from participating in community life, engaging in healthy activities, or accessing health care services when needed. Thus, people who live in poverty are particularly at risk for poor quality of care and undesirable health outcomes.
- Racial and ethnic diversity has increased. An increase in the percentage of people who identify as two or more races accounts for most of this increase having risen from 2.9% to 10.2% between 2010 and 2020.
- In 2020, Hispanic adolescents (37.0%) had lower levels of access to depression treatment than non-Hispanic White adolescents (49.1%).
- Living in proximity to primary care services could improve a person's likelihood of receiving high-quality care for chronic disease. However, many communities in the United States report limited or no access to primary care, especially non-metropolitan communities.

In addition to the reporting for specific quality metrics surrounding health equity, organizations such as the Lown Institute are starting to hold hospitals and organizations accountable for the degree of equity evident in their provision of health care services. The Lown Institute maintains an annual hospital index for diversity and equity. In 2022, over 3,600 hospitals were evaluated with 66 receiving straight As in equity, value, and outcomes (America's Most Socially Responsible Hospitals 2023). This suggests that just 2% of the hospitals included within the index demonstrate exemplary practice regarding health equity and diversity.

## Effective Strategies

Since the concept of health disparity and inequity was identified as being a significant problem in the American health care system, there have been a wide range of strategies deployed to increase awareness, improve quality of care, and decrease the burden of social determinants of health. The effectiveness of such strategies must oftentimes be tailored to the specific demographics or issues faced within the context of a given region, population, or disease. While the same health disparities are generally applicable to most areas of the United States, there are often differences to the severity in which they effect populations within a given region. For example, there may be discernable difference in the severity of diabetes between white and nonwhite patients in rural versus urban environments. With this in mind, physician leaders and health care organizations must be intentional in their strategy and implementation. This requires specific awareness of disparities that impact the population that an organization serves, be those geographic, demographic, socioeconomic, or disease specific.

### *Cultural Awareness*

In order to gain an understanding of where disparities lie and how to appropriately address them, there must be a high degree of organizational cultural awareness and competency. People, populations, and cultures can perceive and receive health care in vastly different ways. This represents the spectrum from the perception of pain, views on childbirth, acknowledgment of treatment options, educational level, among many other factors. Physician leaders should seek to equip themselves and their teams with the tools to be cognizant of cultural differences and adequately address them in ways befitting individual patient needs.

Ignorance of cultural differences can be amplified by unconscious bias. These are the biases that are present in each of us, that impact how we interact with others, most often without our awareness. These can express themselves in nonverbal responses to an individual's skin color, or inappropriate assumptions about an individual's likelihood to follow through on treatment recommendations based upon the clothes they are wearing. Such erroneous assumptions may not be a direct reflection of an individual's overt prejudice, but instead demonstrate how inequity in health care is further perpetuated.

Physician leaders should begin by raising awareness of implicit biases, and should consider personal and team-based unconscious bias training. A 2018 systematic review conducted by the Equality and Human Rights Commission found that unconscious bias training programs are an effective strategy to reduce racially biased attitudes (Atewologun et al. 2018). In addition to formal training programs, there are other resources publicly available such as Harvard's Project Implicit. Project Implicit is a not-for-profit organization focused on researching unconscious or implicit bias and providing the cognitive tools aimed at combatting bias. They offer an implicit bias test directly on their website for those seeking to assess their personal bias (Project Implicit). Increasing this type of awareness in a clinical setting is an essential step for physician leaders and organizations seeking to minimize health care disparities.

## *Stratify Data to Identify Areas of Need*

Health care organizations must understand the demographic and cultural circumstances within the populations they serve, and use objective data to drive decision-making and monitor improvement. Improvement strategies to mitigate health disparities may be successful for some populations, but may not benefit every group. In fact, it is possible that emphasis on improvement targeting a given population could cause balancing measures to negatively impact another. There must be a narrowed focus to address specific quality measures within specific underrepresented patient groups. Data can help to identify variation in care and outcomes, and can be subdivided based upon patient and population factors.

Specific health needs within populations served may already be identified through the Community Health Needs Assessment (CHNA). Community health assessments have been carried out for decades by a wide array of public health entities such as local health departments and social service agencies as a tool to identify key health needs and concerns within a given community. With the passage of the Affordable Care Act, all nonprofit hospitals are mandated to complete a CHNA every three years. One of the primary challenges has been that while hospitals and health systems have gone about conducting and reporting the CHNA, there have been minimal and mixed results in terms of efforts to actually address the issues outlined. For health care organizations to begin eliciting meaningful change within the communities they serve, there must be more structured, intentional planning processes surrounding the efforts pre- and post-assessment. Physician leaders should use resources, such as the Association for Community Health Improvement's assessment toolkit, which encompasses a nine-step process to ensure appropriate action is taken. The toolkit can be referenced in Figure 11.1.

After assessing population and community-specific needs and variation, key quality measures can be established to track and improve these needs. Such measures should be stratified by variables including race, ethnicity, language spoken, and others. Physician leaders should seek this cycle of studying their population, identifying variation and disparity, articulating goals for improvement, implementing initiatives, and tracking success. At regular intervals, a restudy of

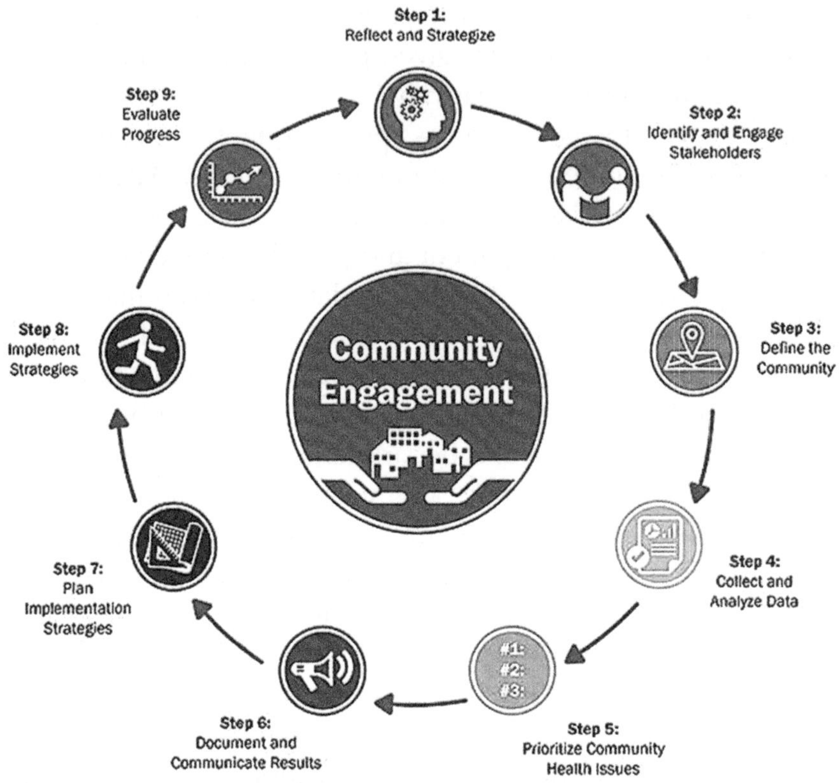


**Figure 11.1 Community health assessment toolkit. (AHA Community Health Improvement, 2017.)**

the population is essential to identify any newly emerged or previously unrecognized disparities.

## *Community Partnerships*

Community partnerships represent another avenue for physician leaders and health systems to reach patient populations who may be suffering from identified health disparities. For just about every aspect of health care, cultivating community partnerships and building upon these relationships represent positive action. Meeting these demographic groups where they are in specified settings has the opportunity to enhance both engagement and trust.

Examples of such community partnerships and engagement would be for a community-based hospital to partner with an underrepresented minority-owned business or religious organization. Barber shops, grocery stores, and gas stations have been frequently trusted and valuable locations for non-traditional health care delivery and education. Churches, social halls, and community outreach groups can be strong partners as well. These locations can be used for everything from point-of-care hemoglobin A1C testing for demographics that are disproportionately suffering from uncontrolled diabetes, to vaccine administration, to healthy cooking demonstrations.

## Case Study: A Health Equity Report

An excerpt of a health equity report produced by a regional health system is shown in Figure 11.2. The complete health equity report is posted on the organization's website to be

| Health Disparities by Race/Ethnicity | | | | |
|---|---|---|---|---|
| Measure | White | Non-White | Disparity (Absolute % Difference) | Relative % Difference |
| Newborn Exclusive Breast Milk Feeding (%) | 45.5% | 34.1% | 11.4% | 28.6% |
| Poorly Controlled Diabetes (HbA1C ≥ 9) | 8.7% | 12.3% | 3.6% | 34.3% |
| ED Throughput Time (Admitted ED-1b) | 405 Minutes | 421 Minutes | 16 Minutes | 3.9% |
| Medicaid Patient Timely Follow-Up Compliance (%) | 72.30% | 64.60% | 7.70% | 11.2% |

**Figure 11.2 Measure and relative differences of health disparities by race/ethnicity.**

transparent. This organization analyzed over two dozen quality measures and stratified the results by race/ethnicity and language spoken. The table shown in Figure 11.2 identifies disparities or differences in results between white and nonwhite patients for four quality measures. The organization then established improvement teams for each quality measure led by a physician and administrative leader. The physician leader of each team reviewed the data, shared the data with the team, developed a driver diagram with the team of potential drivers, received unconscious bias training, and started implementing various interventions. This similar process was conducted for the quality measures from the previous health equity report. From that improvement work, two disparities were reduced: Sepsis core measures and preterm births.

The role of the physician leader in this example is not too dissimilar from other quality improvement efforts. It requires analyzing data, leading a team with strong communication, providing education, setting goals, and implementing improvement efforts. They must identify and then raise awareness of the reality of what otherwise may be unrecognized disparities within the day-to-day work of their teams. Physician leaders must be able to clearly articulate the reason for improving specific disparities, develop targeted goals for each, and engage champions to support this work.

## Lessons Learned

1. **Health disparities are not new, though their transparency has only emerged in recent years**. Systemic inequities over the course of decades have culminated to form health disparities that are directly impacting the health status and well-being of historically marginalized populations. Addressing such inequities for one group has the potential to elevate care for all. Health inequity

must be addressed through comprehensive policy change, evidence-based practice compliance, and awareness and minimization of unconscious bias.

2. **Change cannot be expected unless the current systems of care delivery perpetuating health inequity are appropriately addressed**. Action must be taken and progress must be measured based on the disparities pertinent to each individual organization. As such, it is critical to find the cracks in care delivery that inadvertently exacerbate health disparities. This is no simple undertaking and will oftentimes require systematic overhaul of processes in place.
3. **Health disparities are oftentimes difficult to pinpoint**. Data must be utilized to drive effective quality improvement initiatives. Awareness alone is insufficient, and objective data should be followed with measurable action steps and metrics. There must be fundamental emphasis throughout assessment, data analysis, and meaningful improvement.

## Action Steps and Strategies to Lead

1. **Implement appropriate training mechanisms**. With an understanding that cultural awareness and competency are effective in addressing unconscious bias, physician leaders should implement tools to equip their team members for success. Unconscious bias may take root regardless of conscious practices. Bringing about awareness and recognition is the first step in facilitating meaningful change. Physician leaders should implement unconscious bias and cultural competency training into their orientation and team development plans.
2. **Stratify your data**. Physician leaders and organizations must understand the demographics they are serving.

Within differing demographic groups, efforts must be made to understand how health disparities uniquely impact varying populations. Study and transparently shared data on outcomes between identified populations and subpopulations. Targeted improvement initiatives should be informed by objective data, rather than feel. Efforts to restudy and restratify groups will continually reveal disparities that can be acted upon for meaningful change.

3. **Launch improvement teams**. Health disparities are multifactorial. Seeking to mitigate these through traditional committees or long-standing infrastructure may not be sufficient to yield the right perspective or improvement. Rather, new teams should be formed and designed specifically for targeted disparities. Where possible, team members should include those that can speak for and from impacted constituencies.
4. **Leverage community partnerships**. In many cases, the social determinants must be addressed outside of traditional clinical settings. Leveraging community stakeholders and organizations must be a top priority for any physician leader or health care organization with a commitment to mitigating health disparities. The building and nurturing of community relationships can make a significant impact in addressing the systematic issues plaguing underrepresented minorities and groups.
5. **Strive for truly transformational improvement**. The extent of iniquities in the U.S. health care system are profound. Physician leaders and organizations should not settle with small or incremental improvements. Such limited progress will not address current issues, and may only allow others to be revealed in time. Rather, physician leaders should boldly seek to wholly eliminate inequity within their organization and populations served.

## References

Agency for Healthcare Research and Quality. National Healthcare Quality and Disparities Report. AHRQ. 2022. Accessed March 12, 2023. https://www.ahrq.gov/research/findings/nhqrdr/nhqdr22/index.html

Agency for Healthcare Research and Quality. Project Implicit. 2023 Accessed March 20, 2023. https://www.projectimplicit.net/

America's Most Socially Responsible Hospitals. Lown Institute Hospital Index. 2023 Accessed March 19, 2023. https://lownhospitalsindex.org/lists/2022-social-responsibility/

Association for Community Health Improvement. Community Health Assessment Toolkit. 2017. www.healthycommunities.org/assesstoolkit

Atewologun, D., Cornish, T., Tresh, F. Unconscious Bias Training: An Assessment of the Evidence for Effectiveness. Equality and Human Rights Commission Research Report Series. 2018.

Editors of Scientific American. Clinical Trials Have Far Too Little Racial and Ethnic Diversity. *Scientific American.* 2018;319(3):10.

Institute of Medicine (US) Committee on Understanding and Eliminating Racial and Ethnic Disparities in Health Care. *Unequal Treatment: Confronting Racial and Ethnic Disparities in Health Care*, eds. Smedley, B. D., Stith, A. Y., & Nelson, A. R. National Academies Press, Washington, DC, 2003.

Ma, M.A., Gutierrez, D.E., Frausto, J.M., Al-Delaimy, W.K. Minority Representation in Clinical Trials in the United States: Trends Over the Past 25 Years. *Mayo Clinic Proceedings.* 2021;96(1):264–266.

Mann, C., Striar, A. How Differences in Medicaid, Medicare, and Commercial Health Insurance Payment Rates Impact Access, Health Equity, and Cost. *Commonwealth Fund.* August 17, 2022. Accessed March 20, 2023. https://www.commonwealthfund.org/blog/2022/how-differences-medicaid-medicare-and-commercial-health-insurance-payment-rates-impact

# Chapter 12

# Addressing Variation in Utilization

## The Evidence

Variation is not a new phenomenon. In a now-classic study conducted in 1938, Dr. J. Allison Glover uncovered geographic variations in tonsillectomy procedures in schoolchildren in England and Wales. Dr. Glover was unable to identify a cause for the variation other than providers' preferences in performing surgery (Ballard et al. 2022). Decades later, in 1973, Jack Wennberg, who would become a pioneer and leading researcher in variation in health care, published his first paper on small-area variation (Wennberg 1973). Since then, identifying and explaining variation has been the subject of many studies, including the Dartmouth Atlas of Healthcare, a series of reports dedicated to analyzing health care utilization in the United States (Newhouse and Garber 2013 and Ballard et al. 2022). As Wennberg was popularly known to posit, "geography is destiny" (Brooner and Skinner 2022).

Variation in health care spending and utilization generates interest and concern because of its implications for cost and

 DOI: 10.4324/9781003402831-12

quality. There are many documented instances of systematic variation in Medicare spending and utilization that are seemingly unrelated to health outcomes. In these instances, higher costs do not necessarily correlate with higher quality (Combes and Arespacochaga 2013). Furthermore, research has demonstrated that unexplained variation persists even when controlling for individuals' age, sex, income, race, and health status, and that it is significant (Newhouse 2013). In 2022, Medicare spending per beneficiary averaged at $10,281, and ranged from a low of $7,654 in Honolulu, Hawaii, to a high of $15,186 in The Bronx, New York (Cooper et al. 2022).

As health care costs continue to grow, the potential for savings by reducing unwarranted variation is increasingly becoming a focus of policy-makers and health care leaders. One recent 2019 study suggested that 30% of national health care spending could be considered waste, including overtreatment or low-value care costing roughly $100 billion and further failures in care delivery and care coordination at over $150 billion and $75 billion, respectively (Shrank et al. 2019). Given the potential to provide care that is higher quality at a lower cost, physician leaders must develop competencies in identifying and addressing unwarranted variation within their teams and systems.

## *Understanding Warranted vs. Unwarranted Variation*

Not all variation is inappropriate. Variation may be warranted or unwarranted. Warranted variation occurs because of differences in patient preference, disease prevalence, or other patient-related factors. Essentially, variation of this sort can be positive when care is appropriately individualized to a given patient or unique clinical context. Alternatively, unwarranted variation is not explained by patient preference or condition. Unwarranted variation implies inefficiency including underuse, overuse, or misuse of services (Gnadinger 2014 and Ballard et al. 2022). Potential causes of unwarranted variation include underuse of effective care, misuse of preference-sensitive care, and overuse of supply-sensitive care (Ballard et al. 2022). Preference-sensitive care includes treatments that involve significant trade-offs that affect the patient's quality or length of life, but for which there is no clear evidence-based recommendation for practice. Such treatment decisions should reflect patients' personal values and preferences, and when carried out with shared decision-making can contribute to reducing costs (Veroff et al. 2013). In many instances, however, there is unwarranted variation in the use of preference-sensitive care due to a failure to accurately communicate the risks and benefits of alternative treatments. As a result, the treatment choice is not based on the patient's values and preferences, but on those of the physician.

Research suggests that the extent and degree of unwarranted variation in the United States is a result of the empirical nature of clinical practice and the lack of a foundation in evidence-based medicine. No facility is exempt; even top academic medical centers and metropolitan areas experience unwarranted variations in delivery and outcomes of care (Arora and True 2012 and Song et al. 2022). To provide high value, patient-centered care, leaders must guide their facilities to recognize the systematic underuse, misuse, or overuse of care and to modify practice patterns to provide care that is evidence-based and consistent with patient preferences and values.

There are many reasons to reduce unwarranted variation. Specifically, payment reform and new reimbursement models are designed to reward high value care. Reimbursement is increasingly tied to quality and patient experience outcomes. Facilities that are over- or under-providing care will be penalized under value-based reimbursement. As the health care system shifts from a fee-for-service model to one based on value, providers will be incentivized to deliver appropriate, effective care at a reduced cost to maximize reimbursement and minimize financial penalties. Furthermore, reducing unwarranted variation can improve quality of care and lead to increased patient satisfaction—both important components in the triple aim of health (Berwick et al. 2008). Finally, health care consumers will continue to have increased access to provider and facility-level data, costs, and outcomes. Transparent sharing of variation, through the form of publicly shared benchmarking and comparative data, has the potential to revolutionize how, where, and from whom patients seek care. Physician leaders must be attuned to this reality not only for the good of patient care but also for the success of their providers and systems.

In recent years, many stakeholders in health care have sponsored initiatives or educational campaigns promoting evidence-based care and reduction of unwarranted variation. Two examples are the Choosing Wisely Campaign and the American Hospital Association's education related to the appropriate use of medical resources.

## *Choosing Wisely®*

Of the more than five billion tests performed in the United States each year, it is suggested that upwards of 40–60% may be unnecessary (Koch et al. 2018). Further, when asked, physicians will report that one out of every five tests that they order is not indicated. Such unnecessary testing is most often done for a variety of reasons, including patient preference or pressure, fear of liability, difficulty accessing prior medical records, ease of ordering, and heuristic bias, among others. To combat this, the ABIM Foundation's Choosing Wisely® Campaign, begun in 2012, promotes conversations between patients and providers in order to choose care that is evidence-based, not duplicative, free from harm, and truly necessary. The result has been a compendium of recommendations on

"Things Providers and Patients Should Question." These lists provide evidence-based recommendations for patients and providers to discuss regarding decision-making on the most appropriate care for each individual patient. These recommendations include information such as whether tests and procedures are appropriate in specific situations. In addition to these lists, participants in the campaign have developed patient-friendly materials that use plain language to educate patients on various medical topics, as well as resources on physician-patient communication. These resources empower patients to understand their condition and to initiate conversations with their physicians regarding the appropriateness of care. Physicians can also access a suite of communication education models to help them engage with their patients in these conversations.

Choosing Wisely has engaged over 80 medical specialty organizations and published over 600 recommendations of overused tests and treatments that physicians and patients should question and discuss concerning their necessity. The key for physician leaders will be how to use awareness of these resources to drive their organizations and teams. Studies have shown variability of the potential impact of the range of recommendations, and that leaders should target interventions with greatest potential to improve cost, lower harm, and reduce further testing (Ganguli et al. 2022).

## *The Safer Dx Checklist*

A large component of unnecessary utilization derives from poor diagnostic accuracy and lack of decision support tools. Clinicians, particularly those practicing outside of team-based models, have the potential to order a multitude of tests to generate more information and rule out a broader spectrum of possible disease. Some of this occurs when single clinicians are held solely accountable to produce a diagnosis. The fear of diagnostic error or delayed diagnosis can greatly motivate overordering of tests (Brady et al. 2022). In 2022, a joint team from the Center for Innovation in Quality, Effectiveness, and Safety (IQuESt), and Institute for Healthcare Improvement (IHI) developed the Safer Dx Checklist to share ten High-Priority Organizational Practices for Diagnostic Excellence. Physician leaders should use this self-assessment tool to understand the current state of diagnostic practices, identify areas to improve, and track progress toward diagnostic excellence over time within their organizations. Figure 12.1 outlines the ten recommended practices, which focus on increasing team communication, distributing accountability through team-based care, and involving patients and families in decision-making. Steps to success including developing a multidisciplinary team that review's the organization's status, crafting specific action plans, and periodically reviewing checklist results with organizational leaders and the governing board to engage them in diagnostic safety improvement efforts (Singh et al. 2022).

## Strategies for Success

Many recommendations and evidence-based tools are useful in reducing unwarranted variation. For example, tools that facilitate shared decision-making between providers and patients not only ensure high quality of care for the patient but also make more efficient use of clinicians' time (HRET 2011). In 2011, the Health Research and Educational Trust published an action guide for health care leaders on understanding and managing variation and outlined five steps for clinical leaders aiming to reduce unwarranted variation (Figure 12.2) (HRET 2011).

| The Safer Dx Checklist | Implementation Status | | |
|---|---|---|---|
| 10 High-Priority Practices for Diagnostic Excellence | Current state of organization's practice | | |
| | Full | Partial | Not Implemented |
| 1. Health care organization leadership builds a "board-to-bedside" accountability framework that includes structure, capacity, transparency, time, and resources to measure and improve diagnostic safety. | | | |
| 2. Health care organization promotes a just culture and creates a psychologically safe environment that encourages clinicians and staff to share opportunities to improve diagnostic safety without fear of retribution. | | | |
| 3. Health care organization creates feedback loops to increase information flow about patients' diagnostic and treatment-related outcomes. These loops, which include clinicians and external organizations, establish mechanisms for capturing, measuring, and providing feedback to the diagnostic team about patients' subsequent diagnoses and clinical outcomes. | | | |
| 4. Health care organization includes multidisciplinary perspectives to understand and address contributory factors in analysis of diagnostic safety events. These perspectives include human factors, informatics, IT system design, and cognitive elements. | | | |
| 5. Health care organization actively seeks patient and family feedback to identify and understand diagnostic safety concerns and addresses concerns by codesigning solutions. | | | |
| 6. Health care organization encourages patients to review their health records and has mechanisms in place to help patients understand, interpret, and/or act on diagnostic information. | | | |
| 7. Health care organization prioritizes equity in diagnostic safety efforts by segmenting data to understand root causes and implementing strategies to address and narrow equity gaps. | | | |
| 8. Health care organization has in place standardized systems and processes to encourage direct, collaborative interactions between treating clinical teams and diagnostic specialties (e.g., laboratory, pathology, radiology) in cases that pose diagnostic challenges. | | | |
| 9. Health care organization has in place standardized systems and processes to ensure reliable communication of diagnostic information between care providers and with patients and families during handoffs and transitions throughout the diagnostic journey. | | | |
| 10. Health care organization has in place standardized systems and processes to close the loop on communication and follow up on abnormal test results and referrals. | | | |

**Figure 12.1 IHI safer Dx checklist: Ten high-priority practices for diagnostic excellence. (Baylor College of Medicine.)**

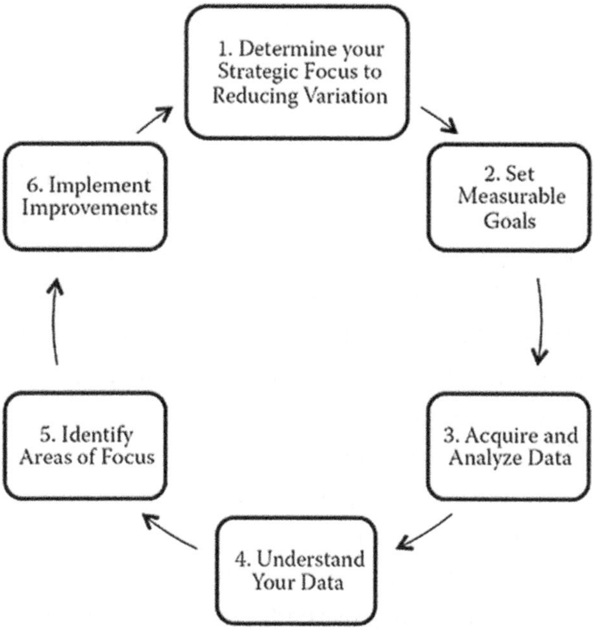


**Figure 12.2 Steps to understanding and addressing variation. (Health Care Leader Action Guide: Understanding and Managing Variation. Health Research & Educational Trust. Chicago, IL, February 2011. www.hret.org/variation.)**

1. **Determine your strategic focus for reducing variation**. Leadership must be clear on the strategic imperative for reducing readmissions: To reduce operational costs, reduce spending on hospitalization, improve patient safety and satisfaction, or strengthen shared decision-making and patient engagement.
2. **Set measurable goals**. Adhering to the adage "what gets measured gets managed," leadership should set measurable goals related to the aim of reducing variation and track progress toward those goals on a regular basis.
3. **Acquire and analyze data**. The first step in addressing variation is to identify it. To do so, organizations must have high-quality data on their own performance as well as local, regional, state, and national data for comparison.

Data acquisition and analysis is necessary to identify and prioritize opportunities to reduce variation. The collection process should focus on a few critical metrics that are most relevant to the operational or clinical processes under scrutiny. Data should be collected from both internal and external sources, and should incorporate multiple sources to minimize the potential shortcomings of various data sources. Sources for comparison and benchmark data include the Dartmouth Atlas, University Health System Consortium, Premier, and the Veterans Health Administration.

4. **Identify areas of focus**. One of the crucial roles of the physician leader is to prioritize interventions to manage variation. Once variation is identified, leaders should investigate (a) whether the organization's performance varies in a way that positively or negatively impacts patients, the health system, and the community and (b) the drivers and root causes of variation. If it is determined that the variation should be addressed, leaders can identify interventions to reduce variation. Based on national trends, the following areas may yield the greatest opportunity for improvement: Readmissions, emergency room utilization, intensive care unit utilization, obstetrics utilization, surgical procedures, appropriateness of admission, diagnostic and treatment procedures, imaging, and end-of-life care. Alternatively, leaders may use the following to guide the decision of which areas' initiatives to prioritize: Those areas with the highest volume of services, that have the greatest financial impact, that are most likely to result in avoidable injury, or that have been identified by leadership as a high priority for the organization.
5. **Implement improvements**. As with any improvement initiative, there should be substantial planning before any intervention is implemented. The following questions can help guide the planning process:

- *Communication*: Has there been visible and sufficient communication focused on the initiative? Are communications frequent, relevant, and compelling?
- *Consensus*: Is there adequate buy-in among senior leaders, mid-level managers, and clinical staff at the point-of-care to address the issue? Has utilization management and reduction of unnecessary treatment become part of everyone's job (including the front line)? Or are these efforts isolated and being encouraged only by a few managers?
- *Leadership*: Is there sufficient leadership to drive improvement and internal decision-making that supports change and innovation?
- *Accountability*: Have improvement initiatives on variation been tied to overall performance metrics? Will senior leaders of key areas be evaluated on their ability to drive improvement?
- *Timelines*: Has the organization categorized and established several levels of targets (i.e., short-, medium-, and long-term goals and strategies?) Has the organization's leadership agreed on the improvement initiative's timeline and does it include identified milestones?
- *Micro-centers for change*: Have demonstration sites been selected to serve as models?
- *Utilization improvement officers*: Are there a sufficient number of utilization experts throughout the organization who can act as resources? Are there available training programs and resources that are designed to maintain the focus and drive for improvement?
- *Overarching guidelines*: Has the organization adopted the appropriate and current CMS, AHRQ, or other federal guidelines related to utilization? Does the organization's plan look three to five years ahead to maintain a competitive position in the industry?

## Case Study: Reducing Opioid Overprescribing

Barry R. Meisenberg, MD, serves as chair of the Department of Medicine at Anne Arundel Medical Center (AAMC). In 2017, a rapid increase in opioid-related deaths were reported by news sources, leading to states of emergency in local and national jurisdictions. Across the United States, opioid prescriptions delivered in the context of every day clinical care were found to have grown 300% in the 20 years preceding 2012 (Guy et al. 2017). The reaction to this public health emergency predictably centered on criminal justice actions and harms reduction. Dr. Meisenberg and leaders at Anne Arundel Medical Center believed that health systems were accountable for responding to this crisis, working with their prescribers and improving utilization of therapeutic use of opioids.

Reacting to the public health messaging, a small team including an undergraduate summer research intern executed a pilot study analyzing prescribing variability at hospital discharge following a single type of surgical procedure, thoracic lobectomy. This analysis revealed both non-clinical variability and idiosyncratic prescribing, as the amounts of opioid prescribed at discharge in milligram morphine equivalents (MME) did not correlate with the amounts of opioids required during the patient's initial post-op period (Figure 12.3). It was recognized that order sets and Enhanced Recovery after Surgery (ERAS) protocols generally did not include a discharge opioid order, or when they did, it was a one-size-fits all, large amount. Convenience for patients and doctors in avoiding the necessity of making and responding to calls for refills was a major driver of high discharge amounts.

Because opioid prescribing was not a regulatory quality metric, no standing health system report, resources, or team were available to examine the problem. Resources for a deeper and wider program of assessment and action had to be cobbled together from existing resources in different

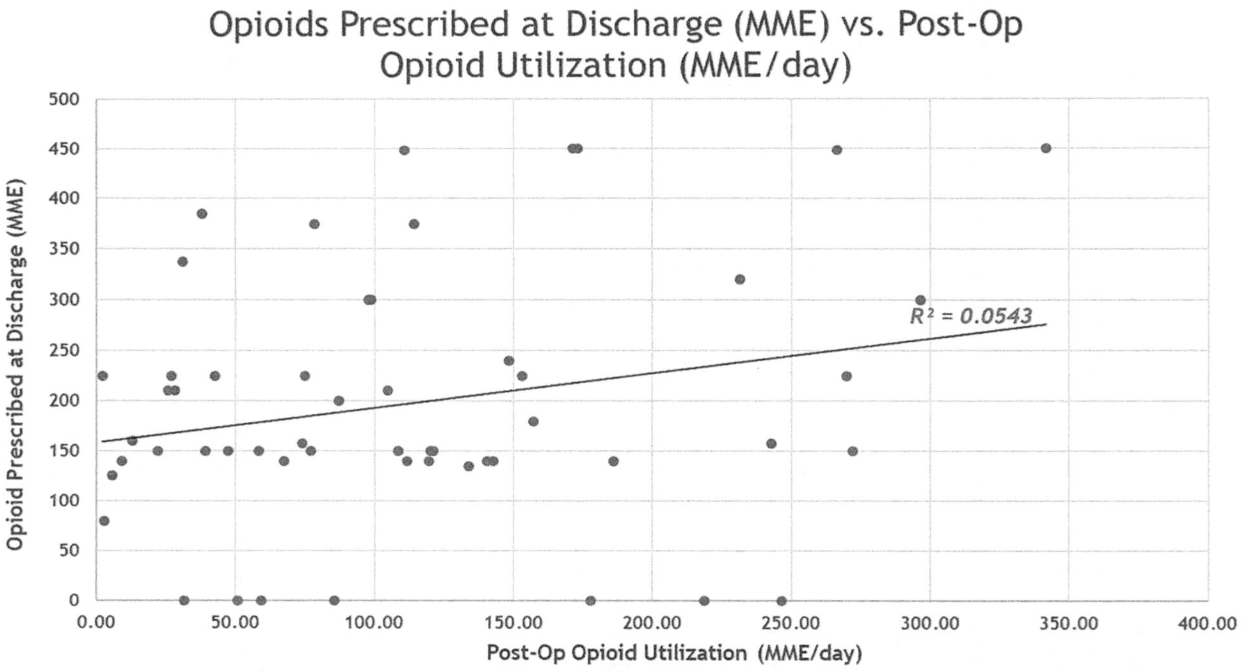


**Figure 12.3 Post-lobectomy prescribing at baseline. (Anne Arundel Medical Center, Annapolis, MD.)**

departments. For this project, major leadership energy and expertise was found in Jennifer Grover PA, DHSc (performance improvement) and Dan Korpman M.S. (Information systems). These leaders created a de novo initiative including instructing the electronic medical record (EMR) and analytic software tool what formulary drugs were considered opioids to be counted and how to convert prescription amounts into MME automatically. A new multidisciplinary and multidepartment opioid prescribing task force was created and led by these individuals.

Recognizing that there were linkages between prescribing and adverse patient and community outcomes due to diversion, the AAMC team began a pilot review of prescriptions from various health system departments and found lack of adherence to prescribing best practices, some of which are facilitated by electronic medical record set up such as prescription defaults to high dose of opioids as the default choice.

To generate the motivation to take corrective actions, a series of "reverse" detailing educational sessions were held with medical staff at various venues including departmental meetings, "Grand Rounds" and medical staff meetings. The most relevant teachings derived from peer-reviewed journals are shown in Figure 12.4.

To empower program leaders with actionable data, a report was built using a software application that pulled prescribing data from the EMR, converted these prescriptions to a morphine milligram equivalent (MME) and assigned the prescription to an individual in particular departments. The program was enabled to calculate the total MME per prescription and MME per clinical encounter to allow for adjustments in clinical volume. Leaders were asked to validate the assignment of prescribers into their department and validate that they had similar clinical practices with those being compared, for example, similar types of procedures or patient population.

| Education Topics Reviewed with Medical Staff | |
|---|---|
| **Topic** | **Comment** |
| 1. Epidemiology of overdose events, overdose deaths, and overall opioid prescribing | 1. Comparison of US opioid prescribing with nations of similar demographics. Role of marketing re pain as a growing medical problem |
| 2. Why hospital and physicians bear some responsibility for the increase in opioid prescribing | 2. Hospitals and physician offices were the sites of cynical marketing disguised as medical education |
| 3. Dose intensity of the initial prescription is associated with long-term use. | 3. A small but significant percentage of opioid naive patients become long-term users of opioids. These data were the base for CDC recommendation to restrict duration of initial prescriptions for acute problems |
| 4. Association of medicinal opioid with future fentanyl and heroin use | 4. Most abusers of fentanyl and heroin began with prescription opioids; their own or someone else's. |
| 5. Data shows that patients do not use anywhere near all the opioids prescribed. The left over amounts are subject to diversion. | 5. Do not prescribe for the top 80th percentile of use; prescribe at a lower amount and be available for additional therapy as needed (easier with newly available e-prescribing with two factor identification). |
| 6. The public is newly wary of over prescribing and will appreciate the limits based on "best practices" | 6. Our own data confirms this; no drop-off in patient satisfaction with pain management after dose reductions protocols installed. |
| 7. Our own data show marked variation in frequency of opioid prescriptions after an encounter and dose. | 7. Data review by individual departments to benchmark each prescriber with those of peers. Data can be presented blindly or with identities revealed as needed. |

**Figure 12.4 Education topics reviewed with medical staff. (Anne Arundel Medical Center, Annapolis, MD.)**

Some leaders created new practice guidelines and a modified Delphi approach to best practices using patient survey data, published reports, or CDC guidance. These guidelines were built into the EMR as either default prescriptions (for instance, 5 oxycodone pills vs. 30), or attached to order sets for inpatient or same-day surgeries. Adherence to the new guidelines and order sets were tracked and reported to clinical leaders for benchmarking. Other adjustments to the EMR included embedding patient educational material about opioid alternatives and safe storage, facilitating referral for substance abuse counseling, and tracking tools for opioid use during an inpatient stay in order to right-size discharge prescriptions (another best practice). Simultaneously, the health system used its communication assets to boost public messaging from public health authorities about opioid alternative and safe storage.

Data monitored by the opioid prescribing task force included total MME per encounter, MME per prescription for the health system, department and prescriber, and the frequency of an opioid prescription after an ED encounter or an ambulatory visit, the number of new (as opposed to renewal) opioid prescriptions. Other data also included simultaneous prescribing of opioids and benzodiazepines. With all the prescribing reduction initiatives in place, the health system monitored for evidence of untoward results, including increase in return to the emergency department for inadequately treated pain and reduction in pain control and patient satisfaction after an encounter.

Data revealed that 15 months after the initiative commenced, MME per encounter was reduced by 58% resulting from a combination of 34% less MME per prescription and a 38% lower incidence of an opioid prescription after an encounter (Figure 12.5). Moreover, frequency of encounters that were accompanied by an opioid prescription decreased in both the emergency department, 24% to 12%, and primary care clinics, 2.5% to 1.4%.

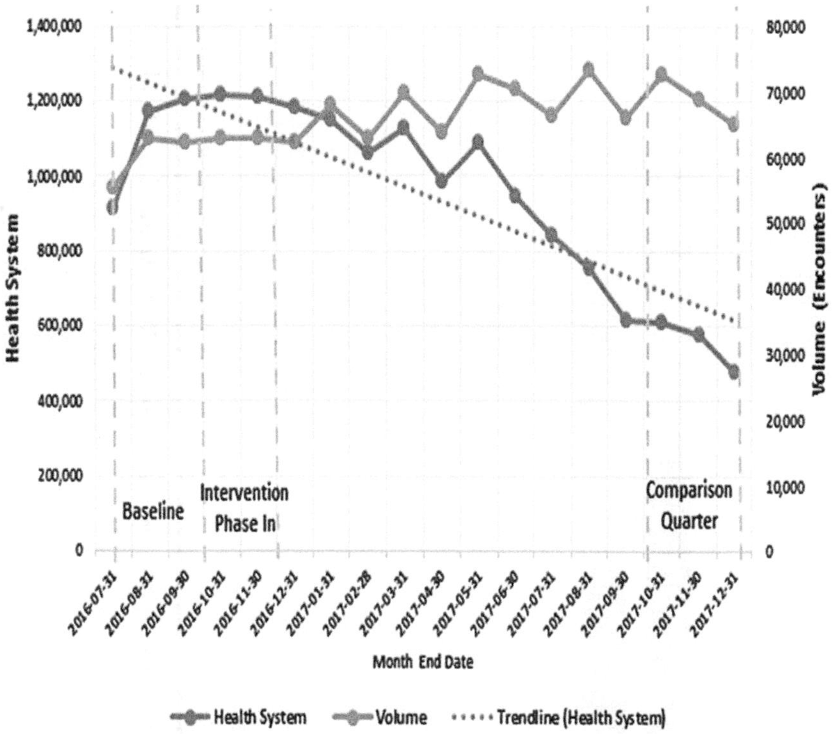


**Figure 12.5 Reduction in health system prescribed MME and clinical encounter volume over time (Anne Arundel Medical Center, Annapolis, MD.)**

Contrary to many quality initiatives where results slide toward the baseline after attention wanes, these results have improved even further over time as more surgeries were included in the reduced prescribing initiatives. These improvements are likely now "baked in" due to fixed changes in policies such as limits on short-term prescription amounts, EMR defaults to lower MME amounts, and changes in physician attitudes reinforced by external guidelines from pharmacies and insurers. Five years after the initiative began, the average MME per prescriptions have been reduced by 45% from baseline and the overall reduction in MME is 75%, (excluding cancer and palliative medicine patients), as depicted in Figure 12.6.

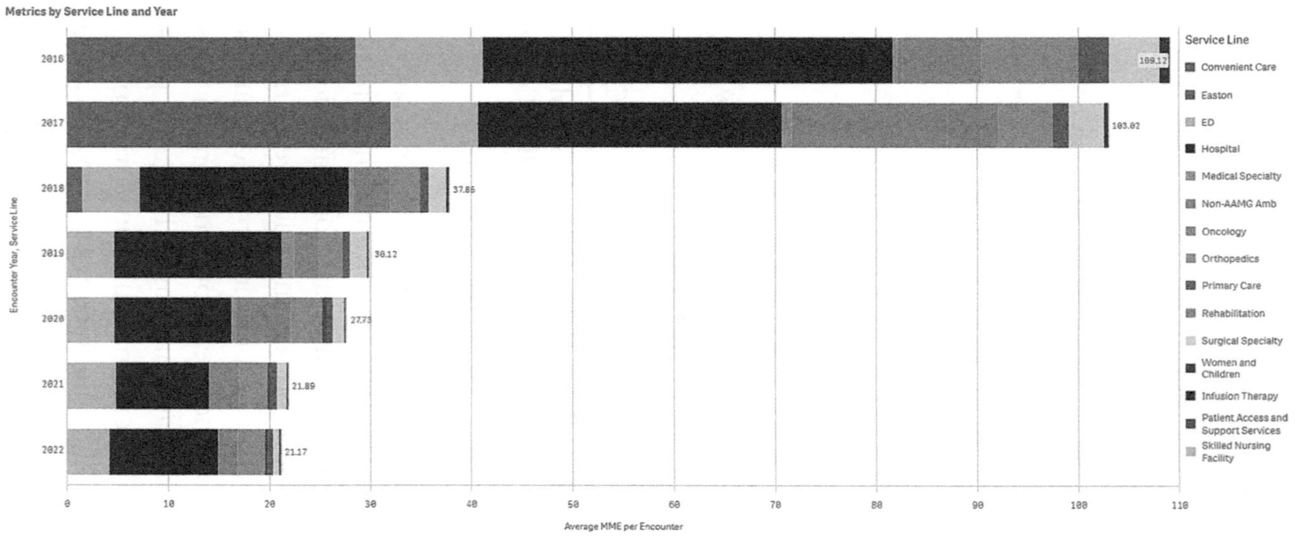


**Figure 12.6 Average MME per prescription and overall prescription by service line. (Anne Arundel Medical Center, Annapolis, MD.)**

Dr. Meisenberg noted elements of success included having an engaged leader with the ability to mobilize health system resources regardless of departmental lines. Likewise, a health system that supports such flexibility. It was necessary to collect accurate and timely prescriber-level and department-level data delivered to or easily accessible by accountable physician leaders. These leaders then address outlier prescriptions and outlier prescribers. Lastly, to utilize the EMR as a "force for good" to guide prescribers to preferred behaviors. With regard to balancing measures, their team is aware of the need to monitor systematic underdosing of patients in clinical situations where non-opioid measures are inadequate.

## Lessons Learned

Given the influx of new research related to the extent and causes of variation as well as many ongoing initiatives to identify and reduce unwarranted variation, there is immense, ongoing learning in this area of research and practice. The following insights from research and initiatives over the past decade should inform future efforts in this area.

**Defining Variation: Warranted vs. Unwarranted**. Not all variation is unwarranted or inappropriate (Ballard et al. 2022). Any variation must be investigated to determine whether it is appropriate. Initially, there may be resistance from clinicians when unwarranted variation is identified. As a physician leader, your role is to drive consensus through data, evidence, and guidelines.

**Generating Clinician Buy-In**. Particularly for initiatives that target practice variation, clinicians may be resistant to change. Clinicians often believe that variation is explained by the specific demographics of their patients; they are sicker, older, or poorer and cannot be compared to others. Alternatively, you may receive resistance to "cookbook medicine," or fears that implementing clinical guidelines and protocols will eliminate the value of physicians in diagnosing and treating patients. For these reasons, it is important to involve clinicians from the beginning of the project in identifying opportunities to reduce variation, developing guidelines or protocols, and implementing those recommendations. It is important to choose clinicians who are opinion leaders and who will be good ambassadors for the initiative. Persuasion and engagement should rely heavily on ongoing data and feedback and in comparison to published evidence and guidelines.

**More than adherence to clinical protocols and evidence-based guidelines**. Though reducing variation often does involve the development of and adherence to clinical protocols and evidence-based guidelines, those are not the only strategies. Despite the growing body of evidence-based treatments, there are still many conditions for which the recommended course of action is preference-sensitive. That is, there are important trade-offs between treatment options and a significant impact on quality of life, yet there is no evidence-based recommendation. In these instances, the course of treatment should be determined by the patient's values and preferences, and only once the patient has been given access to all the appropriate information. Thus, in many instances, reducing unwarranted variation involves the intentional engagement of patients in shared decision-making (Veroff et al. 2013).

**Regional intervention vs. targeting decision-makers**. The National Academy of Medicine Report on variation in health care spending recommends targeting decision-making, particularly at the point of care with patients, to reduce variation (Alston et al. 2014). While the Choosing Wisely campaign has promoted individual provider education and decision support, to move the needle on global utilization, physician leaders must drive systemic action. The Safer Dx Checklist can be used by organizations to assess their state of diagnostic processes and seek improvement and quality. To date, many policy interventions that aim to reduce variation have included geographically based payment policies to encourage high-spending regions to behave more like low-spending ones. Additionally, regional multistakeholder initiatives have made significant progress in addressing the local economic, social, political, and environmental drivers of health care utilization. This is one important approach. At an organizational level, key approaches include promoting clinical and financial integration and maintaining robust information systems, including electronic health records. More global initiatives at the organizational level, promoted by physician leaders and system leadership, are essential.

## Action Steps and Strategies to Lead

1. **Engage clinicians with data-driven feedback**. In any initiative to improve care delivery, physicians and clinical stakeholders should be engaged early and often. As a physician leader, you can convene a group of peer physicians to review data and hypothesize drivers of unwarranted variation. Often, the solution may be the development or adoption of an evidence-based clinical guideline. Clinicians must be engaged throughout the development and adoption process to generate buy-in. All decision-making should be based on evidence and reinforced through data (HRET 2011).
2. **Standardize operational processes using quality-improvement interventions**. Variation may be addressed by standardizing processes through quality-improvement initiatives. Interventions and tools such as checklists, Lean, Six Sigma, and Plan–Do–Study–Act (see Chapter 2) can guide projects to improve quality, patient satisfaction, and efficiency (HRET 2011).

3. **Implement evidence-based clinical guidelines and appropriateness criteria**. Greater adherence to evidence-based guidelines would result in fewer unnecessary treatments, lower cost, and an increase in appropriate, high-quality care. Appropriateness criteria for certain procedures are important components of evidence-based guidelines and can be used to improve care on a prospective basis.
4. **Initiating and sustaining a culture change toward safety, improvement, transparency, and excellence**. Efforts to reduce variation in utilization should be integrated into everyday processes. External benchmarks by top-performing states have been established and they provide examples of collaborative leadership. Aside from clinical and administrative stakeholders, patients can also play an integral role in helping reduce unwarranted variation. By communicating with patients and learning why they needed to undergo surgery or utilize emergency department services, needed resources or education in the community can be identified in order to reduce unnecessary medical utilization (HRET 2011).

## References

ABIM Foundation. Choosing Wisely®: An initiative of the ABIM Foundation. 2023 Accessed March 23, 2023. https://www.choosingwisely.org/

Alston, C., Berger, Z., Brownlee, S., Elwyn, G., Fowler, F.J. Jr., Hall, L.K., et al. *Shared Decision-Making Strategies for Best Care: Patient Decision Aids*. 2014 NAM Perspectives. Discussion Paper, National Academy of Medicine, Washington, DC, 2014. Accessed February 17 2023. https://nam.edu/perspectives-2014-shared-decision-making-strategies-for-best-care-patient-decision-aids/

Arora, A., True, A. What Kind of Physician Will You Be? Variation in Health Care and Its Importance for Residency Training. The Dartmouth Institute for Health Policy and Clinical Practice.

October 2012. Accessed February 15, 2023. https://data.dartmouthatlas.org/downloads/reports/Residency_report_103012.pdf

Ballard, D.J., Graca, B., et al. Variation in Medical Practice and Implications for Quality. In *The Healthcare Quality Book: Vision, Strategy, and Tools*, eds. Maulik S. Joshi, Elizabeth R. Ransom, David B. Nash, Scott B. Ransom (5th Ed). Health Administration Press, Chicago, IL, 2022, 65–94.

Barnett, M.L., Olenski, A.R., Jena, A.B. Opioid-Prescribing Patterns of Emergency Physicians and Risk of Long-Term Use. *New England Journal of Medicine*. 2017;376(7):663–673.

Berwick, D.M., Nolan, T.W., Whittington, J. The Triple Aim: Care, Health, and Cost. *Health Affairs*. 2008;27(3):759–769.

Brady, P.W., Marshall, T.L., Walsh, K.E. Promoting Action on Diagnostic Safety: The Safer Dx Checklist. *The Joint Commission Journal on Quality and Patient Safety*. 2022;48(11):559–560.

Brooner, K., Skinner, J. Geographic Variations in Spending and Utilization Across Payer Types. The Dartmouth Institute for Health Policy and Clinical Practice. August 2022. Accessed February 15, 2023. https://www.dartmouthatlas.org/wp-content/uploads/Spending_Util_Variation_3payers_083022.pdf

Combes, J.R., Arespacochaga, E. *Appropriate Use of Medical Resources*. American Hospital Association's 2013 Physician Leadership Forum, Chicago, IL, 2013.

Cooper, Z., Stiegman, O., Ndumele, C.D., Staiger, B., Skinner, J. Geographical Variation in Health Spending Across the US Among Privately Insured Individuals and Enrollees in Medicaid and Medicare. *JAMA Network Open*. 2022;5(7):e2222138.

Ganguli, I., Thakore, N., Rosenthal, M.B., Korenstein, D. Longitudinal Content Analysis of the Characteristics and Expected Impact of Low-Value Services Identified in US Choosing Wisely Recommendations. *JAMA Internal Medicine*. 2022;182(2):127–133.

Gauld, R, Horwitt, J., Williams, S., Cohen, A.B. What Strategies Do US Hospitals Employ to Reduce Unwarranted Clinical Practice Variations? *American Journal of Medical Quality*. 2011;26(2): 120–126.

Gnadinger, T. New Health Policy Brief: Geographic Variation in Medicare Spending. *Health Affairs Blog*. 2014. Accessed March 23, 2023. http://healthaffairs.org/blog/2014/03/06/new-health-policy-brief-geographic-variation-in-medicare-spending/

Guy, G.P., Zhang, K., Bohm, M.K., et al. Vital Signs: Changes in Opioid Prescribing in the United States, 2006-2015. *Morbidity and Mortality Weekly Report*. 2017;66(26):697–704.

Health Research & Educational Trust American Hospital Association. *Health Care Leader Action Guide: Understanding and Managing Variation*. Health Research & Educational Trust, Chicago, IL. February 2011. www.hret.org/variation

Joshi, M.S., Hatzigeorgiou, M. Overview of Healthcare Quality. In *The Healthcare Quality Book: Vision, Strategy, and Tools*, ed. Maulik S. Joshi, Elizabeth R. Ransom, David B. Nash, Scott B. Ransom (5th Ed). Health Administration Press, Chicago, IL, 2022, 5–31.

Koch, C., Roberts, K., Petruccelli, C., Morgan, D.J. The Frequency of Unnecessary Testing in Hospitalized Patients. *American Journal of Medicine*. 2018;131(5):500–503.

Newhouse, J.P., Garber, A.M., Graham, R.P., McCoy, M.A., Mancher, M., Kibria, A. Eds. *Variation in Health Care Spending: Target Decision Making, Not Geography*. National Academies Press, Washington, DC, 2013.

Newhouse, J.P., Garber, A.M. Geographic Variation in Health Care Spending in the United States: Insights from an Institute of Medicine Report. *JAMA*. 2013;310(12):1227–1228.

Shrank, W.H., Rogstad, T.L., Parekh, N. Waste in the US Health Care System: Estimated Costs and Potential for Savings. *JAMA*. 2019; 322(15):1501–1509.

Singh, H., Marinez, A., Mushtaq, U., et al. The Safer Dx Checklist 10 High-Priority Practices for Diagnostic Excellence. Baylor College of Medicine. 2022. Accessed February 17, 2023. https://betsylehmancenterma.gov/assets/uploads/Safer-Dx-Checklist.pdf

Song, Z., Kannan, S., Gambrel, R.J., et al. Physician Practice Pattern Variations in Common Clinical Scenarios within 5 US Metropolitan Areas. *JAMA Health Forum*. 2022;3(1):e214698.

Surgical Care and Outcomes Assessment Program (SCOAP). Surgical Checklist Initiative. 2014. http://www.scoap.org/checklists

Veroff, D., Marr, A., Wennberg, D.E. Enhanced Support for Shared Decision-Making Reduced Costs of Care for Patients With Preference-Sensitive Conditions. *Health Affairs*. 2013;32(2): 285–293.

Wennberg, John and Alan Gittelsohn, Small Area Variations in Health Care Delivery, *Science*. 1973;182(4117):1102–1108.

# Chapter 13

# Improving Care Coordination and Reducing Readmissions

## The Evidence

In 2009, a study by Joynt and Jha published in the *New England Journal of Medicine* concluded that readmissions among Medicare beneficiaries were not only costly to the U.S. health care system but also very common. Almost one-fifth (19.6%) of Medicare beneficiaries during the study period were rehospitalized within 30 days of discharge. Within 90 days of hospital discharge, the readmission rate increased to 34%. Most importantly, the study estimated that merely 10% of readmissions were planned, suggesting significant opportunity to reduce the number of unplanned readmissions (HRET 2014). In addition to concerns about quality, readmissions are very costly for the health care system and for patients. In 2018 alone, there were 3.8 million adult hospital readmissions within 30 days, with each costing an average of $15,200 (AHRQ 2021).

DOI: 10.4324/9781003402831-13

It has been estimated that up to 27% of these readmissions could otherwise be preventable and that the cost of Medicare alone amounts to over $17 billion (Auerbach et al. 2016 and CMS 2016). In the years that have followed, significant emphasis from payers, patients, and systems has been placed on improving processes for care coordination, hospital discharge, and ultimately reduction in readmission.

Prior to 2012, hospitals were reimbursed in full for readmissions under the fee-for-service system. Thus, hospitals were not incentivized to reduce readmissions, but rather to increase the number of patients admitted in order to maintain revenue and operations. As discussed in Chapter 5, in 2012, the Centers for Medicare and Medicaid Services implemented the Medicare Hospital Readmissions Reduction Program to correct this misalignment of incentives. This program has been aimed to correct the perverse incentives of the fee-for-service system to reward high-quality care and reduce readmissions, though many challenges remain. Encouragingly, research and pilot programs have demonstrated effectiveness of interventions such as patient education, predischarge assessment, care coordination strategies, and strategies to target social determinants of health in reducing unplanned readmissions.

Recent data suggests that the resources, attention, and investment in reducing readmissions are beginning to yield results, with a 2018 MedPac report suggesting a 17% reduction in risk-adjusted readmissions. The report identified trends including the shift of less-complex cases to outpatient settings and reduction in observation cases, with overall improvement in mortality (MedPac 2018). Hospital quality does matter, as research shows that independent of patient factors, the highest-performing hospitals do have significantly better readmission rates when compared to the lowest performing (Krumholz et al. 2017). Increasingly, however, the onus for reduction of readmission is moving from the acute care setting of free-standing hospitals into communities and the hands of comprehensive care coordination programs. Likewise, studies have shown that disparities in care do have an impact on health including readmission and access to care coordination (Silvestri et al. 2022). Among this, minority and vulnerable populations are more likely than their white counterparts to be readmitted within 30 days for a host of chronic conditions. (CMS 2016). Chapter 11 details the efforts to address disparities in care, and physician leaders need to recognize the impact of these on readmissions and incorporate these in planning at all levels.

Physician leaders in any system must be aware of the clinical and financial implications of robust care coordination. In terms of evaluating readmissions, leaders should first consider how these impact their specific organization and patient population. Recognizing that some readmissions are necessary and appropriate, efforts should be focused on those that can be improved or eliminated.

The following are examples of some specific programs:

## Boston Medical Center Reengineered Discharge

Project Reengineering Discharge (Project RED) is an intervention developed by researchers at the Boston University Medical Center that is based on 12 discrete, mutually reinforcing components (Figure 13.1) that aim to improve communication and streamline the multiple components that contribute to a successful discharge. The initial implementation of Project RED resulted in a 30% reduction in readmissions and emergency room visits. As a result, the Agency for Healthcare Research and Quality funded the creation of a toolkit that enabled others to adopt and replicate the success of the program. This toolkit is available free of charge online at www.bu.edu/fammed/projectred/toolkit.html.

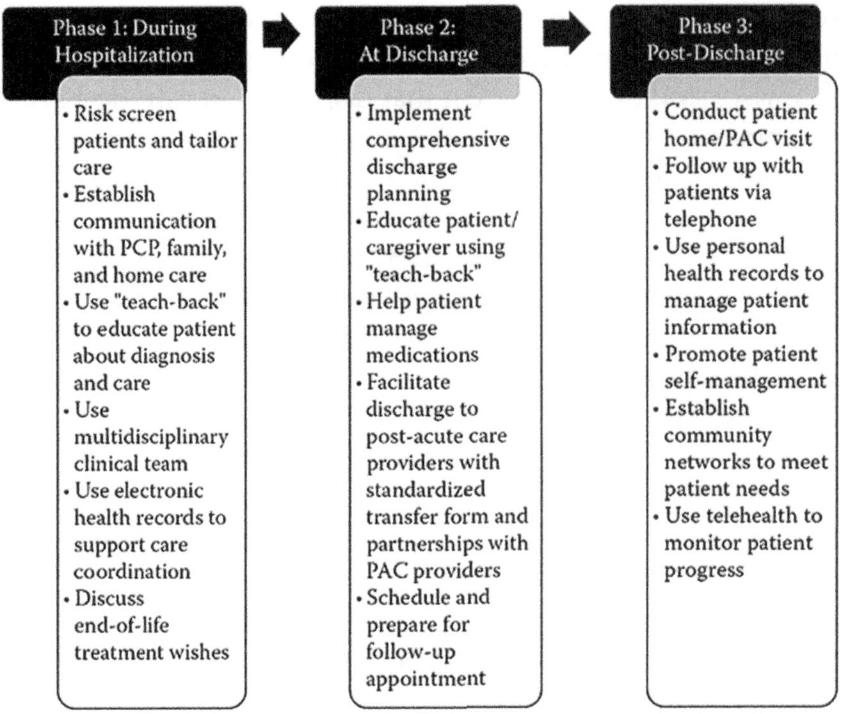


**Figure 13.1 Strategies for improving care coordination and reducing readmissions. (Osei-Anto, A., Joshi, M., Audet, A.M., Berman, A., Jencks, S. *Health Care Leader Action Guide to Reduce Avoidable Readmissions.* Health Research & Educational Trust, Chicago, IL, January 2010.)**

The key elements of the Project RED approach include patient education, comprehensive discharge planning, an after-hospital care plan, and a post-discharge phone call for medication reconciliation.

## Care Transitions Program

The Care Transitions Program was developed to address the need for an interdisciplinary, patient-centered transition that improves continuity of care across multiple settings and providers. This four-week program pairs older patients that have complex care needs with a Transitions Coach (Coleman 2007). The Transitions Coach, typically a discharge nurse, visits the patient prior to discharge and at home or a skilled nursing facility two to three days post-discharge. In addition, they have three follow-up telephone calls with the patient over the first 28 days post-discharge

The role of the transitions coach is to empower the patient and caregiver to actively build self-management and care skills for the transition process from hospital to home. This includes encouraging the patient to maintain a discharge preparation checklist, a personal health record that consists of interdisciplinary communication elements during the care transition, and set up timely follow-up appointments. Furthermore, they help the patient develop problem-solving and communication skills for addressing common challenges in care transitions (Coleman 2007). A study that evaluated the Care Transitions Program demonstrated that it reduced 30-day readmissions from 11.9% to 8.3% and 90-day readmissions from 22.5% to 16.7%, with an average cost reduction of $500 per patient caseload (Coleman et al. 2006).

Note that the role of the transitions coach is not to provide skilled care or to directly fix the patient's problems, but rather to provide guidance and tools. This intervention is fundamentally a self-management model based on the premise of adult learning and skills transfer and works to sustainably address a patient's current and long-term needs (Coleman 2007).

## Transitional Care Model

Elderly adults who have chronic comorbidities and receive complex therapies are at particularly high risk of experiencing mismanagement of care (Transitional Care Model 2013). Major factors contributing to this risk include uncoordinated care, fragmented communication between providers, inadequate patient and caregiver education, and insufficient access to services. The Transitional Care Model (TCM) was developed to address the transition from a hospital to a post-acute care setting or home.

The TCM equips patients and family caregivers with strategies to more effectively manage patients multiple chronic illnesses. Essential elements of the program include the following:

- A transitional care nurse who uses advanced knowledge and skills to coordinate the care of high-risk patients within and across all health care settings.
- Holistic and comprehensive assessment of each elderly patient's prioritized needs, preferences, and goals.
- Regular home visits by the transitional care nurse (TCN) with ongoing telephone support available.
- Multidisciplinary approach involving the patient, family caregivers, and health care providers as members of the same team.

Studies have proven TCM to be effective in reducing hospital readmissions, improving post-discharge health outcomes, and enhancing patient and family caregiver satisfaction (TCM 2013).

## Strategies for Success

Figure 13.1 outlines interventions to reduce readmissions predischarge, at discharge, and post-discharge. These strategies vary in complexity and the amount of resources required. An organization's existing infrastructure and capacity may or may not support the implementation of these interventions; some may require additional resources, installation of new technologies, formation of new partnerships, or culture change.

In addition to adopting these specific strategies, the role of clinical leaders is to develop a comprehensive, customized approach to care coordination and readmissions reduction at their facility and within their community. The overarching strategies in Figure 13.1 can guide the development of such an approach.

## *Identify Patients at High Risk for Readmission*

Screening patients to identify those at higher risk of readmissions can help tailor interventions to them in a timely manner. No risk stratification tool is perfectly accurate, and patients with highly advanced disease or at-risk socioeconomic situations are at increased risk for unpreventable readmissions regardless. However, risk stratification tools, such as the LACE index and HOSPITAL have shown to be successful at predicting risk of readmission within 30 days (Robinson and Hudali 2017). Upon admission, these tools assess information including the patient's comorbidities, length of stay, number of previous admissions, and emergency department visits during the previous six months. A patient's score assigns them to a risk level, which allows tailored interventions for them promptly after admission. Increasingly, artificial intelligence is being utilized to predict patient risk across a host of care delivery, including risks for acute decompensation while in the hospital and risks for readmission following discharge.

## *Build Self-Management Skills*

Many patients return to the hospital, often repeatedly, because they lack the skills and understanding needed to adequately manage their condition. Initiatives to improve health literacy and patient activation levels, educate patients on their medications, provide clearly written instructions, and educate patients on symptoms and red flags for complications can all improve self-management skills. However, studies have shown that patients immediately forget 40% to 80% of the medical information they receive (Dewalt et al. 2010). To ensure that the health care team communicated information clearly to the patient and family about self-management skills, the teach-back method is an effective tool that should always be used prior to discharge. The method involves asking a patient or a family member to explain in his or her own words what they need to know or do to care for the patient. In order to competently use teach-back, the care team member should use plain language, a caring tone of voice and attitude, comfortable body language and eye contact, and non-shaming, open-ended questions that avoid yielding simple "yes" or "no" answers. To recheck understanding, the team member can ask them to reexplain the information or clarify information if it was initially misunderstood. Evidence has shown that teach-back improves patient-provider communication and patient outcomes (Dewalt et al. 2010). Furthermore, in a study on patients with heart failure, patients who underwent the teach-back method correctly answered 75% of self-care teach-back questions 84.4% of the time while hospitalized. During follow-up calls, seven days following discharge, 75% of teach-back questions were answered correctly 77.1% of the time (White et al. 2013).

## *Discharge Planning*

Care coordination is a significant challenge and one of the primary drivers of readmissions. In order to adequately prepare a patient for a transition to home, a skilled nursing facility, or other post-acute care setting, the provider must develop a discharge plan, ideally at the start of a patient's hospitalization. Discharge planning is a complex process that involves determining the appropriate post-discharge site of care, a patient's functional self-care abilities, medication reconciliation, and should produce a discharge summary. Medication reconciliation is a process that verifies a patient's list of medications prior to hospital discharge, by identifying medications that have been added, discontinued, or changed. In order to perform accurate medication reconciliation, a care team member should have an accurate: (1) pre-admission medication list, (2) list of medications that the patient is taking at the time of discharge, and (3) knowledge of medication changes during hospitalizations and the reasons for the changes. It is critical to perform an accurate medication reconciliation for a successful discharge transition. In a 2012 systematic review, medication reconciliation was associated in most studies with a decrease in potential and actual adverse drug events. Furthermore, many initiatives focus on medication reconciliation in order to prevent avoidable readmissions. The discharge summary is the primary communication tool between hospital and post-acute care providers and should communicate the hospitalization outcome, the patient's disposition, and the necessary provisions for follow-up care (e.g., appointments and care need specifications).

## *Follow-Up and Community Resources*

Many hospital readmissions are unavoidable; however, many readmissions are due to factors that occur either during or after the transition from the hospital to post-acute care. These factors include premature discharge or failed handoffs, insufficient follow-up, adverse drug events, and patient falls. To keep patients from returning, it is essential for hospitals to not only identify and educate patients about resources but also to truly connect patients with the community-based resources they can access for support. Many patients are readmitted because of social or economic barriers including lack of transportation, inadequate nutrition, lack of social support, or inability to access a pharmacy to fill prescriptions. While hospitals have a role in preemptively identifying these barriers, they can work with a variety of partners within the community, connecting patients with those organizations and social services agencies that can help. Chapter 14 focuses on the value of community partnerships and how organizations can work with others within the community to improve overall health. Multifaceted interventions that are comprised of follow-up telemonitoring, home visits, scheduling convenient follow-up appointments for the patient, and follow-up medication reconciliation with a clinical pharmacist over telemedicine are effective strategies for assessing and addressing patient status, needs, and barriers to adequately receiving and self-administering care following hospital discharge.

## Case Study: Increasing Access and Improving Care Coordination

The following case studies illustrate how two systems approached sizable gaps in patient access and needs for coordinating care to improve outcomes and reduce readmissions.

Jonathan Jimenez, MD, MPH is executive director of NYC Care, which launched in 2019 as a health care access program at NYC Health + Hospitals, the largest public health care system in the nation. Undocumented and some low-income Americans are excluded from health insurance and contribute disproportionately to emergency presentations and hospital readmissions, including hundreds of thousands of New York City residents. Barriers to receiving medical care in the ambulatory, versus inpatient, setting were identified as lack of primary care homes, integrated information technology systems, care coordination, customer service, access to care, and public awareness. NYC Care is a health care access program designed to close these gaps.

First, the program targeted the population excluded from health insurance through eligibility criteria. New York City residents ineligible for health insurance or who cannot afford insurance are eligible for NYC Care. Upon enrollment, they are offered a primary care home at NYC Health Hospitals. An integrated, system-wide electronic medical record allowed searching for appointments system-wide. The program committed to offering patients new to NYC Health + Hospitals a primary care appointment within two weeks. Enrolled members were mailed a member manual and membership card with their name, the name of their primary care provider, and the fee scale they can expect to pay on the back. A 24-hour customer service line was established to answer questions about the program and initiate enrollment.

The launch of integrated EMR system-wide also allowed NYC Care members to benefit from electronic referrals for specialty care and procedures, including United States Preventive Services Task Force (USPSTF) recommended screenings. For patients who already had a primary care home outside of NYC Health + Hospitals, they could enroll in NYC Care to access those specialty services that are typically out of reach for the uninsured. With a new EMR and membership card, NYC Care members could take advantage of all services provided at NYC Health + Hospitals facilities, which included 11 hospitals and 56 clinics. A small administrative team was hired to maintain program operations, communicate program services and benefits with the public, and pursue key performance indicators.

All services, from the call center to the medical care, are available in multiple languages via diverse staff and telephonic interpretation. Member materials are available in more than 13 languages. To ensure those typically excluded from health care due to lack of insurance would enroll, NYC Care contracted with community-based organizations across the city to answer questions about the program, perform strategic outreach, and facilitate enrollment. Additionally, a multilingual marketing campaign leveraged community and ethnic media, social media, and other local outlets to spread the word about access to primary and preventive care for the uninsured. The program was awarded the Bernard J. Tyson National Award for Excellence in Pursuit of Healthcare Equity by the Joint Commission.

The program attracted tens of thousands of members in its first year and, by the summer of 2021, had reached over 80,000 active members. By the fall of 2021, over 100,000 active members were enrolled in NYC Care. Historical electronic medical record data showed that 50% of members had not seen a primary care physician in the prior three years. Members were also taking advantage of services. In 2021, 75% of members saw their primary care provider at least once, and 50% saw them twice or more. In 2022, NYC Care members had completed 187,524 primary care visits and 454,194 specialty visits. More than 90,000 members had a USPSTF recommended cancer screening.

NYC Care strove to deliver equity in health care access and health outcomes. Investments in primary care access led to halving of the time to next available appointment from 2015 to 2022. In addition, preliminary analyses showed that hypertension and diabetes control was comparable between NYC Care members and the general NYC H+H population. Moreover, subgroup analyses demonstrated that after six months in NYC Care, 53% of members with diabetes and 40% of members with hypertension experienced an improvement in their hemoglobin a1c and blood pressure measurement, respectively. Likewise, we expect that improved chronic disease control will lead to reduced admissions and readmissions among this population.

For physician leaders, NYC Care shows value of reorganizing to simplify access to care for the uninsured, investing in primary care access, and partnering with the community, whether it is local media or community-based organizations. Many NYC Care members were not aware of the affordable high-quality care available to them, and community-based organizations had to be there for them to believe in the benefits of the program. What's more, all patients want a doctor to call their own and are thrilled to have a primary care home. By investing in timely access to primary care and connecting patients directly to primary care homes at first touch points, we can make their desire a reality.

## Case Study: Improving Access and Preventive Care

Michael Hanak, MD, is associate chief medical officer for Population Health at Rush University Medical Center in Chicago. Rush University System for Health is a large academic medical center located in Chicago that employs a multispecialty medical group comprised of clinicians delivering care on its main campus as well as at a variety of outpatient locations around the city. In 2018, the medical group recognized that only 8% of its eligible Medicare beneficiaries had completed an Annual Wellness Visit (AWV). This compares to approximately 59% of national eligible beneficiaries that receive the service. This variation at Rush suggested sizable clinical and operational barriers to improving performance of this common measure in value-based plans. Health care organizations and payers alike recognize the opportunity, and studies show that patients are more likely to complete recommended screenings, and their health care spending is significantly reduced within two years of completing an AWV. These visits typically incorporate screening, counseling, and selected examination or preventive health services, which support an upstream shift in intervention when treatment is less expensive and often more effective. Consequently, directing patients to engage in preventive care and AWV encounters have become a foundational element of most value-based plans.

Dr. Hanak and the team at Rush began by assessing the situation and identifying barriers to fulfillment of AWV. Among these were the prolonged physician time required to document and gather data for each encounter, alternative patient agenda items raised during scheduled AWV, lack of perceived value in the visit by patients, and transportation and scheduling. There was a clear need to address the narrative around the utility of the visits, as well as streamline the process for patients and clinicians alike. While AWVs were prioritized by payers, clinicians viewed the encounters as detrimental to visit efficiency and broader access to other visit types. Furthermore, local practices lacked adequate staffing and time to conduct necessary outreach, assist with required documentation, and facilitate additional requests brought by patients who did not understand the visit to be purely preventive in nature.

Throughout the project, the team at Rush prioritized streamlining of workflows in which information was captured and documented, seeking to offload as much as possible from the clinician. The top of license practice was viewed as foundational to the promotion of team-based care in this improvement initiative. Gathering of screening data and standardized risk assessments were removed from the point-of-care to allow more time for the clinician to respond to the information and address patient concerns. The grid containing this information in the electronic health record was modified to ease the burden of data entry, while flowing easily into pre-templated notes. Rush constructed a pre-visit team with patient navigators conducting registry-based outreach and scheduling, while nurses completed the majority of the required elements of the AWV ahead of time. In the day(s) that follow collection of this information, the patient

attends their visit with the clinician (in-person or virtually) where a few final elements are completed. Patients are afforded the advantage of reviewing medication and responding to questions in the comfort of their own home, with the opportunity to consult family or caregivers in the process. Social determinants of health screenings take place and resources are able to be identified prior to their clinical interaction.

At Rush, clinicians were thrilled to have many tedious aspects of the visit already covered so attention could be focused on intervention and follow-up. The institutional standard of 40 minutes for this visit allowed for ample time to review additional health concerns and assign standard evaluation and management (E&M codes) charges in addition to the AWV revenue, creating a financial opportunity in addition to payer-sponsored incentives and downstream sustainability through patient attribution resulting from AWV completion.

The outcome of the project was an increase in the performance rate of completed beneficiaries with an AWV from 8% in 2018 to 42% in 2022. More than two-thirds of these visits are now dual-coded as a combined AWV and E&M visit, enhancing revenues by nearly 40% on these visit types (and more than twice this for clinicians capable of shortening their AWV to 20 minutes). Patients were pleased not to have to complete the screening questions on their own (which is allowed by Medicare) and interact with a licensed health care professional in triaging other needs during their call. Clinicians also benefited from having specific screening orders prepopulated in the electronic health record, thus saving time during the visit. Ongoing challenges with labor shortages resulted in intermittent declines in outreach volume and represented a primary driver of underperformance in some areas. Access at busy primary care sites and restrictions on the number of extended visit slots allocated to certain practices were also barriers to scaling and improving performance.

## Lessons Learned

1. **Engage multiple stakeholders across the continuum of care**. To successfully reduce readmissions, any initiative must include entities across the continuum of care. This may include representatives from the hospital, primary care, hospice, home health, and long-term care settings. It may also include social services, behavioral health, and community-based organizations that target the social determinants of health.
2. **Engage patients, families, and caregivers**. Patients, their families, and their caregivers are crucial partners in reducing readmissions. The patient and his or her designated family member or caregiver should be included in discussions throughout the care episode. Clinicians must be especially attuned to the needs, concerns, and potential barriers voiced by the patient or his or her family members. Common barriers include lack of transportation to a follow-up appointment, incomplete inventory or medication reconciliation, a lack of access to nutritious foods, or other nonmedical causes. Clinicians should listen to the concerns of the patient to recognize and address those avoidable barriers early in the process.
3. **Prioritize interventions**. As with any improvement project, organizations should start small and incrementally add interventions once others have become integrated into the workflow. This will help prevent improvement fatigue. Figure 13.1 provides key interventions to implement during hospitalization, at discharge, and post-discharge. Hospitals can begin with the

during-hospitalization and at-discharge processes and expand to the post-discharge interventions once they have identified partners in the community as willing participants.

## Action Steps and Strategies to Lead

1. **Start with the data**. Any improvement project, particularly one focused on readmissions, should begin with a thorough examination of the organization's data to identify root causes, patterns, and drivers of readmissions. Physician leaders should stratify and examine data:
   - *For different conditions*: Examine correlation with patient's severity, such as diagnosis and significant comorbidities.
   - *By practitioners*: Assess readmission rates by physician to determine appropriateness or if any practitioner type is associated with unexpected readmissions.
   - *By readmission source*: Examine rates by provider source (e.g., skilled nursing facility and rehabilitation center) to determine the places from which patients are most frequently being readmitted.
   - *At different time frames*: Readmission rates can be examined at time points such as 7, 30, 60, and 90 days. Earlier time points may reveal gaps in effective transitions to the ambulatory setting, whereas later time points could demonstrate flaws with follow-up care and patients' understanding of discharge instructions.

   Patterns in the data will reveal which processes to target. Eventually, sophisticated risk stratification and prediction tools can also help facilities identify patients at high risk of readmission before they are discharged, so that additional measures may be taken as appropriate. Using data and targeted analysis can ensure that interventions are both cost-efficient and effective.

2. **Assess and prioritize your improvement opportunities**. The physician leader's role is to prioritize interventions and devote resources accordingly based on what the data reveals. Leaders should prioritize interventions that leverage immediate opportunities for improvement within the hospital. For example, leaders could focus on specific patient populations, stages in the care-delivery process, leveraging other quality-improvement efforts in other areas, or building on the organization's established strengths.
3. **Engage key stakeholders**. Reducing readmissions and improving care coordination requires working with partners inside and outside the hospital. Physician leaders must engage partners across the care continuum, not only in the implementation process but in the development process as well. Stakeholders should be included in the planning from the beginning of the project to create buy-in and to develop the best strategies. Stakeholders may include patients, physicians, pharmacists, social services, nutritionists, physical therapists, community providers, community-based organizations, and local government. Community partners become increasingly important as interventions move beyond the hospital walls. Community organizations are often better equipped than hospitals to address nonmedical factors that put patients at risk of readmission, such as behavioral, health literacy, and cultural issues.
4. **Monitor your organization's progress**. As with any quality-improvement initiative, monitoring efforts is the key to sustaining progress in reducing readmissions. Monitoring could shed light on which individual strategies are efficacious and help guide leaders in implementing additional strategies.

## References

Auerbach, A.D., Kripalani, S., Vasilevskis, E.E., et al. Preventability and Causes of Readmissions in a National Cohort of General Medicine Patients. *JAMA Internal Medicine.* 2016;176(4): 484–493.

Benbassat, J., Taragin, M. Hospital Readmissions as a Measure of Quality of Health Care: Advantages and Limitations. *Archives of Internal Medicine.* 2000;160(8): 1074–1081.

Berenson, R.A., Paulus, R., Kalman, N.S. Medicare's Readmissions-Reduction Program—A Positive Alternative. *New England Journal of Medicine.* 2012;366(15):1364–1366.

Berkowitz, R.E., Fang, Z., Helfand, B., Jones, R.N., Schreiber, R., Paasche-Orlow, M.K. Project ReEngineered Discharge (RED) Lowers Hospital Readmissions of Patients Discharged from a Skilled Nursing Facility. *Journal of the American Medical Directors Association.* 2013;14(10):736–740.

Centers for Medicare & Medicaid Services. Guide to Reducing Disparities in Readmissions. 2016. Accessed February 19, 2023. https://www.cms.gov/About-CMS/Agency-Information/OMH/Downloads/OMH_Readmissions_Guide.pdfCenters for Medicare & Medicaid Services. Readmissions Reduction Program. http://cms.gov/Medicare/Medicare-Fee-for-Service-Payment/AcuteInpatientPPS/Readmissions-Reduction-Program.html/

Coleman, E.A. The Care Transitions Program. 2007. Accessed March 23, 2023. http://caretransitions.org/

Coleman, E.A., Parry, C., Chalmers, S., Min, S. The Care Transitions Intervention: Results of a Randomized Controlled Trial. *Archives of Internal Medicine.* 2006;166(17):1822–1828.

Dewalt, D.A., Callaghan, L.F., Hawk, V.H., Broucksou, K.A., Hink, A., Rudd, R., Brach, C. *Health Literacy Universal Precautions Toolkit.* North Carolina Network Consortium, Chapel Hill, NC, 2010.

Evercare by United Healthcare. 2010. Physician and Health Care Professional Administrative Manual: Evercare At Home. http://caretransitions.org/

Health Research & Educational Trust. 2014. Readmissions Change Package: Improving Care Transitions and Reducing Readmissions. 2014.

Jencks, S.F., Williams, M.V., Coleman, E.A. Rehospitalizations Among Patients in the Medicare Fee-for-Service Program. *New England Journal of Medicine.* 2009;360(14):1418–1428.

Joynt, Karen E., Jha, Ashish K. A path forward on Medicare readmissions. *New England Journal of Medicine.* 2013;368(13):1175–1177.

Krumholz, H.M., Wang, K., Lin, Z., Dharmarajan, K., Horwitz, L., Ross, J.S., et al. Hospital-Readmission Risk Isolating Hospital Effects from Patient Effects. *New England Journal of Medicine.* 2017;377:1055–1064.

Medicare Payment Advisory Commission (MedPac). Report to the Congress: Medicare and the Health Care Delivery System. January 2018.

Osei-Anto, A., Joshi, M., Audet, A.M., Berman, A., Jencks, S. *Health Care Leader Action Guide to Reduce Avoidable Readmissions.* Health Research & Educational Trust, Chicago, IL, 2010.

Project Red (Re-Engineered Design). A Research Group at Boston University Medical Center. n.d. Accessed March 23, 2023. http://www.bu.edu/fammed/projectred/

Re-Engineered Discharge (RED). *Toolkit.* Agency for Healthcare Research and Quality, Rockville, MD, February 2020. Accessed February 19, 2023. https://www.ahrq.gov/patient-safety/settings/hospital/red/toolkit/index.html

Robinson, R., Hudali, T. The HOSPITAL score and LACE Index as Predictors of 30 Day Readmission in a Retrospective Study at a University-Affiliated Community Hospital. *PeerJ.* 2017;29(5):e3137.

Silvestri, D., Goutos, D., Lloren, A., et al. Factors Associated with Disparities in Hospital Readmission Rates Among US Adults Dually Eligible for Medicare and Medicaid. *JAMA Health Forum.* 2022;3(1):e214611.

Statistical Brief #278. *Healthcare Cost and Utilization Project (HCUP).* Agency for Healthcare Research and Quality, Rockville, MD, July 2021. Accessed February 19, 2023. www.hcup-us.ahrq.gov/reports/statbriefs/sb278-Conditions-Frequent-Readmissions-By-Payer-2018.jsp

Transitional Care Model. Overview of TCM. 2013. http://www.transitionalcare.info/about-tcm

UnitedHealthcare Medicare Solutions. Our Story—Our Difference. 2014. https://www.uhcmedicaresolutions.com/health-plans/special-needs/nursing-homeplacement.html

UnityPoint Health, Picker Institute, Des Moines University, and Health Literacy Iowa. Always Use Teach-back! 10 Elements of Competence for Using Teach-back Effectively. 2013 http://www.ihi.org/resources/Pages/Tools/AlwaysUseTeachBack!.aspx

White, M., Garbez, R., Carroll, M., Brinker, M., Esquivel, J. Is "Teach-Back" Associated with Knowledge Retention and Hospital Readmission in Hospitalized Heart Failure Patients? *Journal of Cardiovascular Nursing*. 2013;28(2):137–146.

Weiss, AJ., Jiang, J. Overview of Clinical Conditions With Frequent and Costly Hospital Readmissions by Payer, 2018. HCUP Statistical Brief #278. July 2021. Agency for Healthcare Research and Quality, Rockville, MD. Accessed June 16th, 2023. www.hcup-us.ahrq.gov/reports/statbriefs/sb278Conditions-Frequent-Readmissions-By-Payer-2018.pdf

# Chapter 14

# Population and Community Health

## The Evidence

Population health, in the most practical and fundamental sense, can be traced back centuries. Grouping patients together by shared symptoms of illness allowed early medical educators the opportunity to study and characterize disease. Plague outbreaks demonstrated inherent connections between health, geography, and transmission patterns. Meanwhile, advancement of public health and patient education have intertwined with opportunities to educate larger groups of patients. Only in recent decades, however, has population health been framed by a clearer definition and purpose within the modern delivery of health care.

With references dating back to the late 1800s and increased relevancy among epidemiologists in the 1970s, population health truly came to the forefront of innovative health care thinking through the work of David Kindig and Greg Stoddart in the early twenty-first century (Appold 2020). Since then, the practice of population health has been widely advanced on a

 DOI: 10.4324/9781003402831-14

multidisciplinary scale across clinical health care settings, through philanthropic initiatives, for epidemiological research, and in efforts surrounding policy among other endeavors. The widespread application of population health in practice has a high degree of overlap between disciplines that will almost certainly expand as issues surrounding population and community health continue to take center stage.

In stark contrast to traditional medical models that rely on the interaction between an individual patient and individual provider and, thus, ultimately the volume of services provided; population health aims to identify and improve health outcomes for a group or groups of patients. In the 2010s, following the passage of the Affordable Care Act and the implementation of Accountable Care Organizations, population health began to be used to describe the panel management of a certain grouping of attributed patients. Clusters of patients can thus be grouped or subdivided within larger overarching populations. In some cases, this is as simple as identifying a cohort for all those patients that have a certain disease state, such as asthma or diabetes. Additional variables, including comorbid disease states, demographics, and geography can be used to narrow the population and enhance complexity. Examples of such groupings could be the identification of a target population that encompasses all patients aged 11–18 that live within a given zip code and have uncontrolled asthma. Population health represents this more sophisticated identification and analysis of patient groupings, with the goals of optimizing health outcomes, improving care, expanding access, and lowering cost.

Community health, which does share many goals with population health, should not be confused as being one and the same. While the two disciplines of community and population health do share similarities and will overlap in some instances, they are different nonetheless. Community health, as its wording suggests, takes place outside the walls of traditional institutions of health care delivery, with its roots most often within non-clinical settings. Community health is comprised of the work done through community partnerships and individuals to emphasize the importance of health and well-being within groups defined by geographical location or cultural traits. Meanwhile, population health primarily focuses on the health outcomes and indicators within these groups and is oftentimes influenced by the social determinants of health (SDOH) (Maraccini et al. 2017). Community health interventions are deployed at the broader community-wide level, while population health-based interventions target specific patient populations within a given community.

So why do population and community health matter? Put simply, they bear the potential for larger impact and a more targeted approach. Population health can shed light on the health status of socioeconomically disadvantaged groups who disproportionately suffer from worse health outcomes. Taking a population health approach allows the clustering of large groups and tailoring of initiatives to meet their distinct needs. For example, traditional models approach the care of hypertensive patients by waiting until each arrives one-by-one to a primary care physician, cardiologist, or emergency room. Each patient then receives responsive treatment for their immediate need, which may be medication or health education. A population health approach may instead identify the total grouping of all hypertensive patients within a panel or targeted geographic area, proactively seeking to fill gaps in care for preventive services, disease management, and treatment. These efforts may additionally include screening to clarify the cohort and prevent disease progression. Lastly, population health encourages appreciation for environmental factors that may contribute to high rates of elevated blood pressure within a specified community. Following, targeted initiatives could emphasize prevention and healthy lifestyle interventions that are pertinent to the health of the collective as opposed to the individual. Barriers to address range from issues with transportation needs to financial assistance. Breaking down such barriers to healthy living and desirable health outcomes are at the core of what population health aims to address.

## Population-Based Payment Models

Models of reimbursement are increasingly recognizing measures that characterize the health of populations within value frameworks. As has been discussed, the transition from fee-for service, which has brought inherent waste and fails to recognize quality, has begun with shifts to value (Allen 2018). Fully recognizing success in caring for populations holds the possibility to transition to financial rewards that incentivize providers based on long-term health outcomes of patients and groupings of patients. Likewise, it portends to reward providers that improve health across complex or disadvantaged groups, who otherwise are often neglected in volume-based systems of payment.

Under population-based payment models, health care providers are held accountable to ensure optimal health outcomes for the patients they treat. Population-based payment in practice is oftentimes demonstrated through the treatment of specific states of disease. One prime example of a disease that can be treated through the lens of population-based payment is type 2 diabetes. From the perspective of the physician and population-based payment, the measure of success for this patient population would be to facilitate hemoglobin A1C levels below 9%.

## Per Member Per Month

One method of reimbursement that seeks to provide proactive, up-front payment and incentivize care for full populations is per member per month arrangements. Essentially a form of capitated payment, the per member per month model emphasizes services provided to all patients, as opposed to just those in which a definable and documented service is rendered. This allows consideration for more individualized or novel mechanisms to address illness for that group. For instance, this may include hiring specific members, or seeking population-based efficient interventions. An example of such an arrangement could be the payment of $5 for each assigned patient within a panel for each month of care. This is paid up front and remuneration does not require demonstrating specific action, rather an expectation that improved health and quality will result. At $5 per month for a panel of 2,000 patients, the resulting $10,000 per month would translate to $120,000 per year. Such funds could be dedicated to additional staffing, such as nursing or health coaches, dedicated resources, or patient education. Broadening the scope of high-quality health care services within a given population lies within the essence of what population and community health truly seek to inspire. Payers are starting to identify high-risk and high-cost patient populations, such as those managed on dialysis or patients that have suffered a stroke and to pay to better manage the care of these groups. Models of payment that stress this approach will eventually be more commonplace and will continue to evolve over time in ways that benefit larger, more diverse clusters of patients.

## *Policy Implementation and Implications*

As population and community health have increased in relevance, so too has the federal government's interest in advancing population health-based policy within the United States. These efforts have increased and will assuredly persist as research continues to indicate the effectiveness of population health-based approaches to health care. Health care

currently sits at a crucial juncture in the collective approach to meeting populations where they are, as opposed to waiting until they are sick enough to need emergent or advanced care. Specifically, if upstream interventions that can be deployed within a community are prioritized and incentivized, as opposed to downstream acute care interventions, shifts in policy may drive payment moving from the later to the former.

## *The Affordable Care Act*

Since its enactment in 2010, the Affordable Care Act (ACA) has played a significant role in elevating and conveying the importance of population health within federal policy and procedure. One specific example to illustrate the Affordable Care Act's impact on population health has been through access to health care services. Since the act was passed into law, those covered by health insurance increased exponentially. In fact, as of 2022 coverage as a result of the Affordable Care Act has surpassed an additional 35 million individuals, with an additional 21 million individuals gaining coverage since Medicaid's expansion to low-income adults under 65 years of age (New Reports 2022). Additionally, recent studies have found that gaining insurance coverage through expansion decreased the likelihood of not receiving appropriate health care services by nearly 25% (Glied et al. 2017).

Increasing accessibility to health care is a fundamental goal of population and community health. Making available the means to receive health care services for populations who otherwise were not receiving them directly ties into the cultivation of desired health outcomes for targeted populations needing them the most. As the U.S. population continually increases and ages, innovative policy will increasingly be needed to reach the populations who face a disproportionate share of barriers in achieving optimal health outcomes.

## Accountable Care Organizations

Similar to other value-based and population-based models of reimbursement, Accountable Care Organizations (ACOs) prioritize the treatment of specific patient populations in a manner that brings about quality-centric patient outcomes. As the name would suggest, the groups of physicians or health systems that make up an ACO take upon the responsibility to ensure targeted patient populations are receiving high-quality, cost-effective care. From the organizational or provider perspective, ACOs facilitate a mechanism of shared risk in which taking the measures to cultivate positive patient outcomes and keep costs of care low allow for all to share in the generated savings (National Association of ACOs). Optimal patient outcomes are ultimately the goal of ACOs.

## Social Determinants of Health

Health has long been viewed as the presence or absence of disease within an individual. For much of the past two millennia, the overarching goal of medicine was centered around identifying illness, say the acute presence of bacterial pneumonia, and then providing appropriate treatment. As the twentieth century moved forward, contributions to illness outside of immediate pathology have been increasingly recognized. So much so that it is now suggested that traditional medical care, that is, the ordering of lab tests and prescribing medications, impacts perhaps just 10–20% of health outcomes for a population, as outlined in Figure 14.1 (Magnan 2017).

This recognition that health and health care are defined by more than disease is the underpinning of the movement to respond to what have come to be known as social determinants of health (SDOH). The Office of Disease Prevention and Health Promotion defines the SDOH as "The conditions in the environments where people are born, live, learn, work, play,

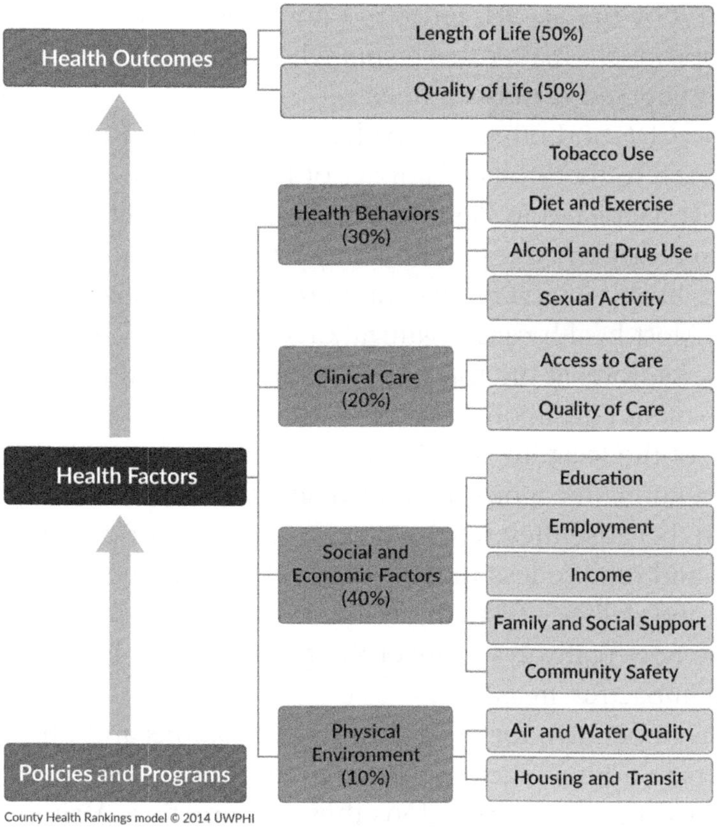


**Figure 14.1 The relative impact of policies, health factors and health outcomes. (County Health Rankings.)**

worship, and age that affect a wide range of health, functioning, and quality-of-life outcomes and risks" (Office of Disease Prevention and Health Promotion). The SDOH and population health go hand in hand. One could even say that a population health approach to improving health outcomes necessitates addressing the social determinants of health. The social determinants are quite diverse and impact different populations in a wide variety of ways. Examples include socioeconomic status, education level, and geographic location. In order to improve population health and mitigate disparities often dictated by the SDOH, emphasis and time must be invested in an appropriate matter that befits what the population or group targeted is most in need of.

The CDC and other groups have recognized a tiered approach to the levels of impact of medical care and patient context. Depicted in Figure 14.2, the public health impact pyramid displays the potential impact of different types of public health interventions compared to traditional clinical ones. Most health care organizations have traditionally focused efforts at the top of the pyramid, clinical intervention and patient education, and these are recognized as having some of the least impact. At the base of the pyramid are interventions recognized with potential for highest impact on health, because they reach entire populations of people at once and require less individual effort. Innovative organizations and delivery systems should seek to transition to or devise new pathways to meet the goals of these lower and more impactful areas.

It is imperative for health care organizations and physician leaders to address factors that have the largest degree of impact within the populations they are targeting. A simple example may be an elderly patient who lives alone and has multiple admissions to the local hospital with acute heart failure. The traditional medical model would wait until she arrives and prescribe treatments to decrease the retained fluid and thus offload the burden on her heart. Considering the SDOH and her individual risk factors may reveal that she cannot afford an air-conditioning unit or transportation to be present for outpatient appointments. The cost to address both of those variables would be significantly less than that of even a single day in the hospital, let alone multiple readmissions.

Coupling population and community health alongside a recognition of the SDOH, physician leaders need to seek to best understand where their patients live, learn, work, and play.

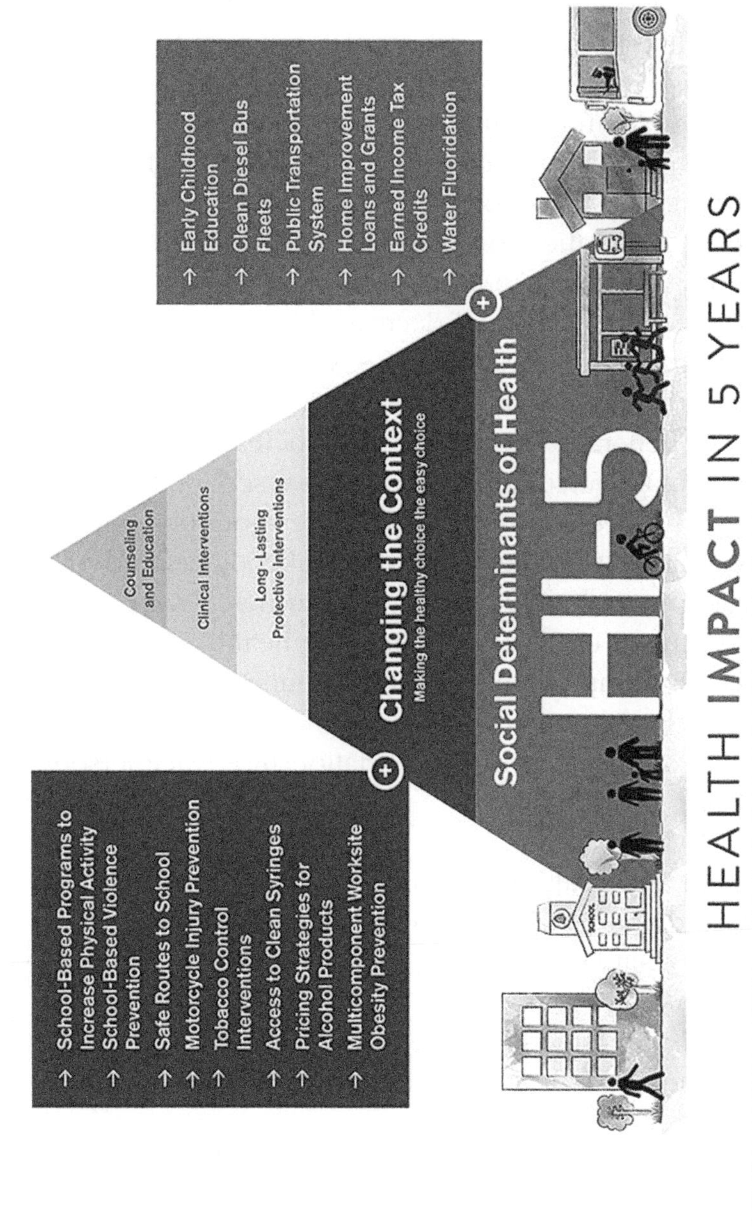


**Figure 14.2** **The CDC HI-5 health impact (CDC).**

## Community Engagement

Most health and the experience of most illness occur outside of the walls of any hospital or health clinic. The greater duration of the lives of most members of a community occur in the schools, barber shops, churches, grocery stores, and places of employment. Thus, the opportunity to impact health, prevent disease, educate, inspire, and transform the health of a group of people should parallel the locations for which they spend the most time. Engaging more directly within any community to improve health offers the potential for enhanced access to care, decreased barriers to patients, and a proactive approach. Likewise, when communities are engaged meaningfully, it increases the voice and vision of that group, and generates the potential for increased trust.

To maximize outcomes from initiatives serving to improve population and community health, there should be integration of community engagement. Relevant stakeholders and pillar organizations can be recognized and partnered with to truly elicit meaningful changes in population health. The Institute for Healthcare Improvement (IHI) has outlined essential items that should be taken into consideration when looking to cultivate meaningful community relationships (McPherson et al. 2021):

1. Health and health equity are cut from the same cloth.
2. Expand your understanding of what engagement is.
3. Know what you are trying to accomplish through forged partnerships.
4. Establish and pursue shared priorities.
5. Draw upon each other's strengths.

Consider a population-based approach to pediatric asthma, such as in a community with a high prevalence of this disease among a given community. Outside of treating this asthma solely in a clinical setting, there should be ample evaluation of the factors that contribute higher incidence and how they can be better served as an overarching group instead of the individual. Different entities within the community would need to work together to mitigate rising pediatric asthma incidence. Perhaps there is a factory in town distributing high levels of pollution into the air. Maybe there is one park or one neighborhood that has a remarkably high prevalence of asthma compared to other areas, and local environmental factors should be investigated. Partnering with the local health department can help with investigation, outreach to nearby schools to spread education and awareness, while hospitals and physician practices serve to provide medical treatment. A population health approach to the problem would include these differing entities, all with a degree of stake in the issue, coming together to work on solution. Identifying those who can play a part in improving the collective health of large groups or populations cannot be understated.

The benefits of well-established partnerships will certainly be evident over time. The possibilities of optimizing community partnerships are endless and can overlap in multiple different ways. There may be organizations to be leveraged that provide complementary services within a service area or region. It is important to understand this so that these complimentary services can be leveraged in a way that establishes the broadest scope without creating duplicative work. Thorough assessment of available services to be leveraged must be conducted to establish target populations and pinpoint current gaps. Partnering with these complimentary services yields the potential for a higher collective degree of output. Such shared success is possible while simultaneously encouraging work that can be done to fill identified gaps in other areas pertinent to population and community health.

## Data Utilization

Proper utilization of appropriate data is often pertinent to crafting successful population health initiatives. As physician leaders, it is well understood that data is utilized to elicit and demonstrate changes in health patterns and trends. Such a line of thinking can be directly translated into larger populations or groups.

Looking again at pediatric asthma, for example. One such tool to collect and analyze relevant data would be geomapping or hotspotting areas in which the highest incidence of children, and specifically children with asthma, are currently present in a given community. An analysis of such geomaps would yield where clusters of pediatric asthma patients reside or spend significant amounts of time within the community. Targeting these specific populations may play a role in expediting progress toward desirable health outcomes. A step further would be to geomap children that are diagnosed with an asthma exacerbation, such as those that are seen in urgent and emergent settings. These may be markers for poor control, and may reveal otherwise hidden SDOH that could mitigate further exacerbations if addressed.

Another illustration of data utilization in the context of population health could be the development and monitoring of disease registries for patients served. From a clinical standpoint, physicians can accomplish a great deal when properly utilizing the information yielded from disease registries. One example could be a database of all patients seen with type 2 diabetes. Physicians responsible for the care of these populations could run a report that sheds light on all patients who have not had their A1C tested within the last year. As a follow-up item appropriate efforts can be made to order tests for the percentage of patients the report yielded who had not had their A1C tested. Furthermore, dashboards could be developed with targets for the groups such as a total percentage of patients with controlled A1C levels. Follow-up could be provided to these patients in the form of healthy living tips sent directly through their patient portal. Taking these steps as physician leaders creates a path to optimal health outcomes for the patients impacted by chronic disease.

## Case Study: Improving Models for Managing Chronic Kidney Disease

The following case study highlights how one organization is targeting a specific population of patients defined by disease state, with emphasis on scale, best practices, technology, and innovation.

Farhad Modarai, DO, is the chief clinical officer of Population Health at Strive Health, a value-based kidney care company that is revolutionizing kidney care through innovative value and population-based delivery approaches. Dr. Modarai is leading a vast clinical team across more than 20+ states and 60,000+ eligible patients as of 2023. While population health is traditionally considered for a single community or geographic area, Figure 14.3 depicts how Strive serves a targeted population that is disease-based, and has a more distributive geographic footprint. The core aim of the care delivery model is to impact the population of patients with kidney disease by targeting subgroups with opportunities to prevent the progression of chronic kidney disease, help patients transition safely to dialysis when they do progress, and optimize care including kidney transplants.

For a variety of reasons, the current status quo in kidney care delivery focuses heavily on end-stage disease and

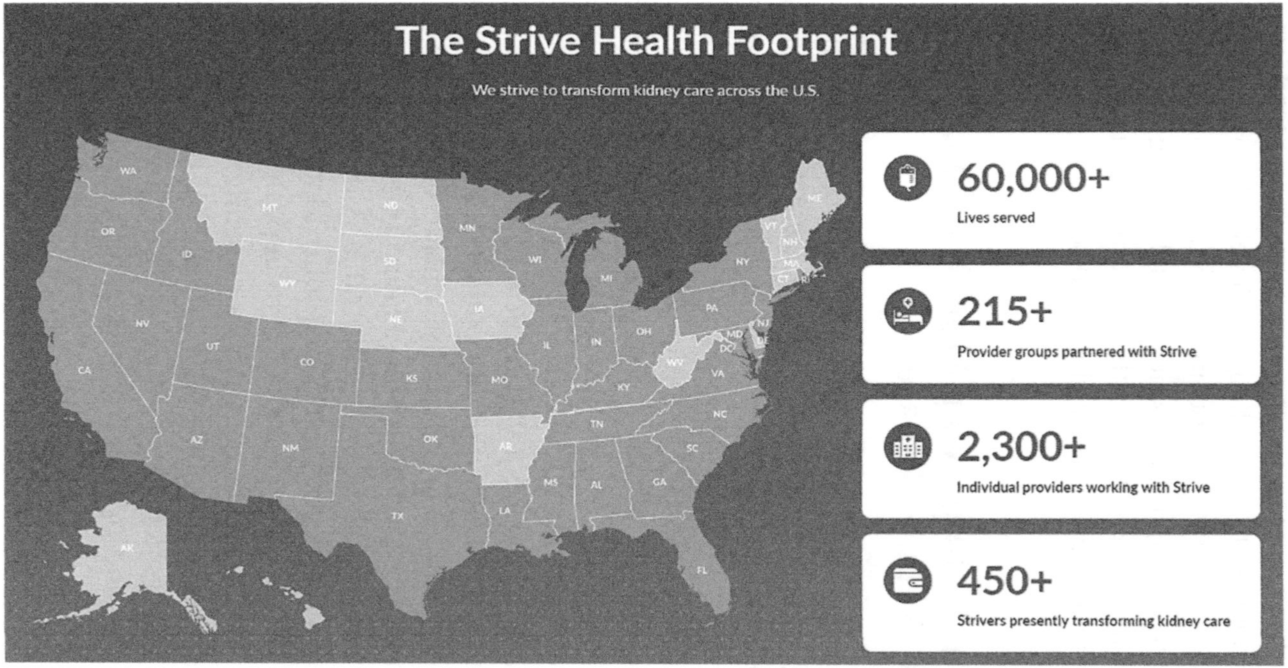


**Figure 14.3 Strive health U.S. delivery footprint (Strive Health).**

in-center dialysis, both of which result in diminished outcomes and are costly to the health care system. One of the most significant challenges in kidney care is the lack of integrated care models, as many kidney patients require care from a variety of specialists, including nephrologists, cardiologists, endocrinologists, and others. However, these specialists often work in silos, leading to fragmented care and suboptimal patient outcomes.

To overcome this challenge, Strive deploys a high-touch care model with personalized care plans that is informed by proprietary data analytics to improve patient outcomes and reduce health care costs. The care team consists of a multidisciplinary team, including nephrologists, nurses, social workers, and dietitians, who seek to provide high-quality care to patients. This means that they do not replace the existing nephrology or primary care providers, and, in fact, they intentionally work to create integrated workflows and care plans with patients' existing care teams.

Strive emphasizes care for the full spectrum of kidney disease patients, the majority of which are usually classified as chronic kidney disease (CKD) Stages 3, 4, and 5, providing the opportunity to stabilize and slow down the rate of progression of kidney disease. The Optimal Dialysis Starts program is one of Strive's programs that uses data to identify high-risk patients who are progressing quickly toward end-stage disease. This data-driven approach allows Strive to prioritize enrollment, and once enrolled, patients receive detailed assessments to identify their level of understanding of their condition, how well their comorbidities are managed, how optimized their lifestyle interventions are, and whether they are aware of options when the need to transition to dialysis would be appropriate. The program tracks many measures of success, such as how many patients transition to home-based dialysis, which is a safer and more affordable approach. For optimal outcomes, the key is to aggressively stabilize and control comorbidities, which leads to much lower morbidity and mortality profiles in the months following a successful transition to dialysis.

The outcomes observed to date have been promising, with Strive reducing hospitalization rates, complications, and readmissions among their population of CKD patients, while delaying the need for dialysis or transplantation. Patients enrolled in Strive's program have seen a 67% increase in optimal dialysis starts and a 52% greater home modality rate, as depicted in Figure 14.4. Patients have reported higher

## Strive Metrics: Analysis Details

AUTHOR: STRIVE HEALTH

**67% increase in optimal starts**

Compares the rate of optimal starts for patients enrolled in the Strive program to that of unenrolled patients across all active Strive markets. Optimal starts is defined as a planned start of renal replacement therapy by receiving a preemptive kidney transplant, initiating home dialysis, or initiating in-center hemodialysis via AVF or AVG.

**36% reduction in 30-day hospital readmissions**

Compares the 30-day hospital readmission rate for patients enrolled in a Strive health system ACO program to a three-year historical benchmark.

**49% reduction in hospitalizations among high-risk patients**

Compares the all-cause hospitalization rate for Complex patients who are engaged in the Strive program to a historical benchmark. "Complex" is the highest-risk tier in Strive's composite risk scoring model, which uses factors such as the Charlson Comorbidity Index, CDC Social Vulnerability Index, and prior hospital visits

**47% greater Peritoneal Dialysis (PD) Start Rate compared to national average**

Time Period: 1/1/2021 - 5/1/2022. Patients have been Optimal Start Candidates for 3 months, are plan eligible and enrolled in Stive programs at the time of dialysis transition, and have known transition modality. Compared to USRDS, 2021 Report Highlights: https://adr.usrds.org/2021/end-stage-renal-disease/1-incidence-prevalence-patient-characteristics-and-treatment-modalities

**52% greater Home Modality (Home Hemo + PD) Start Rate compared to the national average**

Time Period: 1/1/2021 - 5/1/2022. Patients have been Optimal Start Candidates for 3 months, are plan eligible and enrolled in Stive programs at the time of dialysis transition, and have known transition modality. Compared to USRDS, 2021 Report Highlights: https://adr.usrds.org/2021/end-stage-renal-disease/1-incidence-prevalence-patient-characteristics-and-treatment-modalities

**Figure 14.4 Strive health outcomes (Strive Health).**

satisfaction with their care, and providers have seen improvements in the quality of care they deliver.

Implementing a population-based approach to kidney care still faces barriers, such as the lack of standardized care protocols, the need for data sharing and interoperability between different providers, and limited availability of resources and funding. For physician leaders operating outside of traditional health care delivery models or organizations, there are specific lessons to be learned from Strive Health's approach. These include the importance of identifying and addressing targeted high-risk populations using a data analytics approach, which can allow for a more focused care delivery program. The Optimal Dialysis Starts Program is one such program supplementing existing shortcomings among traditional care models. By adopting a population-based approach and partnering with payors and providers, physician leaders can drive improvements in care quality, patient outcomes, and cost-effectiveness.

## Action Steps and Strategies to Lead

1. **Identify target populations to address**. Physician leaders must carefully consider and characterize populations to be served. For your organization, first consider what represents the totality of patients or lives that are served, or could be served, through your services. Next, review how these populations can be subdivided through variables including comorbidities, geography, demographics, and other variables. Physician leaders should consider the clinical elements and risk that is inherent among these groups and target interventions that can have the highest impact.
2. **Review barriers to health that are shared among the target population**. Once a target population has been identified, physician leaders should make an

assessment of barriers that exist, with an awareness of the potential impact of SDOH. Ask what issues disproportionally impact certain groups and what specific health inequities are present that can be addressed. What may be a barrier to one group may not be to another. For meaningful change to happen, it is imperative to understand the contextual factors behind the populations being served.

3. **Develop a community minded strategy**. Physician leaders should look for opportunities to partner with community organizations. If there is a population to be served, particularly one that has been traditionally marginalized, it is possible that some organization already exists to seek to support that group. Before acting, seek out an understanding of the current scope and environment of services and other organizations that already work with the targeted population. Likewise, partnership with community organizations has the potential to engender trust and distribute workload.
4. **Move interventions upstream**. Physician leaders must consider the opportunity to impact health in a proactive, as opposed to the traditional reactive, model. Population and community health move health care away from the passive models of waiting for patients to show up and ask for services. Population minded organizations and leaders actively seek to impact the health of the communities that they serve, emphasize the importance of preventive medicine, disease management, and meeting these groups where they live, work, and play. Physician leaders will increasingly be necessitated to identify health gaps within the diverse set of populations they are intended to serve. Proactive thinking to meet the needs of the whole as opposed to the individual is part of a well-rounded approach to population health.

## References

Allen, M. Unnecessary Medical Care is More Common Than You Think. *ProPublica*. 2018. Accessed February 19, 2023. https://www.propublica.org/article/unnecessary-medical-care-is-more-common-than-you-think

Appold, K. Confused about Population Health? You've Come to the Right Place. *Managed Healthcare Executive*. 2020. Accessed March 5, 2023. https://www.managedhealthcareexecutive.com/view/confused-about-population-health-you-ve-come-to-the-right-place

Frieden, T.R. A Framework for Public Health Action: The Health Impact Pyramid. *American Journal of Public Health*. 2010;100(4):590–595.

Glied, S., Ma, S., Borja, A.A. Effect of the Affordable Care Act on Health Care Access. *Issue Brief Commonwealth Fund*. 2017;13:1–11.

Health and Human Services. New Reports Show Record 35 Million People Enrolled in Coverage Related to the Affordable Care Act, with Historic 21 Million People Enrolled in Medicaid expansion coverage. *HHS.gov*. April 29, 2022. Accessed February 19, 2023. https://www.hhs.gov/about/news/2022/04/29/new-reports-show-record-35-million-people-enrolled-in-coverage-related-to-the-affordable-care-act.html

Kindig, D., Stoddart, G. What is Population Health? *American Journal of Public Health*. 2003;93(3):380–383.

Magnan, S. Social Determinants of Health 101 for Health Care: Five Plus Five. *National Academy of Medicine*. 2017. Accessed February 19, 2023. https://nam.edu/social-determinants-of-health-101-for-health-care-five-plus-five/

Maraccini, A. M., Galiatsatos, P., Harper, M., Slonim, A.D. Creating Clarity: Distinguishing Between Community and Population Health. *American Journal of Accountable Care*. 2017;5(3):27–32.

McPherson, M., Callender, S., Lewis, N. Working with Community Partners. *Healthcare Executive*. 2021;36(5):40–41.

Social Determinants of Health – Healthy People 2030. n.d. Accessed February 19, 2023. https://health.gov/healthypeople/priority-areas/social-determinants-health

# Chapter 15

# New Payment Models: Value-based Purchasing

## The Evidence

Over the course of the last half century, the United States has seen rapid and unabated growth in health care spending. The percentage of gross domestic product spent on U.S. health care increased from 5.0% in 1960 to 18.3% in 2021 (CMS 2022b). Further rising costs are simply unsustainable, and thus the system and core payment mechanisms must shift. Much of the observed increases have been attributed to the predominant fee-for-service method of reimbursement, which incentivizes providers to deliver a greater volume of services without respect to quality of care. The fee-for-service method also propagates the delivery of care in silos. It does not reward providers for efforts to better coordinate care or for the maintenance of health as individuals or in populations. In short, it encourages doing more things to more patients, thus increasing cost, without any accountability for quality or outcome.


DOI: 10.4324/9781003402831-15

Given the negative consequences of fee-for-service, payers in the U.S. health care system have implemented a host of alternate payment methodologies to seek to improve quality and contain costs. These alternate payment mechanisms typically involve increased risk for organizations, both financially and operationally. Figure 15.1 provides a map of current and potential payment methodologies and the degree of associated risk. Though many of these reimbursement models may sound new, most are simply new versions of a previous iteration that have been tested or even implemented prior to the current era of health care reform. Additionally, several of the "new" models, though they have different names, are simply modified versions of the fee-for-service model.

The relationship between payers and providers will continue to evolve in the years ahead, as partnership and consolidation around shared goals has the potential to lower costs for all. In many instances, this means alignment around targets for reduction and an inherent shared financial risk between the two. However, payers are increasingly

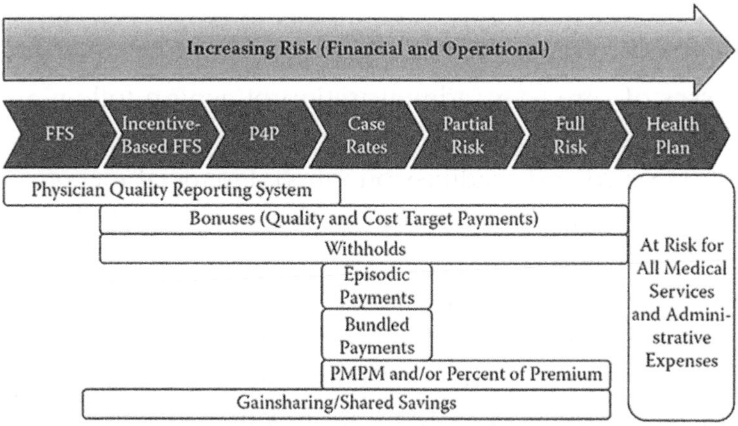


**Figure 15.1 Range of value-based arrangements on the risk continuum. (Value-Based Contracting. Health Research & Educational Trust and Kaufman, Hall & Associates, Inc., Chicago, July 2013. www.hpoe.org.)**

entering the world of directly providing care, often through joint ventures or outright purchase of provider groups or organizations.

## Pay-for-Performance

One of the most basic modifications to the fee-for-service model is pay-for-performance. Pay-for-performance involves the use of a series of explicit financial incentives to deliver predetermined services to achieve a given standard of care. It is an attempt to realign the legacy fee-for-service model to incentivize the delivery of safe, high-quality care. Proponents of pay-for-performance programs acknowledge that in order to achieve greater value in health care, physicians will be required to change practice patterns. Pay-for-performance programs use financial incentives that reward these changes in behavior and practice patterns.

Pay-for-performance programs can be designed along three dimensions: The nature of the quality goal, the form of the financial incentive, and the competitive nature of the program. Quality goals can include benchmarks in health care infrastructure (e.g., electronic health records and patient registries), processes of care (e.g., administration of aspirin following acute myocardial infarction), and medical outcomes (e.g., blood pressure and readmission rates). Financial incentives may take the form of a bonus, penalty, or both, all of which are tied to performance.

Incentives may also vary based on whether the pay-for-performance initiative is structured as a competitive or non-competitive program. In a non-competitive program, providers and delivery systems are rewarded for achieving pre-established, absolute thresholds of quality. All providers in the program may receive bonuses if they all achieve these goals. In a competitive program, providers and hospitals compete against each other for a limited number of rewards.

Competitive programs establish clear winners and losers based on relative thresholds of improvement. Pay-for-performance programs can blend these competitive and non-competitive approaches and provide incentives for both absolute performance and incremental improvement.

At the federal level, the Centers for Medicare and Medicaid Services now has an extensive track record of implementing pay-for-performance programs, including initiatives to reduce readmissions and hospital-acquired conditions, programs to increase compliance with clinical processes and projects to improve patient outcomes. Funding for these programs is globally constructed as a percentage withhold of all Medicare diagnosis-related group (DRG) base payments. For example, the Medicare Readmissions Reduction Program penalizes hospitals with excess readmissions by withholding Medicare payments in the next year.

Many commercial payers also have an extensive track record with pay-for-performance programs. Most fee-for-service reimbursement models now include some elements of pay-for-performance. Stimulated during discussions around the time of the ACA, dozens of demonstration projects have become fixtures of the national payment landscape (McWilliams 2022). Legacy fee-for-service agreements without any attachment to quality, safety, or coordination of care are quickly becoming the exception.

## *Accountable Care Organizations and Shared Savings*

Another payment methodology with roots in traditional fee-for-service is the ACO shared savings model. An ACO is an entity, either a single organization or a group of health care stakeholders, that accepts collective responsibility for the quality and cost of care delivered to a defined patient population. Medical groups, physician hospital organizations, or integrated delivery systems can form ACOs. In some instances, many organizations will partner to form a new entity that includes additional stakeholders such as retail pharmacy, home care, and skilled nursing facilities.

In an ACO contract, physicians and hospitals continue to operate under the existing reimbursement model, whether that is fee-for-service, inpatient case rates, or Medicare DRGs. At the end of a predefined time period, reconciliation is conducted to determine if the ACO has achieved certain quality and cost control thresholds. If the pre-established thresholds are achieved, the ACO retains a portion of the savings and can distribute the rest of the savings to its stakeholders however it chooses.

Through the early 2020s, evidence has generally demonstrated savings through ACO models, with at least maintenance, and in some cases improvement in quality of care (Lewis 2022). The Center for Medicare and Medicaid Innovation (CMMI) has developed expanded ACO models that build around specific focuses such as maternal opioid misuse, emergency transport, and in-home therapies. As of 2022, there were just over 1,000 ACOs, with 1,760 public and private ACO contracts, covering more than 32 million lives. ACOs led by physician groups are far more prevalent than those run by hospitals, and they are additionally showing some early better results (Muhlestein et al. 2022).

ACO shared savings contracts have not traditionally altered the underlying method of payment, especially in those cases where fee-for-service for physician payments dominates. Instead, these organizations attempt to provide an additional financial incentive to align providers in the pursuit of higher value care across the continuum for an attributed patient population. The framework for accountability and the ACO model will only continue to advance in the years ahead, as CMS has committed to have all traditional Medicare beneficiaries and the vast majority of Medicaid beneficiaries in an accountable care relationship by 2030 (CMS 2022a). Because the payment method to providers is not altered and the benefit design for patients may remain unchanged, ACOs continue to face a host of challenges in achieving higher value. Two areas of challenge are patient attribution and risk sharing.

## *Identifying an Attributed Patient Population*

In a shared savings program with an open plan design, such as traditional Medicare or a preferred provider organization, one of the foremost challenges in forming an ACO is to identify the correct population of patients to be attributed to the ACO. The ACO is responsible for cost and quality outcomes within this attributed group of patients, so it is very important that the attribution process be done correctly.

There are many methods for determining attribution. Typically, health plan members are attributed to an ACO based on a historical review of utilization and subsequent identification of those providers or health systems that account for the majority of visits or costs for a given population of patients. Attribution rules are typically created as a hierarchical set of conditions so that if a patient cannot be attributed under one set of logic, he or she may be attributed under a different rule. For example, a woman of childbearing age may be attributed to an obstetrician, even if she has only one visit a year with that physician, if there is no other utilization associated with that member. In contrast, an older patient with multiple comorbidities may be attributed to the provider that has the majority or plurality of associated claims, even if they see multiple physicians a year.

The attribution process should be recognized and appreciated for its strategic relevance. Overarchingly, there is no single recognized standard, and this has resulted in a variety of attribution methods employed by differing organizations for a host of purposes. Given the multiple elements for attribution involved, this can lead to variability in measurement for outcome, utilization, and cost. Increasingly, organizations are prospectively linking patients with providers as a means for enabling population health management, accountability, and continuity of care (McCoy 2018).

Attribution fundamentally determines the population for which an ACO is responsible. It is a complex process and should be executed by an ACO analytics team. In an open plan design where members can choose any provider, it is essential that an ACO be attributed a population that has a large proportion of in-network care so that their efforts in managing costs and quality will be effective and accurately reflected in the data. If the attribution process is done incorrectly, the ACO may effectively be "responsible" for patients who do not even seek a majority of their care within the ACO network.

## *Structure of Risk Sharing*

There are two key considerations when establishing an ACO's structure of risk sharing: (1) The potential for downside risk and (2) the option for shared savings. If an ACO assumes downside risk, it may be held responsible for member costs that exceed established market benchmarks. ACOs may be incentivized to accept downside risk through the opportunity to participate in a greater proportion of any shared savings. Though this larger potential upside may be tempting for early ACO entrants, new ACOs often lack the degree of infrastructure and operational maturity necessary to ensure that they will not sustain losses in early reporting periods. Based on this, it is recommended that new ACOs do not initially assume downside risk.

An additional negotiating point between an ACO and the payer is the proportion of savings that the ACO is eligible to share. Some shared savings agreements require a certain threshold of savings to be achieved before the ACO can earn any savings. Alternatively, the percentage of sharing accrued to the ACO may be tiered and based on the level of savings achieved. For example, an ACO may not be eligible to receive savings until at least $2 million worth of overall savings is realized. After this threshold, all savings may be distributed on a 50–50 basis between the ACO and payer for the first $10 million, and if savings are greater than $10 million, the split may be 60% savings to the ACO, 40% to the payer.

Because the underlying reimbursement model is not altered in an ACO arrangement, the shared savings (or losses) are determined at the end of designated reporting periods through a reconciliation process. There is typically some lag in this process, making it difficult to have the kind of timely data and feedback that are necessary to adjust strategies and tactics in response to performance. This lack of real-time monitoring is a common critique of current ACO contracts. Greater investment in data and analytics investment will be required to enable more accurate decision-making by ACOs.

## *Bundled Payments*

Another reimbursement model that may be construed as an "early adopter" model for those working toward population health is bundled payments. In a bundled payment arrangement, providers receive a fixed sum to cover all of the costs associated with an episode of care or care for a specific disease state over time. This incentivizes care coordination and reduction of redundancies and inefficiencies.

On the surface, bundled payments may appear completely novel. However, almost every hospital and health system has had some experience with bundled payments in the form of Medicare DRG reimbursement. Though it excludes physician billing, Medicare's DRG payment system represents a bundle for all services provided during an inpatient stay.

In a bundled payment system, the episode of care can be defined as inpatient procedure, an outpatient procedure, or a chronic medical condition such as diabetes. The bundled payment includes an established time frame. For instance, in a bundled payment for knee replacement surgery, the episode may start up to one week before the procedure and conclude 90 days following the end of surgery. In this example, the bundled payment would cover all inpatient, ambulatory, post-acute, and physician costs over the nearly three-month episode of care required for a knee replacement surgery.

Compared to shared savings and ACOs, organizations typically regard bundled payment as a narrower approach to population health. This model presents opportunities to redesign care, align stakeholders, and reprioritize incentives, but on a more sharply defined scope. Bundled payment should not be considered an easy route to population health. There are many challenges related to bundle definition, rate setting, and splitting payments appropriately.

Defining the bundle can be a difficult process. It requires defining which services to include, defining the beginning and end of the care episode, and defining criteria for patient inclusion or exclusion. These decisions will dictate whether organizations will accept a flat-rate fee or if the bundles will be risk adjusted.

Establishing bundle definitions not only requires hospital leadership to negotiate with the payer but also to have a detailed understanding of historical costs and patterns of utilization within the facility. Many organizations lack these analytic capabilities, and target price determination remains the most significant ongoing issue across payers and organizations alike. From 2018 to 2019, the Medicare Bundled Payments for Care Improvement (BPCI Advanced) initiative saw a $75 million gross decrease in spending, yet after distribution of financial bonuses, the program found a $279 million increase in net spending (Shashikumar et al. 2022).

As in a shared savings model, most bundled payment arrangements do not change the underlying mechanism of payment. Currently, most payers lack the necessary infrastructure to issue a prospective bundled payment for multiple providers. Similarly, most provider organizations lack the capability to accept and process these types of global payments. Additionally, it may not be apparent at the start of an episode of care whether a patient will meet all of the inclusion criteria. As a result, most bundled payments are structured so that existing reimbursement practices are maintained during the episode of care. Physicians bill and are reimbursed on a fee-for-service schedule and the hospital continues its existing method for billing and reimbursement. At the end of some predetermined period, a budget reconciliation is performed on each episode that was eligible for inclusion. Any savings are then split between the providers participating in the bundle. The percentage split of any savings should be established when parties agree to participate in a bundle.

## *Capitation*

The most aggressive form of risk bearing for providers and delivery organizations is capitation. Capitation involves the advanced payment of a fixed amount to cover the provision of a defined set of health services over a fixed unit of time.

The capitated payment is typically defined as a rate per member, per month. The two basic variations on capitation are global capitation and sub-capitation. Global capitation is used in vertically integrated delivery systems or large, multispecialty groups that cover the costs of care for all of the health care needs in a population. In contrast, sub-capitation is available for primary care and some specialty care providers who only provide some portion of a patient's care. In primary care, the capitation model emphasizes the role of the primary care provider as a comprehensive coordinator for the utilization of services.

Compared to the other payment models discussed, capitation represents a fundamental departure from fee-for-service reimbursement. Providing an up-front fee provides direct incentives around cost and utilization and provides explicit incentives to align stakeholders. It also provides an early source of revenue to fund the types of personnel and information technology investments that are necessary to ensure effective coordination across the continuum of care. In ACO and bundled payment models, the shared savings, if any, are not available until after some lag in data and the final administrative budget reconciliation. This limits the organization's ability to reinvest those funds quickly and may mute their impact as an incentive. Capitation provides all payment up front, enabling organizations to plan and invest accordingly.

Capitation does present some unique challenges. It is a form of payment that requires providers to accept risk for all losses from overutilization or adverse risk selection. In addition, it also involves a trade-off by patients in the choice of providers. These aspects, particularly the latter, contributed to the decline in the prevalence of capitation since the 1990s. The more recent resurgence and interest in capitation is largely due to organizations viewing it as a way to gain more of the first dollar of revenue in an era of declining fee-for-service reimbursements.

## Case Study: Bundled Payments

John Bulger, DO is the chief medical officer for Geisinger Health Plan. Geisinger is a large integrated health care system serving over three million patients, with a health plan covering more than 550,000 lives across central and northern Pennsylvania. The system includes an addiction treatment center, a joint venture rehabilitation center, a medical school, residency and fellowship programs, nursing schools, and a research program. Geisinger has a long history of voluntary stewardship with the Centers for Medicare and Medicaid (CMS) testing pay-for-performance and other alternative payment models designed to provide beneficiaries with high-quality, coordinated care. Among these, Geisinger actively participates in the Medicare Shared Savings Program (MSSP) as well as the Bundle Payment for Care Improvement (BPCI) under the CMS Innovation Center.

Under BPCI, payments are predicated on total costs spanning from the time of hospitalization for a given condition or procedure through up to 90 days of post-discharge care. The BPCI model thus designates the participating hospital as the accountable entity for total spending and quality outcomes across the entire episode of care, such as for spinal, cardiac, or joint replacement surgeries, and others. With the launch of their ACO, Geisinger enrolled two hospitals separately in the BPCI program (2014–2017) and five hospitals in the BPCI Advanced (BPCIA) program (2018–2019). Geisinger utilizes a software program with advanced analytics to track 28 episodes across each hospital and MFFS beneficiaries through EHR alignment across the 90-day episode, including post-hospital management by a post-acute care preferred network.

Leaders at Geisinger identified that shorter or eliminated post-discharge lengths of stay at inpatient rehab facilities (IRF) offered opportunity for cost savings (Figure 15.2). Four Geisinger hospitals participating in BPCIA were asked to increase mobility during the immediate post-operative period, and thus target reduction in unnecessary IRF utilization.

Essential elements of the Geisinger BPCIA initiative:

- **Administrators supportive of value-based care** who allow the people and technology resources

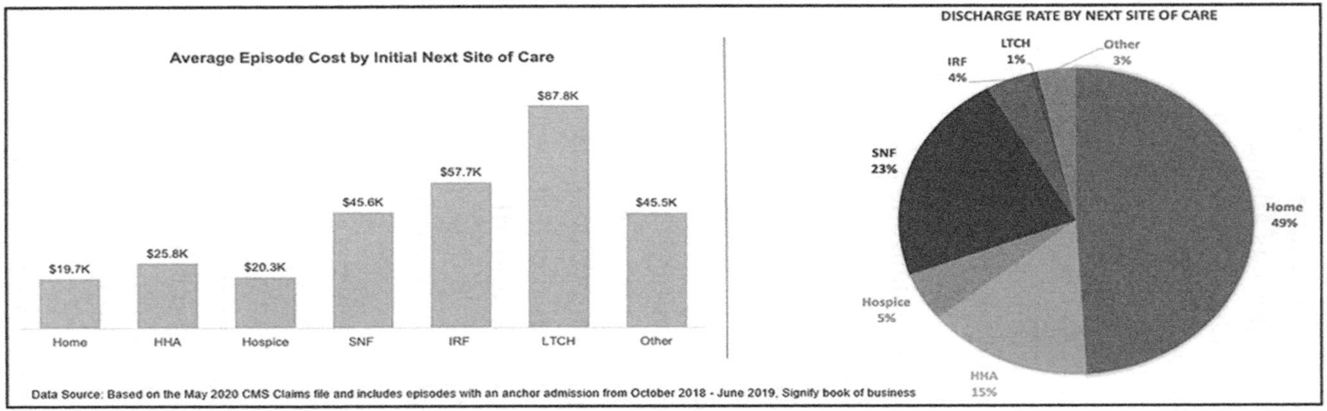


**Figure 15.2** **Average episode cost and discharge rate in 2020 by site of care. (Geisinger Health System, Danville, PA.)**

necessary to promote effective and efficient health care. Geisinger committed to standard mobility scoring tools such as the AMPAC and JH-HLM as well as signing on a BPCIA Convener with EMR software integration to capture real-time performance based upon a working DRG.

- **A resolute project team** includes a project coordinator to organize the project activities and a project director with a strong clinical and quality improvement background to facilitate a charter and clinical redesign.
- **Physician Champions** at the hospital level are willing to engage skeptics and resistors to promote the redesign and aid in change management with teams. The physician champions (both the CMO and the CQO) had a background rich in reliability science and systems theory with impeccable teamship.
- **Change tactics** necessary for change management are reviewed with direct reports by care management, therapy, and nursing directors. This included implementing a mobility campaign with a "home-first" focus and an escalation process for any patient considered for an IRF referral. This escalation process includes active engagement of the patient/decision-maker.
- **Education** with talking points for staff and patients/caregivers explains the benefits of mobility during the hospital stay, discharges to home settings, and requirements for each next site of care destination.
- **An engaged and educated frontline staff** that connects to their directors and are aligned with mobility goals as they are usually first to explain and promote best care practices to patients and their caregivers.
- **Access to reliable data** with benchmarks on past performance and comparatives to peers with analysis.
- **A preferred network** of home health and hospice agencies, skilled nursing facilities, and inpatient rehabilitation facilities. Readmissions, emergency department

visits, and mortalities within 90 days of hospital discharge dates address length of stay and transitions into and out of the sites.

Janet Comrey, RN, serves as director of Payment Transformation with Geisinger, and recommends the following keys to success in the bundled payment initiative:

- **Accountable leaders draft a charter (or Operating Agreement) that is shared with key stakeholders**. The charter outlines the goals, rationale, risks and barriers, and anticipated resources to which the team will commit. It identifies the team and is a living document used to keep the team focused and on track.
- ***Weigh-in* on behalf of stakeholders is necessary for *buy-in* related to any process change**. Since processes of care usually intersect multiple people, service lines, and organizations, where practices are influenced by beliefs, cultural patterns and values, improvement efforts engage all key stakeholders across disciplines, from the front line to the executive suite.
- **The executive suite sets the strategic aims related to value-based care and tags the executive leader(s) to sponsor the work**. Geisinger committed to being prepared to meet the CMS goal to place all Medicare beneficiaries into a two-sided risk arrangement by CY 2030 and appreciate the value of diversifying the MFFS payment portfolio. Resources are allocated to achieve quality and financial targets of alternative payment models spanning both inpatient and outpatient arenas. Population Health and Innovation Institutes prioritize the initiatives.
- **The executive sponsor(s) set the governance and tagged accountable leader(s) to achieve the identified aims and provide necessary infrastructure and supports to remove systemic barriers**. The ACO is

governed by a Fiduciary Board of Managers, which is accountable to manage the costs and quality of a large MFFS population on an annual basis. The BPCIA programs are governed through a hospital-based steering committee and accountable for quality and costs of care for a small MFFS population across a 90-day episode.

- **The success of one program directly impacts the other**. Although governed separately, the BPCI and ACO programs align as 40% of the BPCIA population overlapped with the ACO and workflows were standardized across all-payer populations. Geisinger has established a common director who shares the outcomes with the Quality and Safety Institute that is responsible for Pay-for-Performance and regulatory initiatives. There is additionally a medical home/case management service that partners with primary and specialty care services to manage the populations. Since the majority of Medicare costs occur in the post-acute care arena, prioritizing a preferred network of post-acute providers is key to managing costs and quality.

Although all four hospitals initially reduced IRF utilization, only one hospital was able to improve and sustain a significant reduction in IRF utilization (Figure 15.3). The hospital most successful in delivering value-based care within the BPCIA program was led by physicians and administrators who possessed a strong business acumen, prioritized value over volume, and preached systems theory with reliability science.

Robert Strony, MD, medical director for Provider Relations with Geisinger Health Plan, and other leaders in the plan use a blend of quality improvement sciences to solve problems and innovate. Strony notes that health care systems and accountable care organizations are a collection of multiple complex macro and microsystems, each with their own set of values, culture, priorities, challenges, and logistics. Despite

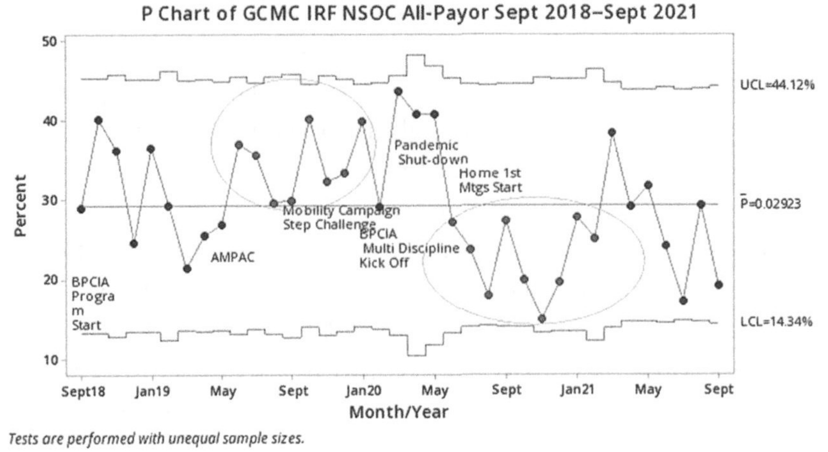


**Figure 15.3 Run chart of percent utilization of inpatient rehab facility 2018–2021. (Geisinger Health System, Danville, PA.)**

this inherent variability, there remains a constant with any improvement effort to achieve success—a desire to improve, skills to execute change, ideas for improvement, and reliable data with analytics.

## Lessons Learned

The implementation of new payment models can involve a dramatic departure from existing reimbursement models, and these transformations are necessary. This may require a new set of core competencies, particularly for organizations that have built their infrastructure and expertise around inpatient care and more volume dependent services. As a result, significant investment may be required to manage care across the continuum of inpatient, ambulatory, and post-acute settings. These investments include information technology, data and analytics, and care management.

## Information Technology

The required IT investments extend beyond electronic medical record capability in the inpatient and ambulatory space. Effective organizations will implement IT solutions that enable data sharing across stakeholders, for example, through internal and external health information exchanges. Investments in disease registries, patient portals, a longitudinal patient record, artificial intelligence, telehealth, and remote monitoring solutions are additional helpful technologies. Organizations should take a gradual approach to selecting and implementing each of these solutions. This will help ensure that each is integrated into the provider workflow in order to maximize the impact on outcomes and costs of care in the population.

## Data and Analytics

To maximize the impact of these IT investments, health care organizations must invest in data and analytics capabilities. This includes the ability to aggregate data from multiple data sources including internal transactional and demographic data, external claims data, and clinical data from EMRs. In order to match data from multiple sources by individual patient, organizations must develop a single master patient index and reconcile the many patient medical record numbers and identifiers across sites of care.

Once the data is aggregated and cleaned, organizations must also have analytic capabilities. This includes the ability to mine information to generate an accurate dashboard of the population along the dimensions of quality, safety, and utilization. Each of these indicators can include clinical integration metrics and measures on emergency department visits, inpatient days, readmissions, and in-network care coordination. In addition to these analytics, ACOs and other organizations must be able to use the data to stratify their populations based on risk. The most basic risk stratification identifies individuals associated with the greatest utilization or cost. This risk stratification enables the organization to perform targeted interventions and to allocate services and resources where they will be most effective and beneficial.

## Care Management

Organizations must develop care management capabilities, especially throughout the ambulatory and post-acute care settings. A care management structure can include outpatient care managers, social work, and community-based health coaches. This will likely require augmentation by alternate providers of care including APPs, patient navigators, home health, and pharmacies. All of these personnel must be integrated into team-based care pathways with clearly identified roles and responsibilities to ensure a seamless experience for the patient.

These are significant investments in people, processes, and technology that may be necessary at the outset of a shared savings or bundled payment agreement. These investments can be challenging given the significant lag in determining any savings or losses in a shared savings contract. There is often no pool of designated funds to pay for any investments in infrastructure or personnel at the beginning of an agreement. In these instances, organizations entering into a new value-based reimbursement scheme may have to invest in existing resources. Alternatively, an ACO could request some up-front funds for infrastructure in their payer agreement, separate against any savings accrual. Either way, organizations should be mindful of the significant up-front costs that are required for success.

Value-based reimbursement models, particularly bundled payments, shared savings, and capitation, require sufficient data so physicians and providers can enter with full appreciation of the risks. This requires not only sharing of data with payers but also developing a true sense of partnership between payers and providers. For some, payer–provider relationships have historically been marked by the routine rituals of difficult negotiations over reimbursement rates. For value-based reimbursement models to succeed, insurance entities and delivery systems must forego past rivalries and enter into truly collaborative arrangements around data sharing, care redesign, and improving the health and well-being of populations.

Much of the discussion has focused on financial incentives for providers and delivery systems. Organizations, however, must also be mindful of the incentives that patients have, particularly in the form of benefit design. Benefit design should be aligned to support care coordination and in-network care. If a patient's plan allows significant out-of-ACO coverage, managing quality and cost is made additionally difficult. Tactics are required to help activate patients in their own care and enable them to be advocates for their own health. The work in patient engagement is nascent and includes many up-and-coming technologies around self-monitoring. Still, tactics for patient engagement should be considered necessary elements for success in a value-based reimbursement environment.

## Action Steps and Strategies to Lead

The transition to value-based reimbursement presents the opportunity to improve population health and possibly offset the decline in traditional fee-for-service revenues. A growing array of payment arrangements are blurring the boundaries among insurers, providers, VBP enablement companies, and other physician management services organizations. Physician leaders must be well versed in the spectrum of these options and willing to engage stakeholders to consider outside the box payment considerations.

In preparation for a value-based contract, leaders should make a few key determinations:

1. **Understand your threshold of risk**. On the spectrum of lowest to highest assumption of risk, bundled payments have the lowest exposure, followed by shared savings and then capitation. These degrees of risk also correspond to the extent of infrastructure and process redesign that are necessary to be successful in each reimbursement scheme. Leaders must understand their organization's appetite to sustain potential losses, measured against the degree of existing infrastructure. Once this threshold of risk is established, an organization can next decide the appropriate reimbursement method to begin the population health journey. Well-designed financial incentives are crucial to promoting accountability and driving action.
2. **Understand your core competencies and the gaps in your capabilities**. Value-based payment is not merely about reimbursement; it is a complete redesign to ensure coordination across the continuum of care. Organizations should take stock of their existing core competencies and identify and understand their gaps in process, people, and technology as they relate to the world of population health. Having this knowledge will provide the roadmap for infrastructure investment and identify key partnerships to establish with other stakeholders in order to be successful.
3. **Involve physicians early and as equal partners in the conversation**. Achieving superior health outcomes in addition to a positive margin in a value-based care environment will require changes in physician behavior

and other aspects of clinical practice. Rather than being the lone captain, physicians become one of many important team players on a multidisciplinary care team. As a result, physician engagement is required for any value-based reimbursement program. It is important to have physician leadership as part of the strategy and throughout the process.

Value-based reimbursement is not just about the dollars. It is fundamentally a paradigm shift from a focus on illness to one of health and wellness; from episodic care to coordination; from discharge to transitions; and from production and volume to performance and value. It is important to keep this underlying rationale and motivation in mind when leading any organization on the path toward value-based care.

## References

CMS. Person-Centered Innovation – An Update on the Implementation of the CMS Innovation Center's Strategy November 2022a. Accessed January 18, 2023. https://innovation.cms.gov/data-and-reports/2022/cmmi-strategy-refresh-imp-report

CMS. National Health Expenditure by Type of Service and Source of Funds, CY1960-2021. 2022b. Accessed February 4, 2023. https://www.cms.gov/research-statistics-data-and-systems/statistics-trends-and-reports/nationalhealthexpenddata/nationalhealthaccountshistorical

Lewis, C., et al. Evidence from a Decade of Innovation: The Impact of the Payment and Delivery System Reforms of the Affordable Care Act. *Commonwealth Fund*. April 2022. Accessed January 18, 2023. https://www.commonwealthfund.org/publications/2022/apr/impact-payment-and-delivery-system-reforms-affordable-care-act#acos

McCoy, R.G., Bunkers, K.S., Ramar, P., Meier, S.K., Benetti, L.L., Nesse, R.E., Naessens, J.M. Patient Attribution: Why the Method Matters. *American Journal of Managed Care*. 2018;24(12): 596–603.

McWilliams, JM. Pay for Performance: When Slogans Overtake Science in Health Policy. *JAMA*. 2022;328(21):2114–2116.

Muhlestein, D., Saunders, R.S., de Lisle, K., Bleser, W., McClellan, M.B. Growth of Value-Based Care and Accountable Care Organizations in 2022. *Health Affairs Forefront*. December 2022. Accessed January 18, 2023. https://www.healthaffairs.org/content/forefront/growth-value-based-care-and-accountable-care-organizations-2022

Shashikumar, S., Gulseren, B., Berlin, N., Hollingsworth, J., Joynt, K.M., Ryan, A. Association of Hospital Participation in Bundled Payments for Care Improvement Advanced with Medicare Spending and Hospital Incentive Payments. *JAMA*. 2022; 328(16):1616–1623.

*Chapter 16*

# The Physician Leader Role in Emerging Models of Care, Disruption, and Innovation

## The Evidence

Leaders should be prepared for innovation and disruption to the extent that these be considered an expected part of their work. Such preparedness requires that physician leaders seek proactive initiatives, looking ahead to anticipate where their organization, markets, and consumers are likely to trend. Likewise, they must be flexible in their own work, and train and lead teams that demonstrate the agility to move through rapidly altering circumstances. As "disruption" and "innovation" are terms that are increasingly used to describe health care transformation, it is important to have a working knowledge of these and to be prepared to lead teams through

DOI: 10.4324/9781003402831-16

success in both. In the most basic sense, much of this text is dedicated to improvement and innovation, which is new or improved policies, practices, systems, products, services, technologies, or delivery methods that improve health care. Meanwhile, disruption results when a specific change or a series of changes upset current systems to the point that incumbents operating within those systems cannot adapt to that change. (Shaw and Chisholm 2020).

Health systems are neither traditionally built nor well suited to deal with disruptive changes, as was evidenced in many areas during the COVID-19 pandemic. This is often due to reluctance to alter existing profit streams, business models, or processes that are perceived as effective "enough" or generating revenue. Existing frameworks and belief systems can also hold back adoption of new processes and technologies. (OECD 2019). Health care governance and policy have also historically struggled to keep pace with such challenges. Similarly, at the team and individual level physician leaders will often confront adversity to change and the desire to continue with the "way things have always been done."

In many ways, innovation is a fundamental and necessary component of the normal operations of successful health systems, scientific research teams, and any efforts to improve care delivery. To take this a step further, the terms utilized in this chapter are not mutually exclusive, and in fact the most forward-thinking organizations are seeking strategies to be active disruptive innovators (Christensen et al. 2015). Physician leaders should seek to work within this paradigm. Afterall, patients and consumer bases will increasingly demand better, more convenient, more cost-effective services and gravitate toward organizations that best meet these. This chapter provides background and context on how areas of the health care sector are evolving through disruption and innovation, and key strategies for physician leaders to be successful in their own organizations.

## *Retail Medicine*

The concept of "retail medicine" involves health care services delivered in the retail store setting including supermarkets, pharmacies, and drug stores. Often nurse practitioners or physician assistants provide care through retail clinics or convenient care clinics. CVS, Walgreens, Target, and Walmart have all invested in retail or convenient care clinics over the past decade.

Retail clinics provide limited yet convenient medical services on a walk-in basis. Common services include vaccinations, flu shots, preventive health services, and treatment for minor ailments such as sore throats, infections, fevers, and sprains. Retail clinics are particularly appealing to consumers because they provide expanded hours beyond the normal workday, including weekend and evening hours. They are typically more convenient, often not requiring a formal appointment and are present in the same shared space occupied for grocery shopping or other routine tasks.

The retail medicine model has existed for decades, but the number of clinics and number of retailers hosting such clinics has proliferated in recent years. As of 2018, there were estimated to be over 2800 retail clinics in the United States, with the number expected to continue to grow. (Knapp et al. 2019).

Several factors are driving this growth, most notably a generation shift. Individuals in Generation X (born between 1965 and 1980), and Generation Y (born between 1981 and 1996) are more likely to visit these clinics, driven by their desire for convenience and easy access. Because these individuals are also generally healthy, the preventive care and treatment for minor ailments provided by retail clinics meet the majority of their medical needs. Beyond the generational pull, however, individuals are also simply beginning to view retail medicine as more responsive to their needs.

The traditional health care delivery system imposes significant burdens on consumers regarding scheduling, inconvenience, and rigid structure. Retail clinics offer the potential for greater flexibility for individuals looking for new, convenient ways to access health care.

Concerning retail medicine, physician leaders, even those that are not currently engaged in retail medicine outfits, should consider:

- How will the evolution of retail medicine impact the health care system in regard to cost, care coordination, patient satisfaction, and clinical outcomes?
- If and how can existing delivery organizations partner or coordinate with these new "organizations" of care delivery?
- How can the current health care system evolve to meet the needs and demands that retail medicine is trying to fill (e.g., access, convenience)?

Particularly for leaders within the traditional health care system, there are important questions to consider:

- Will there be fewer primary care visits because of expanding access through retail clinics?
- How will this impact the utilization levels, the financial viability of medical practices, and the existing physician–hospital relationships?
- How will clinical information be exchanged between retail clinics and other clinicians?
- Will the health system compete or partner with retail clinics?
- If not through retail clinics, how will health systems provide convenient access to consumers outside of the usual care models (i.e., physician offices, urgent care, and emergency rooms)?

Physician leaders must guide their organizations to consider the level of disruption in their current market and their response in light of these questions.

## *Mobile Health*

The advent and widespread adoption of smartphones and tablets has resulted in a proliferation of mobile applications (apps) focused on medicine and health care that promote the "quantified self," collectively known as "mobile health" or mHealth. Examples of mHealth may include smartphone and tablet applications such as Map My Run, an app that tracks distance, time, calories burned, and more. This also includes websites such as WebMD, which provide information related to diagnosis and treatment of disease as well as mobile patient monitoring systems such as Fitbit or Nike Fuel Band, which track users' eating, sleeping, and exercise habits. COVID-19 rapidly accelerated the roll-out of services that disrupt traditional face-to-face interactions in health care. For instance, prior to 2020 only one-tenth of 1% of all Medicare visits were done using telehealth services. The onset of the pandemic witnessed a 63-fold increase in deployment of such visits, and by the end of the year over 53% of all Medicare patients had tried telehealth (Samson et al. 2021).

Mobile health applications allow consumers to easily track health-related data, facilitate self-care, and perform other health and social interactions that previously could only be completed in the presence of a clinician.

Generation Z (born between 1997 and 2010) is the first generation to never know a world without the internet, mobile phones, and the potential for immediate connectivity. Raised with social media and educated with devices in the classroom, this generation demonstrates a facility with technology and a comfort with pursuing health services through technologic means. This generation and others are also increasingly engaged with what has come to be known as the "Internet of Things," described as the network of physical devices that are imbedded with sensors, software, and other technologies for tracking and exchanging data. Such devices range from traditionally fashionable apparel such as watches and rings, to remote health care sensors for blood glucose monitoring and nocturnal heart rate. This wealth of consumer information tracking represents an explosion of health data, and physician leaders will need to consider how they collect, manage, interpret, share, and meaningfully use such remotely assembled information. The growth of mobile health has been compounded by an influx of venture capital investments. Financial markets are making big bets on mobile health gaining greater traction and making a significant impact on health care.

Clinicians and clinical leaders may perceive mobile health applications to be a threat. Mobile health has the potential to erode the ability of health care providers to optimally manage their patients' care if patients move increasingly away from traditional settings due to the impression that mobile devices and apps are adequate substitutes for human practitioners. Mobile health applications also present new opportunities, however, for patients to become more actively engaged in their care. This may result in improved outcomes through better compliance with the care plans prescribed by a physician and greater engagement in social and behavioral activities that have a substantive impact on health status, such as healthy eating and exercise habits. Though there are risks associated with mobile health, there is also infinite potential for positive impact. As a physician leader, there are many opportunities to encourage and embrace consumer use of mobile health applications to maximize the potential of these innovations to improve health. Leaders must align the interests of consumers, mobile health application producers, and the bricks and mortar health care system. For example, leaders should consider initiatives to integrate information from mobile applications with the system electronic health record. Mobile health holds great potential to further engage consumers beyond the medical model, an exciting prospect to change the health behaviors that have such a significant impact on health status.

By the time you read this chapter, there will likely be new innovations in care delivery, consumer engagement, and the ability to impact the health outcomes of populations. As a physician leader, your role is to examine the benefits and risks of opportunities for innovations to maximize your organization's ability to deliver high-quality, low-cost, and patient-centered care.

## Artificial Intelligence

Recent decades have brought use of computers to the forefront of health care transformation, and until recently these served predominately as passive repositories for data, documentation, ordering, and communication. A new generation of active deployment of technology is poised to totally revolutionize how health care is delivered, and ultimately how team members interact within systems and organizations. Artificial intelligence is the use of computers to simulate, predict, and execute intelligent tasks performed by humans. Supplementing this, machine learning (ML) encompasses ways in which computers performing AI can learn through processes and improve, without human input or programming (James et al. 2022). One additional element that will impact health delivery is natural language processing (NLP), in which a computer algorithm decodes conversations, text, or unstructured health data to extract meaning or restructure in a more meaningful format. Such technologies have the potential to impact information available to clinicians at the time of medical decision-making, and to even go a step further and provide targeted point of care decision-making support. These technologies have been used to identify hidden or complex patterns in diagnostic data, to detect diseases earlier, signal patient risk and deterioration, and improve treatments. For instance, a 2020 systematic review and meta-analysis published in Internal Care Medicine showed that individual ML models could accurately predict sepsis onset ahead of time on retrospective data (Fleuren et al. 2020).

Multiple technologies are now readily deployed across the health care landscape to assist with the diagnostic process, including advanced cancer registries, early recognition of diabetic retinopathy, Alzheimer's disease, heart disease, and COVID-19 (GAO 2022). Physician leaders should anticipate how these technologies can impact their own workforce and drive efficiencies and improvement in care delivery. Simultaneously, these do portend to impact the very composition of health care teams—threatening the elimination of many current human-driven positions as well as changing the scope of practice for clinicians. In the coming decade, it is likely that a combination of clinician and AI interface together will be most common, and successful organizations will be those that can strike an ideal balance of the human and computer components of care delivery.

## Case Study: Responding to New and Disruptive Models of Care

Mitchel Schwartz, MD is president of Health Clinical Enterprise and chief physician executive for Luminis Health, a $1.2 billion health system located in Annapolis, Maryland. In this role, he oversees the organization's physician enterprise and accountable care organization initiatives. This interview with Dr. Schwartz describes the ways clinical leaders can respond to new and disruptive models of care.

*Q*: **What is the impact of retail medicine on the practicing clinician in your organization today?**

*A*: Retail medicine can be viewed as a threat or an opportunity. Much depends on the particular medical marketplace in which you work. Retail medicine provides a low-cost access point for patients, when compared to emergency department visits, but it is not equivalent to primary care. If there is a true value-based relationship with an insurer, coordination with this type of provider system should lower costs. In fact, patients who would often be seen in the emergency department can be referred to a lower cost retail option. Physician leaders should not view this as a threat. The clinical leader should be able to understand the potential opportunity retail medicine provides to the health system for preparing for the move to value-based care while offering some financial margin. This orientation is not truly about retail medicine, but is a commentary on the need for health systems to prioritize a focus on access. A tiered approach to access may include telehealth, urgent care, and then primary care.

*Q*: **How should physician leaders and organizations respond to new players entering the traditional health care market?**

*A*: In the past, the primary focus of a health care organization was the hospital. The hospital was designed to care for acutely ill patients, driven by volume and dependent on substantial capital investments. Quality was determined by process measures. New market forces will challenge health care organizations to evolve into a system of care by working with other stakeholders in the community to deliver quality care for low cost. The physician leader must engage with providers, typically those who are based in the community. Those clinicians have been trained in a structure that prioritizes autonomy, independent, task-oriented care. The role of the physician has changed to team leader. That fundamental change requires education, support, and communication. One core competency for physician leaders will be the ability to effectively communicate and educate other clinicians about their changing responsibilities within an evolving health care environment. Reorienting the focus on care coordination as well as access is essential to success in a value-based market, particularly as new and potentially competitive players emerge.

*Q*: **How does your organization respond to mobile health?**

*A*: Mobile health is one novel way to activate and engage patients. In a population health model of care, patient activation is a critical component for success. Mobile health is just one way to manage a large population of patients without having to see patients for the traditional office visit. A smartphone can be used to remind patients about therapy and maintain a record of weights, activity, or serum glucose levels. As with other shifts in health care, this may be perceived as a threat, particularly if there is no value-based payment system. Mobile health offers the clinician a more efficient form of interacting with patients. Real-time patient monitoring will lead to a dramatic increase in clinical data, requiring new clinical workflows and teams, but enable improved, more timely care. This new workflow, managed by a clinical team, may lead to success when reimbursements are dependent on quality metrics and on patients following through on care plans.

*Q*: **What skills would you advise other physician leaders to develop to deal with the challenges and opportunities of retail medicine, AI, and mobile health?**

*A*: The medical landscape is a rapidly changing environment. These disruptive forces are challenges to the status quo. The standard interactions and relationships with patients are quickly evolving, and expectations of the care delivery process are rising. Most patients do not believe the system is functioning and in fact has deteriorated. This destabilization threatens care providers, especially those who are at a point in their careers when change is not perceived as an option. The timeline between strategic thoughts and plans to execution and integration of change has shrunk substantially. Given the speed of change, a physician leader needs to address the issues and opportunities directly. The leader must be able to think broadly, well beyond the scope of a hospital. That strategic thinking must then be distilled into simple, straightforward points that can be easily communicated. The burning platform, the rationale for change, should be a part of that communication. Sustainability is an essential feature to the goal of change management. All too often, improvements once measured are lost without steady consistent management and oversight. Lastly, physician leaders must be able to build a creative team that is committed to continuous learning. The rapid changes underway require a structured learning process that enables the team to maintain a proactive and decisive approach to the market forces impacting their health system. That learning and innovation should include the impact of large language models of AI that will augment, support, and improve our ability to provide care. The role of the frontline clinician will be impacted, as will the patient's experience.

*Q*: **How do you prepare the physician leader for other new models of care?**

*A*: The changes taking place in health care will force all leaders to be more creative in seeking out novel approaches to the challenges of providing value-based care. The responses will have common themes—accepting some amount of financial risk, required process improvement, and a higher level of accountability. Leadership skills will be necessary to help a health system respond to those changes. Change management, which has been codified by Kotter (2014), requires a series of steps that enables leadership to move large organizations toward a defined set of goals. Moving from a superb clinician, recognized for clinical skill, to a leadership position requires training, coaching, and experience. It is a different job, based on the management of relationships, not just direct clinical care. It also includes accountability for the financial stability of the organization. Modeling financial risk, understanding, and managing financial metrics and communicating to others on the team about those challenges has become essential to the physician leadership role. Those clinicians interested in that role can seek out that training in formal leadership academies as we have had here at Luminis. Connecting to a mentor and using smaller projects as a teaching tool will also help a great deal. Physician leaders must be willing to experiment and will, possibly, fail, as that is one aspect of the learning process. Additionally, clinicians typically care for a small group of patients each day. Those interested in leadership positions should be oriented toward building systems that enable other clinicians to thrive in a new environment, thereby expanding their impact by helping to care for a population, within their community.

## Lessons Learned

Regardless of the emerging model of care at hand—population health, retail health, mobile health, artificial intelligence, or other—the physician leader must develop a number of non-clinical leadership skills that will be essential to these and other models of care that will improve the health of the populations we serve.

## Action Steps and Strategies to Lead

Considering the most prominent emerging models of care (retail medicine, population health, artificial intelligence, and mobile health) and the most impactful skills that leaders need to develop (data analytics, change management, and collaboration within and outside of health care), the clinical leader should accelerate the development of these skills and competencies by:

1. **Challenging current assumptions about health care delivery**: Physician leaders must be responsive and proactive toward new generations, new technologies, and new processes. Both retail medicine and mobile health are changing fundamental assumptions that exist within the walls of traditional health care spaces. Physician leaders should equip themselves and their teams to be adaptive, consider new environments, new modalities, and new team members that will all be new additions to the future of health care delivery.
2. **Developing and implementing segmented strategies**: The growth of diversity within our population will require strategies to be more sophisticated and detailed in terms of segmenting populations for care delivery. Consumer segments possess distinct characteristics about motivation and preferences related to seeking care, following up, and adhering to treatment regimens. Physician leaders must have varying strategies for different segments to effectively engage patients and to track and impact their health.

3. **Focusing on care coordination across the continuum**: New care models and reimbursement frameworks are elevating the importance of care coordination. As more players enter health care—and more players will be necessary to effectively impact health status and health outcomes—greater coordination is needed. Handoffs and transitions of information and service are risky, and the most successful organizations and enterprises will be those that are able to facilitate smooth, efficient, and effective transitions. Care coordination and transitions will increase, and successful physician leaders will seek supporting connection and communication between entities.
4. **Seeking out multiple, diverse, and effective partnerships**: Health care delivered in a silo is a model of the past. New entities are emerging within communities, springing from state and national government actions, and even through venture capital investment. Physician leaders should seek to partner with various groups, and negotiate to identify circumstances that benefit multiple overlapping organizations while simultaneously improving patient care.
5. **Actively engaging consumers and patients in their health and health care**: Though there is no turnkey solution to engaging consumers and patients in their health and health care, the number and potential of both emerging and undiscovered opportunities are immense. Physician leaders that partner with their patients through the use of personal health records, sharing of their data with all members of the health care team, using mobile health devices to improve their health behaviors, and working with other health and social service providers will increase their ability to impact their patients' health.

The current and impending changes in health care can cause anxiety. However, the successful leaders of the future will be inspired and excited at the opportunities to improve health and health care in new ways and with new partners. Physicians with exceptional clinical technical skills will become exceptional physician leaders through the development of competencies in data analytics, population health, partnership, and leading change all with a focus on providing high-quality, high-value, and patient-centered care.

## References

Christensen, C., Raynor, M., McDonald, R. What is Disruptive Innovation? *Harvard Business Rev.* December 2015. Accessed February 12, 2023 https://hbr.org/2015/12/what-is-disruptive-innovation

Fleuren, L.M., Klausch, T.L.T., Zwager, C.L., Schoonmade, L.J., Guo, T., Roggeveen, et al. Machine Learning for the Prediction of Sepsis: a Systematic Review and Meta-Analysis of Diagnostic Test Accuracy. *Intensive Care Medicine.* 2020;46(3):383–400.

GAO. Artificial Intelligence in Health Care: Benefits and Challenges of Machine Learning Technologies for Medical Diagnostics, GAO-22-104629. Washington, D.C. September 2022.

Health Research & Educational Trust. Leading Improvement Across the Continuum: Skills, Tools and Teams for Success. 2014.

HHS Press Office. HHS Issues New Report Highlighting Dramatic Trends in Medicare Beneficiary Telehealth Utilization amid COVID-19. U.S. Department of Health & Human Services. July 28, 2020. Accessed March 14, 2023. https://www.hhs.gov/about/news/2020/07/28/hhs-issues-new-report-highlighting-dramatic-trends-in-medicare-beneficiary-telehealth-utilization-amid-covid-19.html

James, C.A., Wachter, R.M., Woolliscroft, J.O. Preparing Clinicians for a Clinical World Influenced by Artificial Intelligence. *JAMA.* 2022;327(14):1333–1334.

Kindig, D., Stoddart, G. What is Population Health? *American Journal of Public Health*. 2003;93(3):380–383.

Knapp, K., Yoshizuka, K., Sasaki-Hill, D., Caygill-Walsh, R. Co-located Retail Clinics and Pharmacies: An Opportunity to Provide More Primary Care. *Pharmacy*. 2019;7(3):74.

Kotter, J. The 8-Step Process for Leading Change. *Kotter International*. 2014. Accessed March 23, 2023. http://www.kotterinternational.com/the-8-step-process-for-leading-change/

OECD. Health in the 21st Century: Putting Data to Work for Stronger Health Systems. *OECD*. Health Policy Studies, OECD Publishing, Paris, 2019.

Samson, L., Tarazi, W., Turrini, G., Sheingold, S. Medicare Beneficiaries' Use of Telehealth Services in 2020 – Trends by Beneficiary Characteristics and Location (Issue Brief No. HP-2021- 27). Office of the Assistant Secretary for Planning and Evaluation, U.S. Department of Health and Human Services. December, 2021.

Shaw, B., Chisholm, O., Creeping Through the Backdoor: Disruption in Medicine and Health. *Frontiers in Pharmacology*. 2020; 10(11):818.

Steinhubl, S.R., Muse, E.D., Topol, E.J. Can Mobile Health Techologies Transform Health Care? *JAMA*. 2013;310(22): 2395–2396.

# Chapter 17

# Compendium of Action Steps

## Chapter 1: The Health Care Landscape

| *Action Step* | *Description* |
|---|---|
| **Communicate the imperative for health care transformation and the steps to achieve it.** | ■ Develop messaging for staff, leadership, governance, patients, and the community.<br>■ Effectively describe how national drivers (i.e., reimbursement changes, demographic shifts) have a local impact.<br>■ Describe how changes and decisions, often difficult ones, are necessary given the larger context of transformation. |
| **Understand the relationship between cost and quality in practice and how to drive value.** | ■ Develop proficiency in measuring and managing costs and quality.<br>■ Identify ways to reduce waste and excess costs to increase value.<br>■ Educate your clinicians on the relationship between cost, quality, and value. |

DOI: 10.4324/9781003402831-17

| *Action Step* | *Description* |
|---|---|
| **Build, deploy, and lead improvement teams across all dimensions of care.** | ■ Teach and empower others in the organization to conduct performance-improvement cycles and lead performance-improvement teams.<br>■ Support a culture of continuous improvement. |
| **Build and lead effective multidisciplinary teams.** | ■ Tear down siloes and work across units, departments, and disciplines.<br>■ Enable clinicians to practice at the top of their licenses.<br>■ Develop effective communication plans and strategies with internal and external partners. |
| **Leverage data to improve clinical and organizational practice.** | ■ Develop competencies in data collection and analysis.<br>■ Use data to drive decisions.<br>■ Build a culture of transparency and continuous improvement guided by ongoing data collection. |
| **Realize the role of the patient as consumer.** | ■ Engage patients and families as partners in care.<br>■ Optimize opportunities to engage patients as consumers to change health behavior and outcomes. |

## Chapter 2: Effectively Implementing Quality and Safety Improvement

| *Action Step* | *Description* |
|---|---|
| **Become proficient in at least one improvement model.** | ■ Become proficient in your organization's model for improvement (e.g., Lean, Six Sigma) and act as a resource for others.<br>■ If your organization does not have a designated method, lead your team, unit, department, or organization to adopt a methodology to promote continuous improvement. |

| *Action Step* | *Description* |
| --- | --- |
| **Create a culture of safety.** | ■ Promote transparency, accountability, and open communication.<br>■ Encourage employees to identify and report mistakes and near misses. |
| **Become data driven.** | ■ Identify improvement opportunities based on data.<br>■ Develop improvement projects with specific, data-driven aims.<br>■ Use measurement and reporting to demonstrate value.<br>■ Support decisions with data. |
| **Empower frontline staff to lead.** | ■ Engage employees—nurses, pharmacists, physicians, and others—in quality-improvement initiatives.<br>■ Defer to expertise—those who work with the process daily often have best knowledge and insights on how to fix a problem.<br>■ Inspire a shared vision, challenge current processes, and enable staff to act. |
| **Provide resources to support improvement work.** | ■ Provide the appropriate financial, human, and time resources that are necessary to achieve an improvement project's aim.<br>■ Advocate to senior leadership on behalf of your teams' efforts. |
| **Lead by example.** | ■ Lead an improvement team yourself and model the skills and behaviors that contribute to successful quality improvement efforts.<br>■ Teach and empower others in the process to build a cadre of improvement leaders within your organization. |

# Chapter 3: Building a Culture of Safety

| *Action Step* | *Description* |
|---|---|
| **Assess your organization's culture.** | ■ Utilize a tool such as the AHRQ Hospital Survey of Safety Culture or Safety Attitudes Questionnaire to determine gaps in safety culture and identify opportunities for improvement. |
| **Actively manage workplace culture, including culture of safety.** | ■ Primary mechanisms that leaders can use to change, embed, and transmit culture are as follows:<br>– What leaders pay attention to, measure, and control on a regular basis?<br>– How leaders react to crucial incidents and organizational crises?<br>– How leaders allocate resources?<br>– Deliberate role modeling, teaching, and coaching.<br>– How leaders allocate rewards and status?<br>– How leaders recruit, select, promote, and excommunicate? |
| **Encourage and reward reporting of safety events.** | ■ Investigate the causes of all safety events and near misses.<br>■ Provide active and ongoing encouragement to staff to report safety events.<br>■ Reward employees who report, especially self-report, safety events, or near misses. |
| **Utilize a nonpunitive policy and decision-making algorithm for assessing individual culpability in safety events.** | ■ Develop and adhere to a nonpunitive policy and process for establishing individual culpability in safety events.<br>■ Algorithms should acknowledge the organization's role in providing the correct policies, procedure, training, and work environment for staff to succeed.<br>■ This process should be a human resources function, not a quality or safety function. |

# Chapter 4: Principles and Practices of High Reliability Organizations

| *Action Step* | *Description* |
|---|---|
| **Continuously monitor organizational culture.** | ■ Recognize that a high reliability organization has a unique cultural and leadership mindset. Commit to and own this mindset.<br>■ Commit to an ongoing evaluation and reinforcement of culture. |
| **Establish and communicate a compelling "why" for the high reliability journey.** | ■ Include aspirational goals and examples of high reliability organizations.<br>■ Relate the "why" back to the mission of the organization. |
| **Educate the organization on the key components of high reliability.** | ■ Sponsor and support organization-wide efforts to educate employees on the key principles of high reliability.<br>■ Demonstrate how high reliability will impact employees' daily work. |
| **Reduce variation in care delivery.** | ■ Serve as educator, highlighting best practices and transparently sharing variation in care.<br>■ Hold team members accountable for consistent, evidence-based care that seeks to reduce variation. |
| **Generate and celebrate quick wins.** | ■ Once the organization understands the "why" and "what" of high reliability, begin to roll out discrete tactics (e.g., the daily huddle) to create a powerful initial and visible example of a new organizational way and rhythm of operating. |

## Chapter 5: Key Quality, Safety, and Efficiency Measures

| *Action Step* | *Description* |
|---|---|
| **Integrate measurement for improvement into organizational culture.** | ■ Allocate non-patient care staff time to focus on performance-improvement projects.<br>■ Provide adequate resources to support improvement efforts.<br>■ Promote a culture that is data driven and focused on performance improvement.<br>■ Lead by example. |
| **Choose a few "big dot" measures to track at the organizational level.** | ■ Guide and define organizational priorities by choosing to focus on a set of key measures. These choices will help staff understand leadership priorities.<br>■ Minimize data fatigue and confusion by focusing on a few essential measures.<br>■ Promote transparency and accountability by creating clear lines of sight between the outcome and process and identify who owns the process. |
| **Connect measurement to action.** | ■ Those who engage with the process on a daily basis often have the best insight into how to fix the process.<br>■ Empowering frontline staff to lead builds organizational capacity, promotes a culture of performance improvement, and enables staff to have greater say in how they do their work. |
| **Monitor the data burden.** | ■ Ensure that data collection processes are efficient, effective, and purposeful.<br>■ Streamline and coordinate data collection.<br>■ Identify when appropriate to discontinue metrics or data collection when impractical or unproductive. |
| **Analyze balancing measures and benchmarking.** | ■ Encourage and guide selection and analysis of metrics that are efficient and effective.<br>■ Work with teams to review benchmarks and frequently consider balancing measures. |

# Chapter 6: Using Data for Feedback and Improvement

| *Action Step* | *Description* |
|---|---|
| **Support teams in developing plans for data collection, reporting, and analysis.** | ■ Data collection and analysis requires commitment and resources.<br>■ Clinical leaders should support teams in developing feasible plans for data collection that are efficient and effective. |
| **Provide ongoing feedback through dialogue and draw clear connections between data and recommendations (i.e., clinical guidelines) or what actions are necessary to improve the process.** | ■ Data is not useful if it is not reviewed on an ongoing basis.<br>■ If clinicians do not understand the data or do not see it as valuable, discontent, skepticism, and rebellion can result.<br>■ Promote transparency, allow dialogue and discussion of the data, including strengths and caveats, and guide colleagues to engage with the data in a way that is productive. |
| **Use graphical methods to display data.** | ■ Find simple, concise ways to display data. Emphasize the relationship between action and results.<br>■ Make the data accessible for all engaged in the improvement initiative. |
| **Explain change and variation in terms of special cause vs. common cause.** | ■ The distinction between special and common cause variation is a core element of using data for improvement.<br>■ Leaders should speak in terms of common vs. special cause variation. |

## Chapter 7: Physician Champions

| *Action Step* | *Description* |
|---|---|
| **Identify stakeholders to constitute a guiding coalition.** | ■ Acknowledge physicians as a key constituency to engage and influence.<br>■ Identify other stakeholders, both internal and external, whose voice should be included in planning and implementing the improvement effort. |
| **Seek guidance and counsel from other physicians.** | ■ Ask colleagues to whom they turn for advice and whose opinion is highly regarded.<br>■ When assessing potential candidates, ensure they are opinion leaders, have strong communication skills, a passion for patient-centered care, and an inherent willingness and adaptability to grow and develop. |
| **Actively guide and assist physician champions.** | ■ Demonstrate the behaviors that promote change.<br>■ Be an active listener, connecting to the "why."<br>■ Utilize storytelling and rely on evidence-based, objective data. |

## Chapter 8: Leading Effective Teams: For Clinical Care and for Performance Improvement

| *Action Step* | *Description* |
|---|---|
| **Define the aims and objectives of the team first and then build the team accordingly.** | ■ Teams should be built according to the purpose or aim.<br>■ Promote collaboration by recruiting multidisciplinary team members.<br>■ For all teams, engage a patient or family member representative. |

| *Action Step* | *Description* |
|---|---|
| **Prioritize training and support for teamwork.** | ■ Provide initial training in specific teamwork skills and ongoing coaching to promote a culture that supports teamwork.<br>■ Designate non-patient care time for team meetings, reimburse individuals for team activities, and develop communication plans and decision protocols that reinforce teamwork. |
| **Engage patients and their families in both care teams and improvement teams.** | ■ Patient and family advisors provide important insights related to quality, safety, and efficiency.<br>■ Teams should be built around and focus on the needs of the patient. |

## Chapter 9: Spreading and Sustaining Improvement

| *Action Step* | *Description* |
|---|---|
| **Find opinion leaders and champions to support spread.** | ■ Physicians and nurses are obvious stakeholder groups, but consider recruiting champions who are nurse assistants, pharmacists, or physical therapists if these groups are key stakeholders in the process at hand.<br>■ Champions must be willing to commit to and advocate for spread efforts. |
| **Consider the implementation/ dissemination model.** | ■ Strategize outreach and education methods based on the target population.<br>■ Consider the hospital's structure, infrastructure, standard operational processes, and potential knowledge gaps. |

| *Action Step* | *Description* |
|---|---|
| **Use data to demonstrate the effectiveness of the implemented practice.** | ■ Track and use data to persuade skeptics.<br>■ Data is a powerful catalyst to spread improvement. |
| **Use stories to engage other leaders and explain the "why" for spread.** | ■ Data is important, but the human aspect of the potential intervention is equally compelling.<br>■ Put a face on data by emphasizing the intervention's potential to save the life of a relative or a friend. |
| **Track spread adoption through data.** | ■ Use two types of measures: those that demonstrate the extent of spread and those that document the impact of the implemented changes.<br>■ Measure the rate of spread—how fast is the organization improving? |

## Chapter 10: Engaging Patients and Families in Safety and Quality

| *Action Step* | *Description* |
|---|---|
| **Determine the current state of patient and family engagement using an assessment tool.** | ■ All improvement initiatives should begin with an assessment of the problem.<br>■ Examples:<br>– Strategies for leadership: patient- and family-centered care—a hospital self-assessment inventory<br>– Patient- and family-centered care—organizational self-assessment tool<br>– Checklist for attitudes about patients and families as advisors |

| *Action Step* | *Description* |
|---|---|
| **Develop a clear vision of how your organization will engage patients and families.** | ■ Communicate and role model this vision.<br>■ Integrate patient and family engagement throughout the organization's culture and work systems. |
| **Demonstrate commitment through providing resources and infrastructure to support patient- and family-centered care.** | ■ Many barriers relate to limited time and resources.<br>■ Leaders must communicate the evidence that supports patient- and family-engagement initiatives and publicly commit to supporting those initiatives.<br>■ Provide resources (financial, time, and infrastructure) to support patient- and family-engagement efforts. |

## Chapter 11: Health Equity and Addressing Disparities

| *Action Step* | *Description* |
|---|---|
| **Implement appropriate training mechanisms.** | ■ Implement tools, such as unconscious bias training and cultural competencies, within teams. |
| **Stratify data.** | ■ Evaluate prevalence of differing demographics among the population served.<br>■ Collect objective measures of inequity and target subpopulations.<br>■ Transparently share data collected for awareness and accountability. |

| *Action Step* | *Description* |
|---|---|
| **Launch improvement teams.** | ■ Develop and foster teams that are specifically tasked and accountable for improvement of targeted disparities. |
| **Leverage community partnerships.** | ■ Investigate potential partners in the community who may already be engaged in support for target populations.<br>■ Seek to move outside of traditional clinical settings and partner with community-based groups. |
| **Strive for transformational improvement.** | ■ Boldly seek to wholly eliminate inequity within their organization and populations served. |

# Chapter 12: Addressing Variation in Utilization

| *Action Step* | *Description* |
|---|---|
| **Engage clinicians with data-driven feedback.** | ■ Engage physicians and clinical stakeholders early and often.<br>■ Convene a group of physicians to review data and hypothesize drivers of unwarranted variation.<br>■ Base decisions on evidence and data. |
| **Standardize operational processes using quality-improvement interventions.** | ■ Quality-improvement methodologies such as Lean, Six Sigma, and Plan–Do–Study–Act can lead to improvements in quality, patient satisfaction, and efficiency. |
| **Implement evidence-based clinical guidelines and appropriateness criteria.** | ■ Target areas where there is not consistent adherence to evidence-based guidelines. |

| *Action Step* | *Description* |
|---|---|
| **Initiate and sustain culture change.** | ■ Promote a culture of safety, transparency, improvement, and excellence.<br>■ Benchmark performance to top performers. |

# Chapter 13: Improving Care Coordination and Reducing Readmissions

| *Action Step* | *Description* |
|---|---|
| **Start with the data.** | ■ Look for patterns, drivers, and root causes.<br>■ Stratify data by condition, practitioner, readmission source, and time frame.<br>■ Target interventions based on what the data shows to be high need. |
| **Assess and prioritize your improvement opportunities.** | ■ Leaders should vocalize organizational priorities and devote resources accordingly.<br>■ Prioritize based on patient population, stages in the care process, or leverage other ongoing improvement efforts. |
| **Engage key stakeholders.** | ■ Work with partners inside and outside the hospital.<br>■ Engage partners in the development and execution of initiatives.<br>■ Move beyond the hospital—community partners are often better equipped to address non-medical factors that impact readmissions. |
| **Monitor progress.** | ■ Monitor data to identify successful strategies.<br>■ Keep the team engaged through showing and celebrating progress. |

## Chapter 14: Population and Community Health

| *Action Step* | *Description* |
|---|---|
| **Identify target populations to address.** | ■ Work with partners inside and outside the hospital. Consider and characterize the totality of patients served, or could be served.<br>■ Review how these populations can be subdivided through further variables. Engage partners in the development and execution of initiatives.<br>■ Move beyond the hospital—community partners are often better equipped to address non-medical factors that impact readmissions. |
| **Review barriers to health that are shared among the target population.** | ■ Monitor data to identify successful strategies. Assess barriers within the population, with emphasis on potential impact of social determinants of health.<br>■ Keep the team engaged by showing and celebrating progress. Understand contextual factors within subpopulations by asking issues and inequities that exits within these groups. |
| **Develop a community-minded strategy.** | ■ Evaluate the current scope and environment of services and organizations that already serve or are available to the target population.<br>■ Seek opportunities to partner with existing community organizations. |
| **Move interventions upstream.** | ■ Move from reactive services to proactive interventions.<br>■ Where feasible, consider the impact of prevention and disease management to mitigate exacerbation.<br>■ Seek to meet patients outside of traditional health care spaces, providing services where they live, work, and play. |

# Chapter 15: New Payment Models: Value-Based Purchasing

| *Action Step* | *Description* |
|---|---|
| **Understand your threshold of risk.** | ■ Bundled payments involve the least assumption of risk, followed by shared savings. Capitation has the most risk.<br>■ The degree of risk corresponds to the extent of infrastructure and process redesign necessary to be successful.<br>■ First, establish a risk threshold. Adopt payment models based on the risk threshold. |
| **Understand your core competencies and the gaps in your capabilities.** | ■ To be successful under value-based payment, organizations may need to redesign care processes to promote coordination across the continuum of care.<br>■ Analyze existing core competencies and identify gaps in processes, people, and technology as they relate to population health. |
| **Involve physicians early and as equal partners in the conversation.** | ■ Physicians must become partners in care teams.<br>■ Engage physicians in leadership roles throughout the process. |

## Chapter 16: The Physician Leader Role in Emerging Models of Care, Disruption, and Innovation

| *Action Step* | *Description* |
|---|---|
| **Challenge current assumptions and mindsets of health care delivery.** | ■ Care delivery is moving beyond traditional settings through retail medicine, mobile health, and population health strategies.<br>■ Shift the paradigm to innovate in ways to partner with and supplement these services instead of resisting or competing.<br>■ Focus on the needs of the patient—how will changing needs affect how health care should be delivered to optimize outcomes? |
| **Develop and implement segmented strategies.** | ■ There is no one-size-fits-all solution.<br>■ More data and greater analytic capability enable stratification and targeted intervention to maximize success. |
| **Focus on care coordination across the continuum.** | ■ Ensure seamless transitions.<br>■ Create new communication methods.<br>■ Engage patients, family members, and caregivers to ensure smooth transitions. |
| **Seek out multiple, diverse, and effective partnerships.** | ■ Move beyond the hospital walls.<br>■ Leverage the skills of community-based organizations.<br>■ Form partnerships inside and outside the health care system.<br>■ Rally around the common goal of providing safe, high-quality, and patient-centered care. |
| **Actively engage consumers and patients in their health and health care.** | ■ There is endless potential to improve patients' health and experience of health care.<br>■ Leverage new technologies (i.e., mHealth, apps, telehealth).<br>■ Engage patients before they are sick and provide ways to stay healthy and maintain treatment regimens to avoid hospital visits. |

# Index

Pages in *italics* refer to figures.


## A

accountability, 160–161
Accountable Care Organization (ACO), 253, 258, 275–277
action steps, compendium of
 clinical leaders, 326
 culture of safety, 314
 disparities, 321–322
 feedback, 317
 health care landscape, 311–312
 high reliability organizations (HROs), 315
 implementing safety improvement, 312–313
 measures, 316
 patient and family engagement (PFE), 320–321
 payment models, 325
 performance improvement, 318–319
 physician champions, 318
 population/community health, 324
 reducing readmissions, 323
 sustaining improvement, 319–320
 variation, 322–323
action, connecting measurement to, 93
active listening, 123–124
Adams, Carrie, 69
administrative databases, 100–101
advanced practice professionals (APP), 120
advocate, physician champion as, 121
Affordable Care Act (ACA), 1, 14, 17, 253, 257
African-Americans, 13
Agency for Healthcare Research and Quality (AHRQ), 151, 180, 197
AHRQ, 50–52
alternative payment models (APMs), 77
American Board of Internal Medicine (ABIM), 88
American College of Surgeons, 111
American Hospital Association Committee on Performance Improvement (AHA CPI), 3–4
American Institutes for Research (AIR), 180

anecdotes, employing, 124–125
Anne Arundel Medical Center (AAMC), 217
Annual Wellness Visit (AWV), 243–246
applications (apps), 299–301
artificial intelligence, 301–302
Asian-Americans, 13
Associates in Process Improvement, 25
attributed patient population, identifying, 277–278

## B

bad apples, 46
barriers, PFE, 189–191, *190*, *191*
bedside, beyond, 187–188
benchmarking, 82–83
Bernard J. Tyson National Award, 242
bias, *see* disparities, addressing
big dot measures, 93
blame and punishment, model, 46
bloodstream infections (BSI), 164
BPCI Advanced (BPCIA), 283
Bulger, John, 282
Bundle Payment for Care Improvement (BPCI), 283
bundle, defining, 279–281
bundled payments, 279–288

## C

capitation, 281–282
care coordination, improving, 240–243
Care Transitions Program, 234–235
case studies
  bundled payments, 282–288
  chronic kidney disease, 265–269
  developing PFAC, 184–186
  enhancing vaccine access, 35–37
  health equity report, 203–204
  high reliability principles, 64–71
  identifying and developing campions, 126–129
  improving access and preventive care, 243–246
  improving organizational culture of safety, 53–56
  improving/enhancing surgical recovery, 110–114
  increasing access and improving care coordination, 240–243
  *On the CUSP: Stop CAUTI*, 163–168
  reducing central line associated blood stream infections, 142–146
  reducing opioid overprescribing, 217–225
  reducing unnecessary testing, 87–91
  responding to models of care, 302–306
catheter associated urinary tract infections (CAUTI), 143
CAUTI Guide to Patient Safety Tool, 164
CDC HI-5 health impact, *261*
Center for Medicare and Medicaid Innovation (CMMI), 276
Centers for Medicare & Medicaid Services (CMS), 232, 283
  national quality strategy goals, 9–10, *10*
central line associated blood stream infections (CLABSI), 142–145, *145*
chaotic unit, 158

Choosing Wisely, 87–91, 211–212, 226
chronic kidney disease (CKD), improving models for managing, 265–269
Cincinnati Children's Hospital, 92
clinical care team, 134–135
commitment to resilience, HROs, 63, 69–70
communication tools, *156*
communicator, physician champion as, 121
community engagement, 262–263
community health, 36, 253–254, 256–257, 260, 262–263, 270; *see also* population health
community health assessment toolkit, *202*
Community Health Needs Assessment (CHNA), 201
community partnerships, 202–203
Comrey, Janet, 286
contribution health plans, defining, 17
contributions, providing opportunities for, 188–189
core competencies, *4*
Core Quality Measures Collaborative, 75
costs, 6–7
coverage, expansion of, 13–14
COVID-19, 15, 36, 144, 176, 296, 299, 302
criteria, 80
critical few, collecting, 91–92
*Crossing the Quality Chasm*, 46
culture of safety, building
  action steps, 57–58
  elements, 48–49
  evidence, 45–49
  lessons learned, 56–57
  strategies to learn, 57–58
  surveys on patient safety culture (SOPS), 50–52
  transparency around safety events, 50
culture, importance of, 45–46
cultural awareness, 199–200
*CUSP:* Stop CLABSI, 157
customer focus, 33

## D

daily organization huddle, 67–69
Darthmouth Atlas of Healthcare, 208
dashboards, 105–106
data burden, monitoring, 93–94
data utilization, population health, 264–265
data, analyzing, 107–109
data, displaying, 103–107
day-to-day leader, 136–137
deference to expertise, HROs, 63–64, 70–71
demographics, 7–8
Department of Defense Patient Safety Program, 137
diagnosis-related group (DRG), 275
direct care level, PFE, 176–178
discharge planning, 238–239
discharge rate, *284*
disparities, addressing
  action steps, 205–206
  community partnerships, 202–203
  cultural awareness, 199–200
  data stratification, 200–202
  definition, 195–198
  health equity report, 203–204
  lessons learned, 204–205
  strategies, 205–206

Donabedian, Avedis, 78
Drucker, Peter, 45

## E

Edson, Barb, 163
education topics reviewed with medical staff, *221*
Electronic Health Record (EHR), 16
electronic medical record (EMR), 218, 220
engagement of people, 34
Enhanced Recovery after Surgery (ERAS), 218
episode cost, *284*
Equality and Human Rights Commission, 200
escalation, 161
evaluation and management (E&M codes), 245
evidence-based decision-making, 34–35
evidence-based information, invoking, 125
executive rounding, 70–71

## F

fee-for-service, payment model, 272–274
feedback, using data for
  action steps, 115–116
  data collection, 99–103
  displaying data, 103–107
  enhancing surgical recovery, 110–114
  evidence, 98–99
  improvement cycles, 110
  lessons learned, 114–115
  strategies, 115–116
first curve, *2*, 2–4
follow-up, 239–240
formation, understanding stages of, 140–142
forming, 141
frontline clinical managers, 163

## G

Geisinger, 114
Geisinger Health Plan, 282–288
Generation X, 297
Generation Y, 297
Generation Z, 299
getting the right people on the bus, 140
Glover, J. Allison, 208
good saves, investigating, 65–66
gross domestic product (GDP), 6–7
Grover, Jennifer, 218

## H

Haidt, Jonathan, 124
Hanak, Michael, 243–246
harm, eliminating, 189
Health and Humans services (HHS), 197
health care
  culture of safety, 45–59
  disparities, 195–207
  feedback, 98–118
  High Reliability Organizations (HROs), 60–73
  implementing quality safety improvement, 25–44
  landscape of, 1–24
  measures, 74–98
  patient and family engagement (PFE), 174–194
  payment models, 272–312
  physician champions, 119–132

physician leaders, 295–310
population health, 252–271
readmissions, 231–251
spreading improvement, 150–191, *191*
teams, 133–149
variation in utilization, 208–230
health equity report, 203–204
Health Information and Technology for Economic and Clinical Health Act (HITECH Act), 15
health information technology (HIT), 15–17
health plan databases, 101
Health Research and Educational Trust, 38
Healthcare Effectiveness Data and Information Set (HEDIS), 81, 100
Healthcare-Associated Infection (HAI), 81
High Reliability Organizations (HROs)
action steps, 72–73
case studies, 64–71
commitment to resilience, 63, 69–70
deference to expertise, 63–64, 70–71
evidence, 60–64
lessons learned, 71–72
preoccupation with failure, 61–62, 65–66
reluctance to simplify, 62, 66–67
sensitivity to operations, 62–63, 67–69
strategies to lead, 72–73
Hispanics, 13
Hospital Consumer Assessment of Healthcare Providers and Systems, 82
Hospital Readmissions Reduction Program (HRRP), 76
household income, 12

## I

improvement, 34
improvement cycles, implementing, 110
improvement, implementing
action steps, 40–42
enhancing vaccine access, 35–37
evidence, 25–35
lessons learned, 37–40
strategies to lead, 40–42
inequities, addressing, *see* disparities, addressing
infant mortality rate, 12
Innovation in Quality, Effectiveness, and Safety (IQuESt), 213
inpatient rehab facility, percent utilization, *288*
Institute for Healthcare Improvement (IHI), 102–103, 136, 151, 186, 213, 262
Institute for Patient and Family-Centered Care (IPFCC), 177–178
integration, 161–162
International Standards Organization 9001, 33–35
Internet of Things, 300

## J

Jimenez, Jonathan, 240
John A. Hartford Foundation, 186
Joint Commission Core Measures, 100

## K


Kaiser Family Foundation, 12–13
Kindig, David, 252
Korpman, Dan, 218
Kotter, John, 129


## L


lab utilization, taskforce on decreasing, *88*
landscape of health care
  first curve-second curve transition, *2*, 2–4
  introduction, 1–6
  physical leader role, 17–20
  transformation, 5–17
leadership, 34
Lean, 28–32, *31*
Leapfrog Hospital Survey, 100
Lee, Jaw W., 35–36
life in the gap, 3
Lown Institute, 198


## M


*Managing the Risks of Organizational Accidents*, 47
*Managing the Unexpected* (Weick), 60
Map My Run, 299
measures
  action steps, 92–94
  collecting critical few, 91–92
  criteria, 80
  data for performance measurement, 77–78
  data sources, 80–83
  driving performance improvement, 84–91
  evidence, 74–84
  metrics of the future, 83–84
  reducing unnecessary testing, 87–91
  selecting, 85–87
  standards, 80
  strategies, 92–94
  types/dimensions of, 78–79
Medicaid, 257
medical record review, 100
Medicare, 8
  Access and CHIP Reauthorization Act of 2015 (MACRA), 77
  Care Compare, 81
  Hospital Readmissions Reduction Program, 232
  Readmissions Reduction Program, 275
  Shared Savings Program (MSSP), 283
MedPac, 232
Meisenberg, Barry R., 217–218
Merit-Based Incentive Payment System (MIPS), 77
Meritus Health, 68–69, 87–91
metrics of the future, 83–84
mHealth, 299
milligram morphine equivalents (MME), 218, 220, 222–223, *223*, *224*
mindful infrastructure, components of, 61
mobile health, 299–301
Modarai, Farhad, 265
Model for Improvement, 25–*27*
models of care, responding to, 302–306
momentum, building, 163
morphine milligram equivalents (MME), 113
*muda*, 31

*mura*, 31
*muri*, 31
must-do strategies, *4*

## N

names and blames, 46–47
National Academy of Medicine, 75
National Healthcare Quality and Disparities Report, 197–198
National Healthcare Safety Network (NHSN), 81–82
National Physician Organizations, 75
National Quality Forum (NQF), 75–76
National Quality Strategy (CMS), 9–10, *10*
National Voluntary Consensus Standards for Hospital Care, 100
natural language processing (NLP), 301–302
near misses, investigating, 65–66
Netflix, 3
never events, 76
*New England Journal of Medicine*, 231
norming, 141
nurse champion, 158
NYC Health + Hospitals, 240–243

## O

observed *versus* expected ratios (O:E), 112
Office of Minority Health (OMH), 197
*On the CUSP: Stop BSI*, 166–168
*On the CUSP: Stop CAUTI*, 163–168
opioids, overprescribing, 217–225
Optimal Dialysis Starts Program, 269
Organization for Economic Cooperation and Development (OECD), 11
organizational culture, 92–93
organizational performance, benefits of measuring, *85*
outcomes, measures, 79
overarchingly nurse practitioners (NP), 120
overprescription, reducing, 217–225

## P

partners, engaging patients as, 188
patient activation, 175
patient and family advisory councils (PFACs), 179–180, 184–186
patient and family engagement (PFE)
  action steps, 192
  barriers, 189–191, *190*, *191*
  defining, 174–176
  developing PFAC, 184–186
  direct care level, 176–178
  key learnings from, 186–189
  organizational design/governance, 179–180
  patient family advisors (PFAs), 180–184
  strategies, 192
patient family advisors (PFAs), 180–184
patient registries, 101
patient surveys, 101–102
Patient-Reported Outcomes Measurement Information System (PROMIS), 100
patients, 7–8

pay-for-performance (P4P), 9–10, 274–275
payment
Accountable Care Organization (ACO), 275–277
action steps/strategies, 291–293
bundled payments, 279–288
capitation, 281–282
fee-for-service, 272–274
identifying attributed patient population, 277–278
insights from research on, 288–291
pay-for-performance, 274–275
shared savings, 275–277
structure of risk sharing, 278–279
payment models, population-based, 255
per member per month, 255–256
performance enhancement team, 135–137
performance measurement, data for, 77–78
performance measures, critical characteristics, *86*
performing, 141–142
personalized performance data, utilizing, 125
Petrick, Anthony, 110
physical leader, role of, 17–20
physician associates (PAs), 120
physician champions
characteristics of, 120–126
developing, 126–129
evidence for involving, 119–112
identifying, 126–129
selecting, 129–131
physician leaders, 136
action steps, 307–309
artificial intelligence and, 301–302
lessons learned, 306–307
mobile health and, 299–301
preparedness of, 295–296
responding to new models of care, 302–306
retail medicine and, 297–299
strategies, 307–309
physician profiles, 104
pilot project, 162
Plan–Do–Study–Act (PDSA), 26–27, *27*, 160
policy implementation, 256–257
population health
Accountable Care Organizations (ACOs), 258
action steps/strategies, 269–270
Affordable Care Act (ACA), 257
community engagement, 262–263
data utilization, 264–265
models for managing chronic kidney disease, 265–269
overview of, 252–255
payment models, 255
per member per month, 255–256
policy implementation/implications, 256–257
social determinants of health, 258–261, *261*
post-lobectomy prescribing at baseline, *219*
preoccupation with failure, HROs, 61–62, 65–66
preventive care, improving, 243–246
problem-solving, 161
process approach, 34
process, measures, 79
Project Implicit, 200
Project Reengineering Discharge (Project RED), 233–234
project sponsor, 137

prospective data collection, 100
ProvenRecovery®, 110–113

## R

readmissions, 76–77
  actions steps/strategies, 247–248
  care coordination, 240–243
  Care Transitions Program, 234–235
  community resources, 239–240
  discharge planning, 238–239
  identifying patients at high risk, 237
  insights from research on, 246–247
  overview of, 231–233
  preventive care, 243–246
  Project Reengineering Discharge (Project RED), 233–234
  self-management skills, 237–238
  strategies for reducing, *234*, 236–240
  Transitions Care Model (TCM), 235–236
Reason, James, 47–48
reimbursement
  models of, 255–258
  new payment models and, 272–294
  transition to value-based, 8–10
relationship management, 35
reluctance to simplify, HROs, 62, 66–67
retail medicine, 297–299
risk continuum, value-based arrangements on, 272
risk sharing, structure of, 278–279
role model, physician champion as, 121
run charts, 106–107

## S

Safer Dx Checklist, 212–214, *214*
Safety Attitudes Questionnaire (SAQ), 53
safety event investigation, 66–67
safety events, transparency around, 50
Schein, Edgar, 45
Schwartz, Mitchel, 302
screening rates, 12
second curve, *2*, 2–4
self-management skills, 237–238
senior leadership, 157–158
sensitivity to operations, HROs, 62–63, 67–69
shared savings, 275–277
simulation, 69–70
Six Sigma, 32–33
smart analysis, 94
social determinants of health (SDOH), 254, 258–261, *261*
spread organizer, 158
spread, improvement
  aim establishment, 154
  challenges, 168–170
  cultural factors of, 151
  *On the CUSP: Stop CAUTI*, 163–168
  executing, 157–159
  monitoring, 157–159
  plan development, 154–157
  preparation, 151–153
  strategies, 170–171
  sustaining, 159–163
  technical factors of, 150–151
standardization, 160
standards, 80
Stoddart, Greg, 252
storming, 141
stratification, data, 200–202

Strive
health outcomes, *268*
health U.S. delivery footprint, *266*
Strony, Robert, 287
structure, measures, 78
surgical recovery, enhancing, 110–114
surveys on patient safety culture (SOPS), 50–52
Safety Attitudes Questionnaire (SAQ), 53
sustainment, improvement, 159–163
Sutcliffe, Kathleen, 60
Swiss cheese model, *65*, 65–66

## T

team
action steps, 147–148
clinical care, 134–135
defining, 133–134
enhancing, 135
implementing science/research on, 137–142
lessons learned from, 146–147
performance enhancement, 135–137
reducing central line associated blood stream infections (CLABSI), 142–145, *145*
strategies, 147–148
understanding stage of team formation, 140–142
Team Strategies and Tools to Enhance Performance and Patient Safety (TeamSTEPPS), 137–139
technical expert, 136
test driver, physician champion as, 121–122
Toyota Production System (TPS), 28–32
transformation
COVID-19 impact, 15
defined contribution health plans, 17
expansion of coverage, 13–14
health information technology (HIT), 15–17
high cost of care, 6–7
leading, 5–6
value-based reimbursement, 8–10
variable quality outcomes, 11–13
Transitions Care Model (TCM), 235–236
Transitions Coach, 235
translator, physician champion as, 121
transparency, 50
Tuckman, Bruce, 141
21st Century Cures Act of 2016, 76

## U

U.S. Census Bureau, 7–8
*Unequal Treatment*, 195
unnecessary testing, reducing, 87–91
unwarranted variation, 209–211

## V

vaccine, enhancing access to, 35–37
value-based purchasing (VBP), 9–10
value-based reimbursement, 8–10
variable quality outcomes, 11–13
variation
action steps, 227–228
Choosing Wisely®, 211–212
insights from research on, 225–227
overview of, 208–209
reducing opioid overprescribing, 217–225
Safer Dx Checklist, 212–214, *214*

steps to understanding/addressing, *215*
strategies, 227–228
strategies for success, *214*, 214–217
warranted *vs.* unwarranted, 209–211
visual management, 161

## W

warranted variation, 209–211
WebMD, 299
Weick, Karl, 60
Wennberg, Jack, 208
workforce, 7–8